The Big Book of Cross-Stitch Designs

The Big Book of Cross-Stitch Designs

Over 900 Simple-to-Stitch Decorative Motifs

The Reader's Digest Association, Inc.
Pleasantville, New York/Montreal/London/Sydney/Singapore

A READER'S DIGEST BOOK

This edition published by The Reader's Digest Association, Inc., by arrangement with the Eaglemoss Publishing Group

FOR EAGLEMOSS
Publishing Manager: Nina Hathway
Project Coordinator: Helen Hawksfield
Copy Editor: Samantha Gray
Art Editor: Phil Gibbs

FOR READER'S DIGEST
U.S. Project Editor: Kimberly Casey
Consulting Editor: Jane Townswick
Canadian Project Editor: Pamela Johnson
Project Designer: Jennifer R. Tokarski
Cover Designer: Mabel Zorzano
Associate Art Director: George McKeon
Executive Editor, Trade Publishing: Dolores York
President & Publisher, Trade Publishing: Harold Clarke

LIBRARY OF CONGRESS CATALOGING-IN-PUBLICATION DATA:
The big book of cross-stitch designs: over 900 simple-to-stitch decorative motifs.
     p. cm.
  ISBN 10: 0-7621-0673-5
  ISBN 13: 978-0-7621-0673-8
   1. Cross-stitch—Patterns. I. Reader's Digest Association.
TT778.C76B55 2006
746.44'3--dc22
                     2006044634

Address any comments about *The Big Book of Cross-Stitch Designs* to:
   The Reader's Digest Association, Inc.
   Adult Trade Publishing
   Reader's Digest Road
   Pleasantville, NY 10570-7000

For more Reader's Digest products and information, visit our website:
   www.rd.com (in the United States)
   www.readersdigest.ca (in Canada)
   www.rdasia.com (in Singapore)
   www.readersdigest.com (in Australia)
   www.readersdigest.co.uk (in the United Kingdom)

Printed in Singapore
1 3 5 7 9 10 8 6 4 2

NOTE TO OUR READERS
The editors who produced this book have attempted to make the contents as accurate and correct as possible. Illustrations, photographs, and text have been carefully checked. All instructions should be reviewed and understood by the reader before undertaking any project. The directions and designs for the projects in this publication are under copyright. These projects may be reproduced for the reader's personal use or for gifts. Reproduction for sale or profit is forbidden by law.

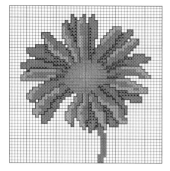
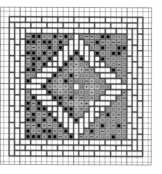
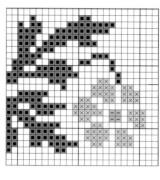
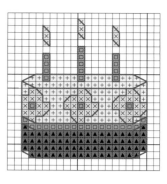

contents

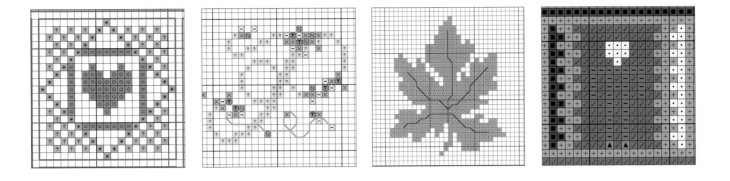

PART TWO:

motifs

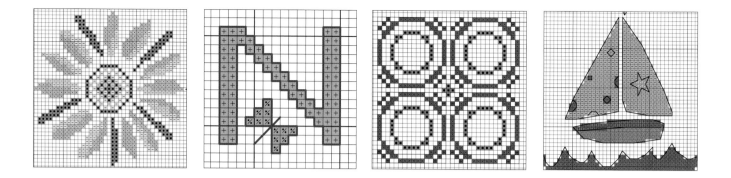

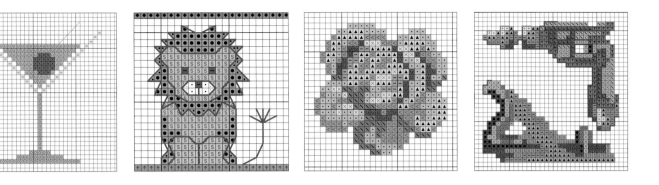

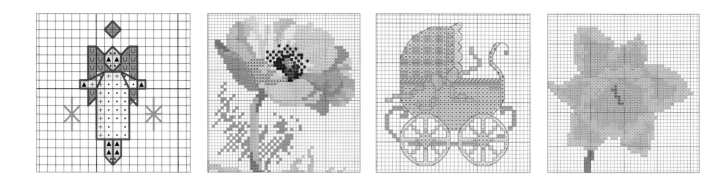

introduction

The great thing about cross-stitch is that it is the easiest embroidery stitch to perfect and the most versatile. You can learn the basic technique in moments, and there is a wealth of designs available, ranging from the very simple to the highly elaborate.

Cross-stitch is a form of counted thread embroidery, which, as the name suggests, involves counting fabric threads. It is usually stitched on evenweave fabric that has easy-to-count threads; the cross-stitches are displayed as clearly marked symbols on charts, so that they also can be counted.

Both the simplicity of the cross-stitch technique itself—each stitch is worked over the same number of threads to form a neat X-shape—and the easy-to-follow charts mean you can stitch designs that are perfect in every detail, even if you are a beginner. It's no wonder that cross-stitch is the world's most popular embroidery stitch.

Believed to be one of the oldest forms of embroidery, cross-stitch spread throughout Europe from the 15th century onward. Designs

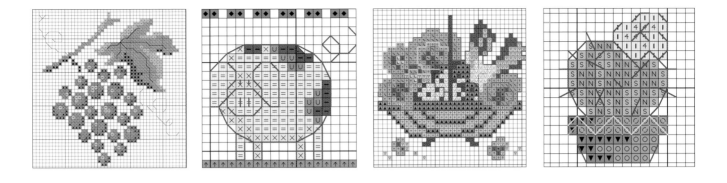

were passed at first from hand to hand and then from generation to generation. By the late 18th century, pattern books in the United States and Europe were inspiring cross-stitchers to work from an ever-expanding pool of designs and motifs.

The Big Book of Cross-Stitch Designs provides a complete guide to the subject and contains hundreds of inspiring ideas taken from traditional and contemporary sources. The six chapters of patterns that make up Part Two of the book present motifs in a variety of ways, and within each chapter you will find samplers —collections of small motifs and alphabets— individual motifs, pictures, borders, and more intricate designs.

Flowers are a popular subject for embroidery, and *Chapter three: Floral Inspirations* offers an extensive collection of natural, traditional, and contemporary flower designs from the garden, while *Chapter four: Nature's Bounty* features motifs that reveal the varied beauty of plants, their foliage, and fruits. *Chapter five: Home Comforts* is a charming record of some of the

everyday objects found at home, from pretty teapots and coffee mugs to garden tools and bunches of herbs.

For animal lovers, a menagerie of motifs is contained within *Chapter six: Animal Magic*, ranging from a whimsical cartoon cow and a little Scottie dog, to evocative portraits of sea horses and cats. *Chapter seven: Kids' Corner* brings together delightful patterns for the nursery and playroom, and child-friendly motifs for clothing and accessories, including clowns, fairies, penguins, and teddy bears.

The final chapter, *Chapter eight: Traditional Arts*, explores traditional and ethnic art forms, and offers a rich selection of authentic motifs taken from sources as diverse as Moroccan tiles, Indian paisley fabrics, and Native American motifs, as well as other folk traditions.

The designers and stitchers who created *The Big Book of Cross-Stitch Designs* have drawn on their knowledge and skills to create a reference work that covers everything a cross-stitcher needs. Now you can benefit from their experience and, above all, enjoy!

how to use this book

Before you start stitching, it's a good idea to read carefully through this section.

This book contains everything you need to know to stitch a perfect cross-stitch design. First browse through *Part Two: Motifs*, chapters three to eight, and think about the type of cross-stitch design you would like to stitch. Experienced cross-stitchers will find hundreds of patterns from which to choose, but if you are new to cross-stitch, start with some of the smaller designs that feature only basic cross-stitch.

prepare first

When you have chosen a design, look through *Part One: Techniques and Materials*. In *Chapter one: Essential Know-How*, you'll learn how to prepare your fabric for stitching, mount it in an embroidery hoop or stretcher frame correctly, and, most importantly, which fabrics are best to use. If you're not sure where to buy the necessary equipment, turn to Resources on page 320, where you'll find a useful list of suppliers.

Chapter one also explains how to select the most suitable thread or floss for working cross-stitch and its variations. All the threads featured in this book are made by the thread manufacturer DMC, as is any yarn used. Please note that threads from other manufacturers, such as Anchor, differ in colour from DMC threads and have different code numbers. Easy-to-follow instructions for other popular embroidery stitches, such as French knots and straight stitches, complete this chapter. They are used in many of the designs to add texture and detail.

Chapter two: Embellishments gives step-by-step instructions for stitching a variety of decorative additions, including making tassels, sewing on sequins and beads, and adding monograms. These stylish embellishments can be added to many of the designs.

get started

Choose a design and then you'll be ready to start stitching. Each design in chapters three to eight comes complete with a cross-stitch chart and clear instructions on how to stitch it. Each chart also includes a materials list, thread key, and size guide.

The size guide shows you instantly the size of the finished cross-stitch design when it is worked on different fabric counts. The fabric count is simply the degree of fineness or coarseness of a fabric, and it is measured by the number of threads per inch (2.5 cm). For example, 14-count fabric has 14 threads to one inch (2.5 cm). Generally speaking, the higher the count the finer the fabric.

If more than one motif is featured in a design, a separate cross-stitch chart is provided for each one. In such a case, each chart will be marked A, B, C, or D, and the size guide will show the dimensions of the largest motif. Please note that if the cross-stitch chart has been turned to enable it to fit the page, the top edge will be marked clearly: **(top)**.

materials

This list includes details of which count of fabric has been used in the photograph that illustrates each design and which size and type of needle to use. Also included is the number of skeins of thread needed and the number of strands of divisible thread.

materials

- ■ **This design uses evenweave fabric, 14-count white Aida, and tapestry needle, size 26.**

- ■ **Stranded cottons, one skein of each colour listed in key. Use two strands for cross-stitch and three-quarter stitch and one for backstitch.**

thread key

This key lists the colours of thread required for cross-stitch and additional stitches, and the colours of beads. (Note that all beads used are not made by DMC.)

thread key

- ⊡ 746 buttermilk
- ⊠ 772 pale leaf green
- ⊟ 818 pale baby pink
- ▲ 963 cream pink
- ◉ 988 mid grass green
- Ⓤ 3326 deep ice pink
- ⊟ 3348 pale moss green
- ⬆ 3821 pale gold
- ☑ 3823 yellow cream

backstitch

- ◪ 988 mid grass green
- ◪ 3326 deep ice pink

cross-stitch chart

Each stitch on the cross-stitch chart is shown as a symbol within a coloured square. On some designs, heavy lines on the chart indicate outlines or special details that are worked in backstitch or straight stitch. Other stitches, such as French knots and the three-quarter cross-stitch, are marked with different symbols, as shown below.

A symbol in a coloured square indicates a single stitch.

Three-quarter stitch is shown by a right-angled triangle.

Backstitch is shown as a heavy line.

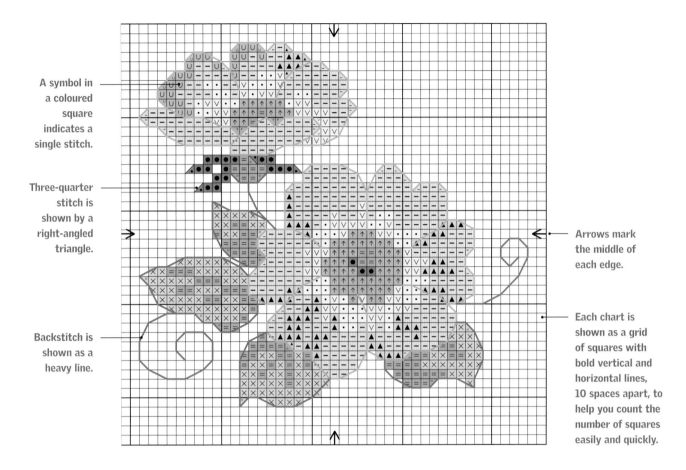

Arrows mark the middle of each edge.

Each chart is shown as a grid of squares with bold vertical and horizontal lines, 10 spaces apart, to help you count the number of squares easily and quickly.

size guide

This easy-to-use chart shows the size of the finished design. Remember that both the number of strands and the number of threads or blocks over which each cross-stitch is worked will vary according to the fabric count of your fabric. You sew over threads with linen fabrics but over blocks with Aida, which is a special evenweave fabric in which the threads have been fused into blocks. For example, if you use an 18-count Aida fabric, the size guide shown below asks for two strands of thread to be worked over one block of fabric threads. The same design worked on 28-count linen requires each cross-stitch to be worked with two strands of thread over two threads of fabric.

This column explains the number of threads to work the cross-stitch over in fabrics such as linen, or, in the case of Aida, the number of blocks to work the cross-stitch over.

This column provides the number of strands of embroidery thread or floss to use for each cross-stitch. DMC stranded cotton, for example, consists of six strands of thread, which can be separated and recombined in groups of two, three, or more, as required.

This column gives you the flexibility to use fabrics of different degrees of fineness or coarseness.

This column gives the actual size the design will be when worked on different counts of fabrics.

size guide			
fabric count	number of threads/blocks	number of strands	size of design
14	1	2	3 1/8 x 2 7/8 in. (8 x 7.25 cm)
16	1	2	2 5/8 x 2 1/2 in. (6.75 x 6.25 cm)
18	1	2	2 3/8 x 2 1/4 in. (6 x 5.75 cm)
28	2	2	3 1/8 x 2 7/8 in. (8 x 7.25 cm)
28	3	3	4 5/8 x 4 1/4 in. (11.75 x 10.75 cm)

PART ONE

techniques and
materials

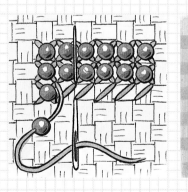

chapter one:

essential know-how

 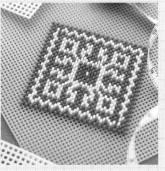  

getting started

Good preparation is essential for professional results.

A few basic tools are required before you begin stitching. As well as fabric, a tapestry needle, threads, and any embellishments listed with each design in this book, you will also need embroidery scissors and an embroidery hoop or a tapestry frame.

Always prepare the fabric before mounting it in an embroidery hoop or a rectangular frame. Embroidery hoops are usually made of wood or plastic and range in size from 4 to 12 in. (10 to 30 cm). Rectangular frames are useful if a design is too big for an embroidery hoop or is to be worked on canvas. They come in varying sizes, and two main types are available—the easy-to-use stretcher frame and the scroll frame.

preparing the fabric

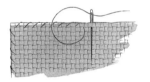

1 Cut the fabric at least 2 in. (5 cm) larger than the design. Overcast or machine zigzag stitch around the raw edges.

2 Find the midpoint of all fabric edges and baste across. The cross marks the middle of the design area.

mounting the fabric in a hoop

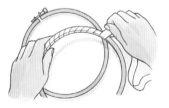
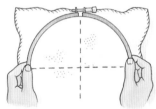

1 Bind the smaller ring with cotton tape to stop the fabric from slipping. Secure the end with a few stitches.

2 Place the fabric over the smaller ring. Ease the larger ring in place so that the fabric is taut. Tighten the outer ring.

mounting the fabric in a stretcher frame

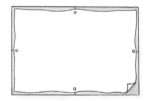
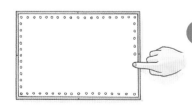

1 Mark the midpoint on each edge of the fabric and on each stretcher bar. Tack the fabric to the stretcher bars at these points, pulling the fabric taut.

2 To secure the fabric, push in tacks at intervals of ¾ in. (2 cm) along each edge, pulling the fabric gently.

TIP

If you are using a stretcher frame, buy the stretcher bars in pairs from a craft store. The bars are available in a range of sizes, usually increasing in 1 in. (2.5 cm) increments. Purchase two bars matching the required length of your fabric, and two matching the required width.

threads

Experiment with threads in different colours and finishes.

Anchor Lamé is a smooth, very shiny, 12-stranded divisible thread.

DMC Flower Thread has a matte finish and is not divisible.

DMC Cotton à Broder has a matte finish and is not divisible.

Anchor Marlitt has a high-gloss finish and is a six-stranded divisible thread.

DMC Rayon is a six-stranded divisible thread and has a high-gloss surface.

DMC Metallic Thread is stranded, with a textured metallic finish.

Danish Flower Thread has a matte finish and is not divisible.

Needle Necessities Floss Overdyed is a six-stranded divisible variegated thread with a slight sheen.

DMC Perle (or "pearl") Cotton has an attractive sheen and is not divisible.

Stranded cottons, for example Anchor and DMC, are six-stranded divisible threads with a subtle sheen.

Stranded cotton has a soft sheen and is the most popular type of embroidery thread for cross-stitch. It comes in a vast range of colours—as do flower threads, which have an attractive matte finish. However, other threads have much to offer, too. For glitter and gleam, there are metallic and lamé threads, and the glossy, brilliant shades of Anchor Marlitt and DMC Rayon threads. Overdyed threads give a variegated finish to a design.

Before you use a new type of thread, make sure it's the right thickness. Divisible threads can be separated and recombined to make thinner or thicker threads. You can also combine lengths of some threads that are not divisible.

TIP

For a smooth finish to your work, always divide stranded threads into separate strands before you start stitching, even if you are using all four or six strands. Then recombine the number of strands you need.

cross-stitch

Easy to learn, basic cross-stitch also has several variations.

Cross-stitch consists of a diagonal cross on the front of the fabric; each cross is composed of two diagonal stitches, worked one on top of the other. It is quickest to work in rows, making sure that the top diagonal of each cross-stitch slants the same way.

Fractional stitches are variations of basic cross-stitch, and they include the half cross-stitch—a single, diagonal stitch—and the three-quarter cross-stitch, made up of a full diagonal and a half diagonal. Such stitches can be used to add details to a design, but their main purpose is to give a motif a smooth outline. For all cross-stitches, weave the loose ends of the thread into the back of the work.

starting and ending a line of stitches

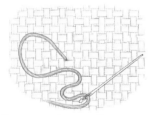

1 Bring the needle up to the front of the fabric from the back to begin cross-stitching. Draw the thread through, leaving a 2 in. (5 cm) tail on the wrong side. This will be secured by the working thread as you stitch.

2 When you have 2 in. (5 cm) of thread left, or you've finished a colour block, take the needle through to the wrong side and run the thread under several stitches. Trim the excess.

working a row

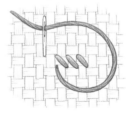

1 To start working from right to left, bring the needle out to the front of the fabric. Insert it one hole up and one to the left, and bring it out to the front again one hole down. Continue like this to form a row.

2 Work from left to right to complete the crosses. Bring the needle out one hole below the top of the last stitch. Insert it one hole up and one to the right. Bring it out one hole down. Continue to form a row.

half cross-stitch

A half cross-stitch is one diagonal stitch. Bring the needle to the front of the fabric and insert it either one hole up and one hole to the left, or one hole up and one hole to the right— depending on the direction shown in the chart.

three-quarter cross-stitch

Single three-quarter cross-stitch fills half the space of a whole cross-stitch. First work a full-sized diagonal. Bring the needle out at the corner of the block, then work a half diagonal. Push the needle down in the middle, over the diagonal.

straight stitches

There are a variety of easy-to-work straight stitches for different effects.

For motifs, individual straight stitches are sometimes used. Backstitch is a very simple straight stitch that is worked in lines. Use it for outlining a shape. You can vary the length of straight stitches, but they must not be so long that they sag or pull.

Whipped backstitch and whipped straight stitch make raised, solid lines and are ideal for curves, such as flower stems and tendrils. They are worked over foundation stitches, which determine their thickness.

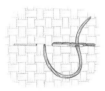

backstitch

Work from right to left. Bring the needle to the front one stitch length to the left of the starting point. Insert it at the starting point and bring it out two stitch lengths away. Pull the thread through.

straight stitch

To work an individual straight stitch, bring the needle to the front. Push it through to the wrong side to make a single stitch of the required length.

straight cluster

To cluster straight stitches, do straight stitches of varying lengths and directions according to the design. Take care to keep the thread tension even, to avoid puckering.

straight flower

To create a simple straight-stitch flower, do straight stitches as desired, working outward from a central circle or oval. Work each stitch in the same way.

whipped backstitch

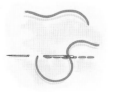

1 Do a foundation row of backstitches, a little larger than usual. Thread the whipping thread onto a tapestry needle, and weave it into the back of the first few backstitches.

2 Bring the whipping thread to the front. Whip it over and under the backstitches without piercing the fabric. To secure the end of the whipping thread, take it to the back and do a few backstitches.

whipped straight stitch

1 Make a straight stitch as shown above. Bring the needle out at the start of the stitch. Whip the thread tightly and evenly around the stitch without piercing the fabric.

2 Insert the needle at the end of the stitch. Continue working whipped straight stitches in the same way.

knots

These traditional embroidery stitches add texture and detail.

Both French knots and caterpillar-shaped bullion knots combine with cross-stitch. You can adjust their size and texture by changing the thread—for example, a round, twisted thread, such as pearl cotton, will give a more raised effect than stranded cotton. Choose a needle that will slip easily through the coils of thread, and begin each knot with two or three tiny stitches at the back of the fabric, under where the knot will be worked. End the thread in the same way each time, directly under the knot.

French knot

1 Work two or three tiny stitches on the wrong side of the fabric. Bring the thread to the front. Holding the thread taut with one hand, wrap it twice around the needle.

2 Pull the thread gently to tighten the twists around the needle. Don't overtighten the twists.

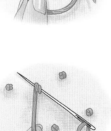

3 Holding the thread taut, insert the needle close to where it originally emerged, and pull the thread through to the back. To do this on Aida fabrics, you might have to push the needle through the blocks—if you put the needle back through the hole it came out of, you will just pull the thread back to the wrong side.

bullion knot

1 Bring the needle to the front at 1. Insert the point at 2, bringing it to the front again at 1. Holding the thread taut, wrap it around the point five to seven times to make a twisted coil.

2 Pull the needle carefully through both the fabric and the twists on the needle, taking care not to distort the twists. This may take some practice.

3 Pull the thread back gently so that the coil of twists lies flat on the fabric. Tighten the thread, and use the needle to pack the twists together.

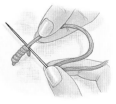

4 To finish the knot, take the needle and thread back through the fabric at position 2.

chain stitches

Decorate designs with chain stitch, or create petals with lazy daisy stitch.

Chain stitch and lazy daisy stitch are both made by looping thread. A basic chain stitch is slightly raised, and you can use it to form lines or curves. It is a versatile stitch that can be worked in thick or fine threads for different effects, and used for outlining or for filling in shapes. When used as a filling stitch, it is worked in rows stitched in the same direction to form a decorative texture. The lazy daisy, or isolated chain stitch, is often worked in groups to look like flower petals.

chain stitch

1 Bring the thread to the front at the top of the stitching line. Form the working thread into a loop and, holding the loop in place with your thumb, insert the needle in the same hole.

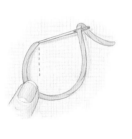

2 Holding the thread loop with your thumb, bring the point of the needle to the front a stitch length away from the starting point. With the loop under the needle, pull the needle through to make the first chain.

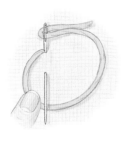

3 Insert the needle next to the emerging thread. Bring the point of the needle out a stitch length away, and pull it through, over the working thread, to make the second chain. Continue in this way.

lazy daisy stitch

1 Mark guide lines in a circle. Bring the needle out at the inner end of a line. Insert it beside the emerging thread and bring it out again a stitch length away, over the working thread.

2 Pull the thread so the loop lies flat. Make a short straight stitch over the loop to anchor it. Bring the needle out to the front, where you want to begin the next stitch. Continue making loops in this way. Finish by pulling the needle through and taking it over the thread to the back.

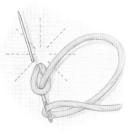

fabrics

Select the right fabric for your design from the wide range available.

Evenweave fabrics are the best choice for cross-stitch. They have an equal number of horizontal (weft) and vertical (warp) threads to every 1 in. (2.5 cm). This number is called the count—the higher the count, the finer the fabric. The threads are easy to see on all but the finest fabrics, so they can be counted accurately to ensure even stitching.

Aida is a special type of evenweave fabric in which threads are fused together to form blocks of various sizes. Each cross-stitch is worked over one block. With other evenweave fabrics, you count individual threads and work cross-stitches over one, two, or three threads. Choose a fabric that best suits the purpose to which you will put your design—Aida is firm and easy to work on, but pure linen is a better choice for more durable items, such as table linens.

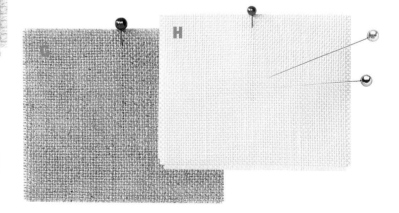

A Binca has a very coarse count per inch—6 to 8—and is often used for teaching children to stitch.

B Aida, the most popular fabric for cross-stitch, has blocks of threads. Usually 100 percent cotton, it comes in 43–51 in. (109–130 cm) widths, in 11, 14, 16, and 18 counts, and in a range of colours.

C Rustico Aida contains linen, which gives it an attractive wheaty finish. It is 51 in. (130 cm) wide and comes in a choice of 14, 16, and 18 counts.

D Hearthstone Aida is a natural beige cotton-linen mix. It is 43 in. (109 cm) wide and comes in 14 count.

E Lurex Aida has metallic threads interwoven in the cotton. It is 51–59 in. (130–150 cm) wide and comes in 14 and 18 counts.

F Belfast is a fine, 32-count pure linen fabric. It is 55 in. (140 cm) wide and comes in an assortment of different colours.

G Cashel linen is a 28-count pure linen fabric. It is 55 in. (140 cm) wide and comes in a range of colours.

H Dublin is a 25-count linen fabric and 55 in. (140 cm) wide. It comes in a small range of neutral colours and blue.

plastic canvas

Create a range of practical items for the home with plastic canvas.

Plastic canvas consists of a plastic sheet punched with regular holes that allow you to cross-stitch in the conventional way. Its rigidity makes it ideal for place mats or coasters, or even jewelry. By stitching together the edges, it is possible to create three-dimensional objects such as small boxes. Plastic canvas requires no preparation, and it is easy to handle for stitching. You won't need a hoop or stretcher frame because the mesh does not distort—and the edges won't fray.

cutting and stitching

1 Using a ruler and permanent marker, mark the design area and the middle point. Cut the canvas, leaving a margin of at least five holes all around. Trim the edges. Stitch the design from the middle outward.

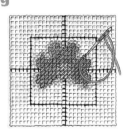

2 When the design is complete, trim the plastic canvas. For pieces that will be edged or joined, leave one row of unworked holes all around the stitching. Don't trim pieces you want to frame.

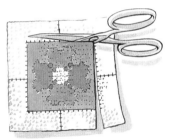

overcast edging

1 Working from left to right, bring the needle to the front through the first hole. Bring the needle out to the front again, one hole to the right, pulling the thread over the canvas edge.

2 Cover an outer corner by working two or three stitches into the corner hole. Don't force through too many stitches or you may tear the mesh. For an inside corner, work one stitch into the corner hole.

braided edging

1 Working from left to right, bring the needle to the front through the first hole. Loop the canvas edge, and bring the needle out through the third hole, then to the front through the first hole again, covering the short thread tail.

2 For the second stitch, bring the needle to the front through the fourth hole. Bring it out to the front through the second hole. Use the fifth and third holes for the next stitch, then the fourth and sixth, and so on.

waste canvas

Using waste canvas makes it easy to work your designs onto many fabrics.

Waste canvas is an evenweave, meshlike fabric, woven from pairs of threads stiffened with starch. With this canvas you can cross-stitch on many fabrics. Simply work the design through the canvas onto the fabric, using the mesh as a stitching guide.

The canvas comes in a range of mesh sizes, from 8 to 16 pairs of threads per 1 in. (2.5 cm). Stitch with a crewel needle—its sharp point will penetrate the fabric weave more easily than the blunt point of a tapestry needle.

Work each stitch over a pair of threads, inserting the needle through the large holes where the pairs intersect. Then remove the threads, revealing the finished design.

using waste canvas

1 Pin the waste canvas in position on the right side of the fabric, making sure that the direction of the fabric threads lines up with the canvas mesh. Baste around the edge of the canvas and from corner to corner.

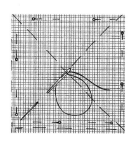

2 Stitch the design through the canvas and the fabric. Work each stitch over a pair of threads, and stitch through the exact middle of each hole with the needle at a right angle to the fabric surface.

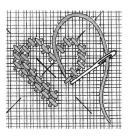

3 Remove the basting, and use embroidery scissors to trim the waste canvas close to the design. Using a damp sponge, moisten the work very slightly. Use only a little water because the starch in the canvas might glue it to the embroidery threads.

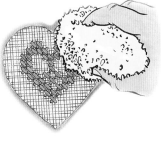

4 Using tweezers, pull out the canvas threads one by one. Remove all of the threads lying in one direction first, then turn the work and pull out the remaining threads. Pull the threads out straight, holding the opposite edge of the fabric firmly.

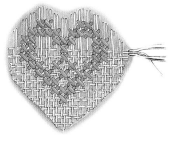

knitted fabrics

Knitted clothes and accessories make a good base for cross-stitch.

Knits are ideal foundations for cross-stitch—the V-shapes of stockinette stitch can be used in the same way as the blocks in Aida or the threads in other evenweave fabrics. Stitch with a thread that is slightly finer than the knitting yarn, and take care not to pull the stitches tightly, as this will distort the knit. Fasten off the thread in the usual way.

Experiment to find new ways of adding interest to plain knits. For quick and easy results, a small motif repeated over a garment looks attractive. Alternatively, try a simple border around a neckline or the hem of a garment. Knitted gloves can also be given a new look with cross-stitch motifs.

cross-stitch on knitted fabric

1 Mark the bottom right-hand stitch of the design area with a safety pin. Insert the needle 1 in. (2.5 cm) below, and bring it out at the bottom left of the marked stitch, leaving a 2 in. (5 cm) tail. Insert the needle from top right to top left of the stitch. This creates the first diagonal of the cross-stitch.

2 After making the first diagonal of the cross over the knitted stitch, bring the needle out at the top left of the stitch. Take out the safety pin. Work a second diagonal to complete the first cross-stitch. Bring the needle out at the bottom left of the next knitted stitch to the left.

3 Continue in this way along the row. Work more rows directly above so that the base of the stitches on the row above share the same holes as the top of the stitches on the row below.

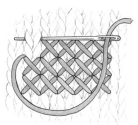

TIP

You can use cross-stitch charts when stitching on knitted fabric, though larger motifs may become a little distorted because the grid formed by the knitted stitches is not perfectly square. If you like, you can correct the distortion by adding extra stitches to the height of the charted design.

chapter two:

embellishments

appliqué

You can appliqué cross-stitch motifs onto clothes, toys, or soft furnishings.

Appliqué means stitching a cut piece of fabric onto a background fabric. It opens up a new range of uses for cross-stitch designs. You can cut them out as a square or rectangular patch, or cut around the shape of the cross-stitch motif. Alternatively, you can decide on the shape of the fabric patch and cross-stitch a simple design onto this shape.

Sew the fabric shape in place by hand by overcasting with tiny stitches in a matching thread. For most fabrics, including evenweaves with a fine count, hem the edges before stitching them in place to prevent fraying. Alternatively, you can deliberately fray the edges of evenweave fabrics (including Aida and higher-count fabrics) to create a decorative fringe.

hemstitched appliqué

1 Draw a shape on the right side of the fabric. Cross-stitch a motif inside this outline. Cut out the shape, adding a ¼ in. (5 mm) seam allowance. Reinforce with running stitches just outside the outline.

2 Clip the seam allowance along the curves. Finger-press the seam allowance to the wrong side, making sure the stitched line is just out of view. Baste in place.

3 Position the shape on the background fabric and baste across it to hold it in place. Sew the shape in place with tiny slip stitches.

fringed appliqué

1 Cut the appliqué to size, with the cross-stitch motif in the middle. Using a tapestry needle, tease out the threads around the edges until you have created an even fringe.

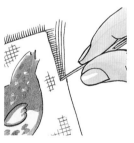

2 Baste the patch in position. Use thread to match the fabric and work small running stitches around the edges, or use a contrasting thread and large, decorative running stitches.

fringing fabric

Frame your designs in a novel way with fringed fabric borders.

To create a decorative border around the edge of cross-stitch designs, try fringing fabrics. This adaptable technique enhances a variety of cross-stitch designs. A self-fringe can be used to add an informal note, soften a hard edge, or form a frame. Fringing a mounting fabric creates a decorative border around the cross-stitch design mounted behind it and is an attractive way to display your work.

Loosely woven medium to heavyweight fabrics, including cotton and linen, are best for fringing. Avoid using very fine fabrics, as these are often tricky to fringe successfully.

creating a fringe

1 Measure around the stitched motif to determine the size of the frame. Draw the frame on the fabric using an erasable fabric marker. Draw another square or rectangle inside the first at the depth of the fringe from the edges of the outer square.

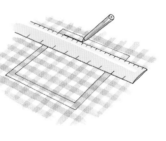

2 Cut diagonally both ways across the inner square or rectangle. Align the stitched motif under the aperture, lifting the flaps to check its position. Pin and baste all around. Topstitch around the edges of the outer square.

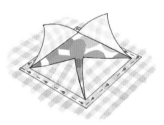

3 Cut along the lines of the inner square. Snip into the corners, nearly to the line of topstitching. Erase the drawn marks.

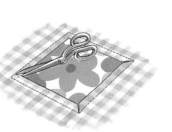

4 Finger-press the flaps back. Using a seam ripper, pull out the threads on each flap back to the line of topstitching.

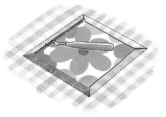

tassels

Use embroidery threads to make tassels for your cross-stitch projects.

It's easier than you might think to create your own tassels. You can use them to decorate cross-stitched home accessories, perhaps using the same embroidery threads.

Once you have mastered the technique, try making tassels from more unusual threads. Use synthetic textured yarns, wool knitting yarns, raffia, or even narrow leather strips, depending on the effect you want to create.

making a tassel

1 Cut cardboard the length of the tassel and about 2 in. (5 cm) wide. Wrap the yarn around it to the desired thickness. Thread a length of yarn onto the tapestry needle and slip it under the tops of the loops; tie them loosely together.

2 Ease the yarn loops off the cardboard. Cut a 30 in. (75 cm) length of yarn. Knot it around the tassel about one third of the way down from the top. Then wrap the end firmly around the tassel, covering the knot.

3 Thread the loose end of the yarn onto the needle and take it up into the middle of the tassel. Cut through the loops with scissors. Trim. Attach the finished tassel to the desired object by making a cord from the same yarn used for the tassel.

beading tassels

1 Thread a fine, sharp needle; knot the thread ends. Bring the needle to the right side of a narrow ribbon. Thread on beads to fit the tassel. Take the thread around the last bead, back up through the line of beads. Secure. Repeat until there are enough for the tassel.

2 Wrap the beaded ribbon around the top of the tassel. Trim the excess, turn in the raw end, and stitch it firmly in place with tiny stitches.

3 Cut a 30 in. (75 cm) length of yarn. Knot it around the top of the tassel; wrap it to cover the knot and ribbon. Thread the end onto a tapestry needle and take it into the middle of the tassel and up through the top. Tie it to the excess yarn, or cover the beaded ribbon with braid or more ribbon.

sequins

Shimmering sequins add highlights and novelty effects to designs.

A vast assortment of sequins is available today. There are flat, round sequins, convex ones with faceted or smooth surfaces, and novelty shapes, such as stars, leaves, and flowers. They also come in a rainbow of colours, including iridescent shades.

You can buy sequins from many craft shops, but for the widest range, try bead shops. You can sew on most sequins with an ordinary needle and thread; for sequins with larger holes, you can also use embroidery threads. Always make sure that you mount the fabric in an embroidery hoop or frame to prevent puckering, and secure the thread with a couple of tiny backstitches behind the sequins.

sunburst sequins

Bring the needle to the front through the middle of a sequin using a contrasting shade of thread, then insert it into the fabric. Bring the needle through the middle and make three or four stitches in a sunburst shape. Take the needle to the back side of the work and secure.

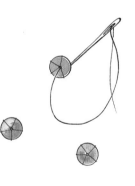

beaded sequins

Bring the needle to the front and thread on a sequin. Ease it down the thread so that it lies flat on the fabric. Thread on a bead and take the needle back through the middle of the sequin. Pull the thread gently from the back until the bead is sitting firmly on the sequin. End the thread as in "Sunburst sequins".

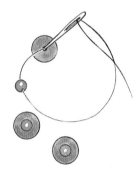

overlapping sequins

Draw a guideline on the fabric with dressmaker's chalk. At the top of the line, bring the needle up through the middle of a sequin, then insert it on the line just below the sequin. Bring the needle out again just below and thread on the next sequin. Insert the needle just below, and continue in this way. End the thread as in "Sunburst sequins".

TIP

Novelty sequins often have a hole at the top so they can dangle from the fabric. To sew them on, bring the needle up through the hole and back down through the fabric a few times, then fasten off behind the sequin.

basic beading

Use beads to add three-dimensional sparkle to your designs.

Beads come in a variety of shapes. Suitable types for embellishing cross-stitch designs include tiny, round rocailles and seed beads, cylindrical bugle beads, and tear-shaped drop beads. Faceted beads have tiny light-reflecting surfaces. Beads are sold in needlecraft and bead shops, and by mail order.

Stitching with beads is simple. Use strong sewing thread or quilting thread that matches or blends with the beads. For an even finish, match the beads to the fabric count. Or you can use larger beads and apply them to alternate stitches or space them farther apart. Small beads have tiny holes, so use the finest embroidery or tapestry needle available.

beaded cross-stitch

Work a row of diagonal stitches. Then, as you complete each stitch in the row with the top diagonal stitch, slip a bead onto the thread before you insert the needle.

working a repeat pattern

Apply beads to the top diagonals of groups of stitches arranged at regular intervals.

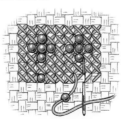

beaded backstitch

Use beads that match or are slightly smaller than the fabric count. As you outline your design with backstitch, apply a bead with every stitch.

applying large beads

To apply beads that are larger than the fabric count and larger than the cross-stitches, work beaded cross-stitch, as shown to the left, but apply beads only to alternate stitches.

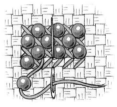

beaded half cross-stitch

Bring the thread out to the front, add a bead, and insert the needle one hole down and one to the left, pushing the bead down the thread so that it lies against the fabric. Bring the needle out one hole up to start the next stitch.

TIP

When you're choosing drop beads for cross-stitch, select beads with holes that run through the tip rather than down the length, so that they will dangle from the fabric.

split-thread beading

Sew beads in place more securely with the help of this useful technique.

When adding beads to an item that will be in regular use and subject to wear and tear—such as a pillowcase, a tote bag, or an item of clothing—the beads must be held in place as securely as possible. Split-thread beading is a technique that holds beads more firmly than ordinary beaded cross-stitch. The beads are threaded on in the normal way as you work the first part of the stitch. Then, as you work the second part of the stitch, you split the thread into two strands and take it around the bead to anchor it in place. While this method requires a little extra time, it extends the range of items you can embellish with beads.

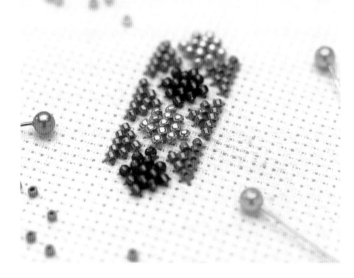

individual split-thread beading

1 Bring the thread out to the front, thread on a bead, and then insert the needle one hole down and one hole to the left. Push the bead down the thread so that it lies against the fabric. Bring the needle out one hole up.

2 Insert the needle one hole down and one to the right and start pulling the thread through. When the thread is nearly pulled through, split the strands over the bead so that a strand lies on either side of the bead; finish pulling the thread through. To end the thread, take several short stitches on top of one another on the back side of your work.

rows of split-thread beading

 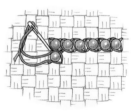

1 Work a row of split-thread beaded cross-stitches, as above. To start the second row, bring the needle out one hole down and one hole to the left. Work a beaded half cross-stitch from bottom left to top right. Bring the needle out one hole down.

2 Insert the needle one hole up and one to the left, splitting the strand over the bead. Bring the needle out one hole down and one to the right, ready to work the next stitch. Continue in this way to the end of the row. To end the thread, take several short stitches on top of one another on the back side of your work.

monograms

Personalize your household linens with elegant monograms.

Monograms are decorative motifs and can transform mundane items. Initials on bed linens, napkins, kitchen linens, or drawstring bags can turn these ordinary accessories into personal gifts that may well become treasured heirlooms.

There's a wealth of charted cross-stitch alphabets to use as sources for personal monograms, but it's also fun to create your own alphabets. You could try charting a cursive script you particularly like or, for a contemporary look, try a strong, blocky script. Books of copyright-free alphabets are an ideal source; you'll also find a range of fonts on home computers—just print out the letters at a large size or enlarge them on a photocopier. As an added bonus, printing an alphabet at a very large scale may bit-map the letters, turning them into a series of block shapes that are perfect for cross-stitch.

Once you've charted the letters, you can experiment with different ways of turning them into elegant personal monograms. Interlocking letters look very attractive, and so do overlapping ones.

creating cross-stitch letters

1 Trace each of your chosen letters onto squared graph tracing paper (available at craft shops). Trim each letter to a neat square.

2 Use a coloured pencil to modify the traced letters into blocks to fit the grid. Create "steps" for curved lines, and use half-blocks to indicate three-quarter stitches to smooth out the curves.

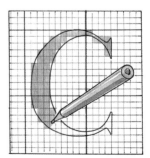

designing monograms

1 Chart each letter on a separate piece of squared graph tracing paper. Cut out each letter neatly. Experiment with different tones for a three-dimensional effect. Lay one letter on top of another and move them around to find the best arrangement.

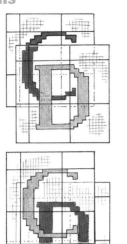

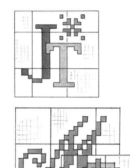

2 Intertwine letters to create flowing monograms, making sure they remain legible. Try elaborating the design with different colours.

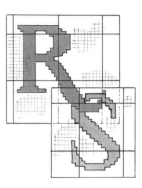

3 Combine letters from different alphabets, or use small decorative motifs to enhance plain letters. Then transfer the final design to squared graph paper, from which you can work the letters in cross-stitch.

TIP

ADDING PERSONAL DETAILS
Instead of creating a monogram, you can use this simple alphabet to add your initials and even the date to your work. You can put together complete names and dates to personalize greeting cards and small sampler designs. Hand- or machine-knitted garments, or other knitted items, can also be adorned with beautiful monograms from this cross-stitch chart. Bear in mind, though, that knitting stitch is rectangular rather than square, so you must make adjustments to the cross-stitch design to compensate for this if necessary.

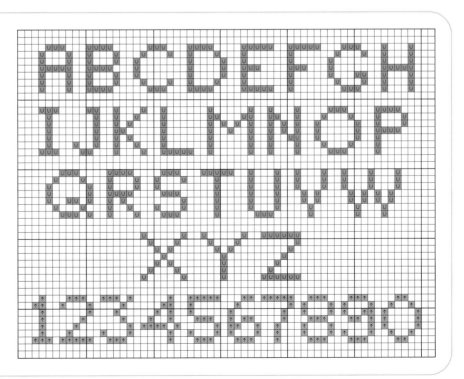

PART TWO
motifs

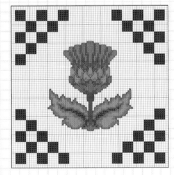
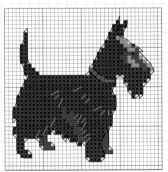
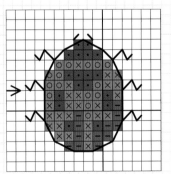

chapter three:

floral inspirations

floral display

This beautiful sampler features flowers chosen for their particular associations—an ever popular style.

stitching the design

1 Overcast the edges of the fabric to prevent fraying. Mark the midpoint of the fabric both vertically and horizontally with basting stitches; mount the fabric in an embroidery hoop (or stretcher frame) (see Getting Started, page 18).

2 Use the size guide below to calculate the size of design that will result from using different fabric counts (see How to Use This Book, page 13). Refer to the cross-stitch chart and thread key, and stitch from the middle outward.

3 Remove the finished design from the hoop and press gently on the wrong side.

size guide

fabric count	number of threads/blocks	number of strands	size of design
14	1	2	10¼ x 7⅝ in. (26 x 19.25 cm)
16	1	2	9 x 6¾ in. (22.75 x 17.25 cm)
18	1	2	8 x 6 in. (20.25 x 15.25 cm)
27	2	2	10⅝ x 7⅞ in. (27 x 20 cm)
27	3	3	16 x 11⅞ in. (40.75 x 30.25 cm)

materials

- The design shown here uses evenweave fabric, 27-count ivory, and tapestry needle, size 26.

- Stranded cottons, one skein of each colour listed in key. Use two strands for cross-stitch.

thread key

- U 159 pale lavender blue
- X 160 mid lavender blue
- Z 407 maple sugar
- – 422 light hazel
- 4 758 mid rose brown
- + 951 pink cream
- T 3012 mid dull green
- < 3013 pale dull green
- N 3045 yellow beige
- ■ 3363 antique green
- O 3836 pale grape

◄ Flowers have long been used as motifs for samplers. Among the many plants featured on this attractive example are the rose, which symbolizes love, the harebell, symbolizing submission, and the forget-me-not, symbolizing true or abiding love.

(top)

fritillaries

Always graceful, these bell-shaped flowers add a feminine touch to both interiors and accessories.

stitching the design

1 Overcast the edges of the fabric to prevent fraying. Mark the midpoint of the fabric both vertically and horizontally with basting stitches; mount the fabric in an embroidery hoop (or stretcher frame) (see Getting Started, page 18).

2 Use the size guide below to calculate the size of motif A that will result from using different fabric counts (see How to Use This Book, page 13). Refer to the cross-stitch chart and thread key, and stitch from the middle outward.

3 Remove the finished design from the hoop and press gently on the wrong side.

size guide

fabric count	number of threads/blocks	number of strands	size of design
14	1	2	2¾ x 3¾ in. (7 x 9.5 cm)
16	1	2	2½ x 3¼ in. (6.25 x 8.25 cm)
18	1	2	2⅛ x 3 in. (5.5 x 7.5 cm)
28	2	2	2¾ x 3¾ in. (7 x 9.5 cm)
28	3	3	4½ x 5½ in. (11.5 x 14 cm)

materials

- The design shown here uses evenweave fabric, 18-count antique white Aida, and tapestry needle, size 26.

- Stranded cottons, one skein of each colour listed in key. Use two strands for cross-stitch and one for backstitch.

thread key

- ⊡ blanc
- ◎ 316 pale old mauve
- Ⓝ 471 pale avocado
- ⊠ 472 light avocado
- ⊞ 762 pale pearl grey
- Ⓤ 928 silver grey
- Ⓣ 989 pale grass green
- ▲ 3347 mid moss green
- ⊟ 3803 mauve

backstitch
- ⊠ 3803 mauve

◀ Here shown adorning the cover of a jewelry roll and the frame of a photograph, fritillaries can also be used to enhance window treatments. Add a border of upright fritillaries to the edge of a ready-made curtain—work them directly onto the fabric over waste canvas, or stitch them onto an Aida band.

(A)

(B)

(C)

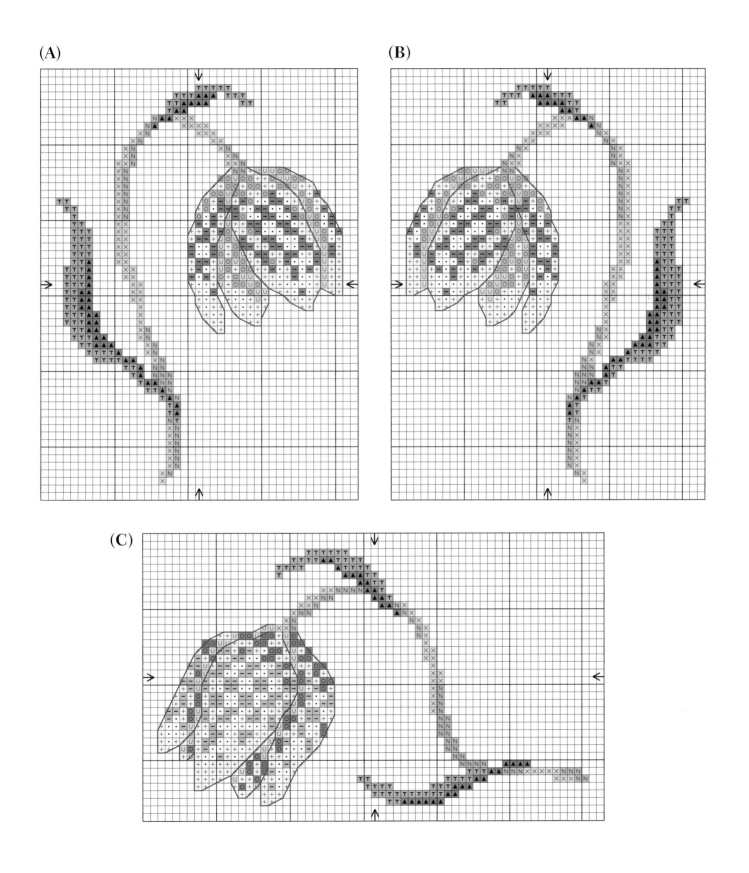

cabbage rose

Ringed by rosebuds and cottage-garden flowers, this design is inspired by traditional chintz fabric.

stitching the design

1 Overcast the edges of the fabric to prevent fraying. Mark the midpoint of the fabric both vertically and horizontally with basting stitches; mount the fabric in an embroidery hoop (or stretcher frame) (see Getting Started, page 18).

2 Use the size guide below to calculate the size of design that will result from using different fabric counts (see How to Use This Book, page 13). Refer to the cross-stitch chart and thread key, and stitch from the middle outward.

3 Remove the finished design from the hoop and press gently on the wrong side.

size guide

fabric count	number of threads/blocks	number of strands	size of design
14	1	2	6¼ x 5⅜ in. (16 x 13.75 cm)
16	1	2	5½ x 4¾ in. (14 x 12 cm)
18	1	2	4⅞ x 4⅛ in. (12.5 x 10.5 cm)
28	2	2	6¼ x 5⅜ in. (16 x 13.75 cm)
28	3	3	9¼ x 8 in. (23.5 x 20.25 cm)

materials

■ The design shown here uses evenweave fabric, 28-count antique white linen, and tapestry needle, size 26.

■ Stranded cottons, one skein of each colour listed in key. Use two strands for cross-stitch and one for backstitch.

thread key

· blanc
‖ 644 creamy beige
T 742 pale sunshine yellow
▽ 760 dusty rose
↑ 772 pale leaf green
⊠ 819 ice pink
⊞ 822 light stone
◉ 987 grass green
▣ 989 pale grass green
⊟ 3326 deep ice pink
▲ 3328 dark salmon
U 3348 pale moss green
■ 3721 brown pink

backstitch

◻ 987 grass green

◀ As well as making a panel on a summer tote bag, this motif would brighten up an evening scarf or bag. Framed, it would make a lovely gift for a friend.

gerberas

The vivid colours of South Africa's brightest blooms are set against white for maximum impact.

stitching the design

1 Overcast the edges of the fabric to prevent fraying. Mark the midpoint of the fabric both vertically and horizontally with basting stitches; mount the fabric in an embroidery hoop (or stretcher frame) (see Getting Started, page 18).

2 Use the size guide below to calculate the size of design that will result from using different fabric counts (see How to Use This Book, page 13). Refer to the cross-stitch chart and thread key, and stitch from the middle outward.

3 Remove the finished design from the hoop and press gently on the wrong side.

size guide

fabric count	number of threads/blocks	number of strands	size of design
14	1	2	9¼ in. (23.5 cm) square
16	1	2	8⅛ in. (20.75 cm) square
18	1	2	7¼ in. (18.5 cm) square
28	2	2	9¼ in. (23.5 cm) square
28	3	3	13⅞ in. (35.25 cm) square

materials

- The design shown here uses evenweave fabric, 28-count white, and tapestry needle, size 26.

- Stranded cottons, one skein of each colour listed in key. Use two strands for cross-stitch and one for backstitch.

thread key

- ▲ 600 dark pink
- ☒ 602 bright pink
- ⊡ 603 pink
- ▣ 702 spring green
- ⊟ 726 daffodil yellow
- ⊞ 727 jonquil yellow
- ⊙ 740 dark tangerine
- ⊠ 907 pale apple green
- ▽ 947 flame orange
- ⊍ 972 sunshine yellow

backstitch
- ◺ 817 poppy red
- ◺ 917 deep raspberry
- ◺ 947 flame orange

◄ These daisylike flowers are stitched in yellows and pinks either as a trio or as an individual motif. For an even bolder effect, stitch gerberas onto coloured fabrics; for example, the yellow gerbera on bright pink or the cerise bloom on yellow.

buttercups

Sunshine yellow flowers with contrasting dark green leaves look good as a single motif or as a border.

stitching the design

1 Overcast the edges of the fabric to prevent fraying. Mark the midpoint of the fabric both vertically and horizontally with basting stitches; mount the fabric in an embroidery hoop (or stretcher frame) (see Getting Started, page 18).

2 Use the size guide below to calculate the size of design that will result from using different fabric counts (see How to Use This Book, page 13). Refer to the cross-stitch chart and thread key, and stitch from the middle outward.

3 Remove the finished design from the hoop and press gently on the wrong side.

size guide

fabric count	number of threads/blocks	number of strands	size of design
14	1	2	4⁷/₈ x 1⁵/₈ in. (12.5 x 4.25 cm)
16	1	2	4¼ x 1³/₈ in. (10.75 x 3.5 cm)
18	1	2	3⁷/₈ x 1¼ in. (9.75 x 3.25 cm)
28	2	2	4⁷/₈ x 1⁵/₈ in. (12.5 x 4.25 cm)
28	3	3	7¼ x 2³/₈ in. (18.5 x 6 cm)

materials

- The design shown here uses evenweave fabric, 16-count white Aida band, and tapestry needle, size 26.

- Stranded cottons, one skein of each colour listed in key. Use two strands for cross-stitch.

thread key

- ■ 502 sea green
- Ⅰ 3771 rose brown
- ☒ 3822 palest gold

◀ Just one buttercup can be stitched onto an Aida band. A row of repeats makes a decorative trim for bathroom and kitchen towels and other accessories, such as tablecloths and napkins.

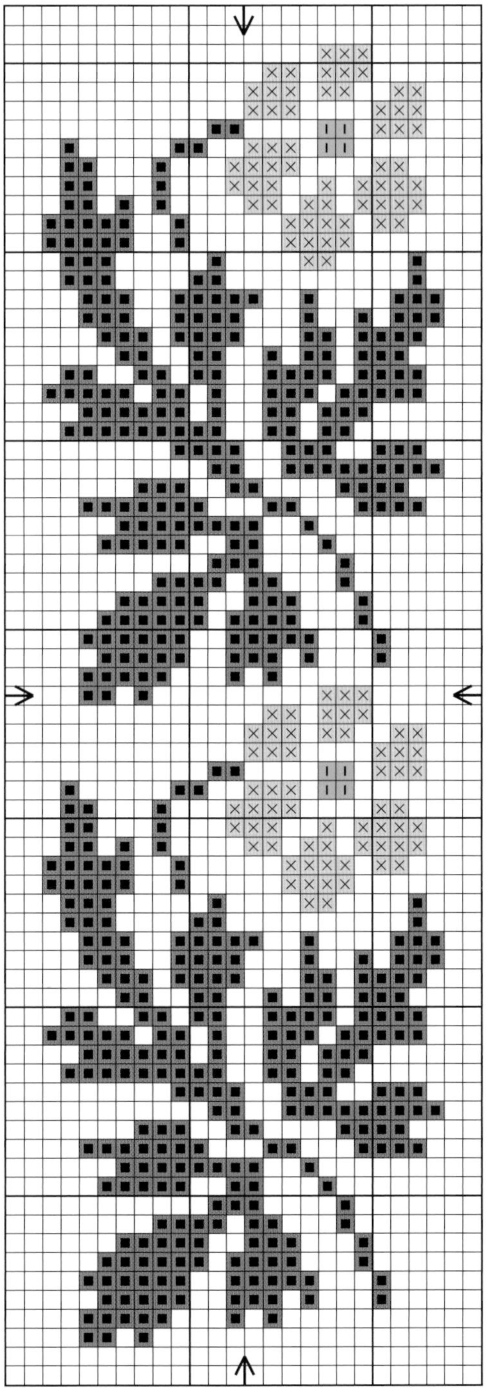

periwinkles

A winding flower stem with curly tendrils is adorned with French knots representing tiny flower buds.

stitching the design

1 Overcast the edges of the fabric to prevent fraying. Mark the midpoint of the fabric both vertically and horizontally with basting stitches; mount the fabric in an embroidery hoop (or stretcher frame) (see Getting Started, page 18).

2 Use the size guide below to calculate the size of design that will result from using different fabric counts (see How to Use This Book, page 13). Refer to the cross-stitch chart and thread key, and stitch from the middle outward.

3 Remove the finished design from the hoop and press gently on the wrong side.

materials

- The design shown here uses evenweave fabric, 28-count white Quaker cloth, and tapestry needle, size 26.

- Stranded cottons, one skein of each colour listed in key. Use two strands for cross-stitch and French knots and one strand for backstitch.

size guide

fabric count	number of threads/blocks	number of strands	size of design
14	1	2	4¼ x 5¼ in. (10.75 x 13.25 cm)
16	1	2	3¾ x 4⅝ in. (9.5 x 11.75 cm)
18	1	2	3¼ x 4⅛ in. (8.25 x 10.5 cm)
28	2	2	4¼ x 5¼ in. (10.75 x 13.25 cm)
28	3	3	6⅜ x 7⅞ in. (16.25 x 20 cm)

thread key

- ▫ 164 palest grass green
- ⊟ 703 lime green
- ▲ 912 deep spearmint
- 4 954 mid spearmint
- ✕ 3807 cornflower blue
- S 3839 pale Delft blue
- U 3840 palest Delft blue
- ↑ 3855 pale apricot

backstitch
- ◸ 703 lime green
- ◹ 792 lilac blue

French knots
- ● 792 lilac blue

◀ The blue-and-violet floral border around this heart sachet echoes the blue of the periwinkles. Filled with potpourri, the sachet can be used to scent drawers of linen or clothes.

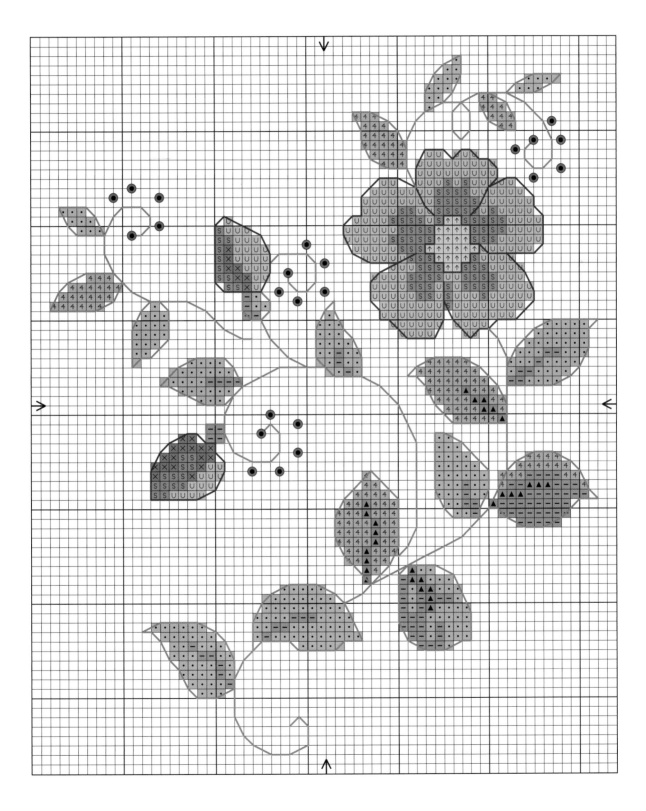

anemone

The blooms of the anemone have an enduring appeal, and a single flower makes an elegant focal point.

stitching the design

1 Overcast the edges of the fabric to prevent fraying. Mark the midpoint of the fabric both vertically and horizontally with basting stitches; mount the fabric in an embroidery hoop (or stretcher frame) (see Getting Started, page 18).

2 Use the size guide below to calculate the size of design that will result from using different fabric counts (see How to Use This Book, page 13). Refer to the cross-stitch chart and thread key, and stitch from the middle outward.

3 Remove the finished design from the hoop and press gently on the wrong side.

size guide

fabric count	number of threads/blocks	number of strands	size of design
14	1	2	4¼ x 7½ in. (10.75 x 19 cm)
16	1	2	3⅝ x 6⅝ in. (9.25 x 16.75 cm)
18	1	2	3¼ x 5¾ in. (8.25 x 14.5 cm)
28	2	2	4¼ x 7½ in. (10.75 x 19 cm)
28	3	3	6¼ x 11¼ in. (16 x 28.5 cm)

materials

- The design shown here uses evenweave fabric, 28-count cream linen, and tapestry needle, size 26.
- Stranded cottons, one skein of each colour listed in key. Use two strands for cross-stitch, half cross-stitch, and French knots and one strand for backstitch.

thread key

- blanc
- ecru
- 153 palest violet
- 165 pale lime
- 209 pale lavender
- 211 pale lilac
- 310 black
- 472 light avocado
- 733 pale olive
- 746 buttermilk
- 772 pale leaf green
- 3042 dull mauve
- 3345 hunter green
- 3347 mid moss green
- 3740 pale aubergine
- 3747 ice lilac
- 3837 dark lavender

half cross-stitch

- 3042 dull mauve

backstitch

- 3837 dark lavender

French knots

- 310 black

An anemone lends itself to being displayed as a pretty picture in a matching frame. This delicate flower could also be used to decorate pillowcases and other bedroom accessories.

floral alphabet

Many traditional samplers combine flowers and letters to create a collection of decorative motifs.

stitching the design

1 Overcast the edges of the fabric to prevent fraying. Mark the midpoint of the fabric both vertically and horizontally with basting stitches; mount the fabric in an embroidery hoop (or stretcher frame) (see Getting Started, page 18).

2 Use the size guide below to calculate the size of design that will result from using different fabric counts (see How to Use This Book, page 13). Refer to the cross-stitch chart and thread key, and stitch from the middle outward.

3 Remove the finished design from the hoop and press gently on the wrong side.

size guide

fabric count	number of threads/blocks	number of strands	size of design
14	1	2	9 x 7¼ in. (22.75 x 18.5 cm)
16	1	2	7⅞ x 6¼ in. (20 x 16 cm)
18	1	2	7 x 5⅝ in. (17.75 x 14.25 cm)
25	2	2	10 x 8 in. (25.5 x 20.25 cm)
28	2	2	9 x 7¼ in. (22.75 x 18.5 cm)

materials

- The design shown here uses evenweave fabric, 25-count antique white, and tapestry needle, size 26.

- Stranded cottons, one skein of each colour listed in key. Use two strands for cross-stitch, backstitch, and French knots.

thread key

- ☑ 340 deep lilac
- ⑥ 367 green
- ⊞ 601 cyclamen
- ⊙ 676 pale old gold
- ⊡ 677 cold cream
- ⊞ 782 mid mustard
- Ⓤ 783 pale caramel
- ◪ 917 deep raspberry
- ⊟ 988 mid grass green
- ⬆ 3348 pale moss green
- ◉ 3607 mid raspberry
- ⬒ 3608 pale raspberry
- ▽ 3609 ice raspberry
- Ⓢ 3689 pale berry pink
- ▽ 3746 purple
- Ⓒ 3747 ice lilac
- ✳ 3806 pale fuchsia

backstitch

- ◸ 367 green
- ◸ 601 cyclamen
- ◸ 782 mid mustard

French knots

- ◼ 310 black

◀ Backstitch is used here to work the letters of the alphabet in a flowing script. Mount your finished sampler in a frame and display it where guests can appreciate it.

(top)

honeysuckle

Twining stems of honeysuckle evoke a cottage garden and will enhance a country-style decor.

stitching the design

1 Overcast the edges of the fabric to prevent fraying. Mark the midpoint of the fabric both vertically and horizontally with basting stitches; mount the fabric in an embroidery hoop (or stretcher frame) (see Getting Started, page 18).

2 Use the size guide below to calculate the size of motif B that will result from using different fabric counts (see How to Use This Book, page 13). Refer to the cross-stitch chart and thread key, and stitch from the middle outward.

3 Remove the finished design from the hoop and press gently on the wrong side.

size guide

fabric count	number of threads/blocks	number of strands	size of design
14	1	2	4¾ x 7⅝ in. (12 x 19.25 cm)
16	1	2	4¼ x 6⅝ in. (10.75 x 16.75 cm)
18	1	2	3¾ x 5⅞ in. (9.5 x 15 cm)
25	2	2	5⅜ x 8½ in. (13.75 x 21.5 cm)
28	2	2	4¾ x 7⅝ in. (12 x 19.25 cm)

materials

■ The design shown here uses evenweave fabric, 25-count raw linen, and tapestry needle, size 26.

■ Stranded cottons, one skein of each colour listed in key. Use two strands for cross-stitch and one for backstitch.

thread key

⊟ 818 pale baby pink
▲ 3346 moss green
⊟ 3354 pale old pink
⊡ 3364 pale old green
◎ 3731 dark old pink
Ⓤ 3770 warm cream
◈ 3859 rose beige

backstitch

◥ 3346 moss green
◥ 3859 rose beige

◀ Two complementary motifs offer the opportunity to be inventive. Here, the finished project's folds of plain fabric are joined by a single button. Either honeysuckle motif could be used on its own to adorn a sachet or jewelry box.

(A)

(B)

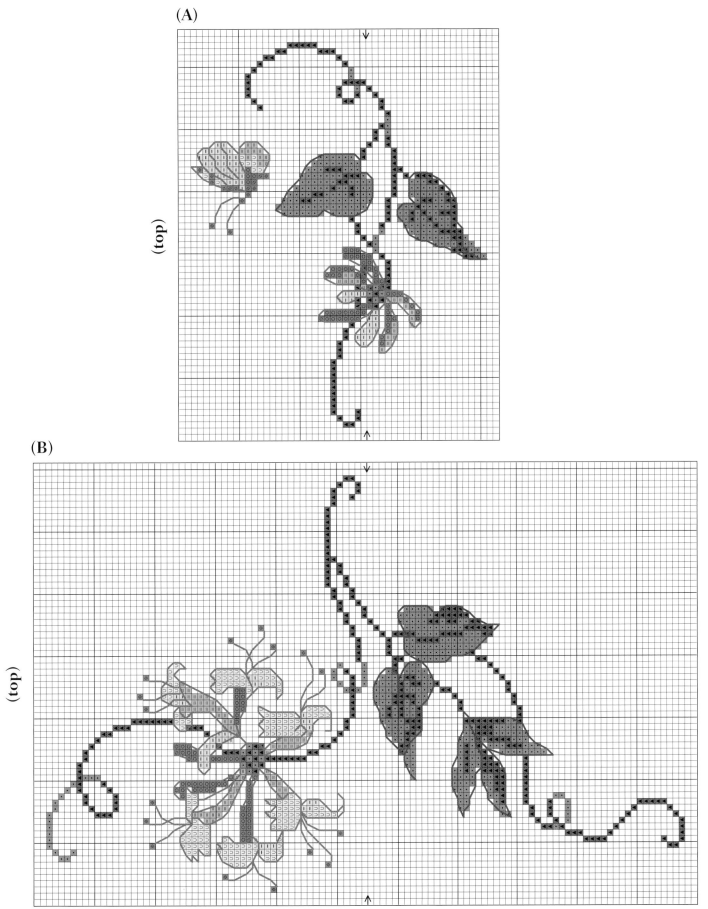

floral mix

Round-, star-, and bell-shaped flowers with slender stems are grouped together in a chic design.

stitching the design

1 Overcast the edges of the fabric to prevent fraying. Mark the midpoint of the fabric both vertically and horizontally with basting stitches; mount the fabric in an embroidery hoop (or stretcher frame) (see Getting Started, page 18).

2 Use the size guide below to calculate the size of design that will result from using different fabric counts (see How to Use This Book, page 13). Refer to the cross-stitch chart and thread key, and stitch from the middle outward.

3 Remove the finished design from the hoop and press gently on the wrong side.

size guide

fabric count	number of threads/blocks	number of strands	size of design
14	1	2	8⅞ x 6⅝ in. (22.5 x 16.75 cm)
16	1	2	7¾ x 5¾ in. (19.75 x 14.5 cm)
18	1	2	7 x 5⅛ in. (17.75 x 13 cm)
28	2	2	8⅞ x 6⅝ in. (22.5 x 16.75 cm)
28	3	3	13¼ x 9⅞ in. (33.75 x 25 cm)

materials

- The design shown here uses evenweave fabric, 28-count beige linen-look, and tapestry needle, size 26.

- Stranded cottons, one skein of each colour listed in key. Use two strands for cross-stitch and one for backstitch.

thread key

- ▼ 301 mahogany
- ⋂ 316 pale old mauve
- Ⓝ 320 poplar green
- ⦿ 349 rust
- ⊙ 351 deep coral
- ⓢ 352 salmon
- ◸ 368 mid green
- ▦ 413 dark pewter
- ⊤ 502 sea green
- ⓤ 742 pale sunshine yellow
- ④ 743 buttercup yellow
- ⊡ 744 primrose yellow
- ⊟ 818 pale baby pink
- ◁ 899 rich ice pink
- ☑ 976 toffee
- ☒ 3688 pink mauve
- → 3716 mid ice pink
- ◲ 3726 mid old mauve
- ↑ 3727 pale old rose
- ⊡ 3816 jade

backstitch

- ◺ 500 dark green

◀ This unusual combination of garden flowers is made up of a yellow daisy, a poppy, a rose, and a fritillary. Such a design would also work well repeated along the edge of a tablecloth.

(top)

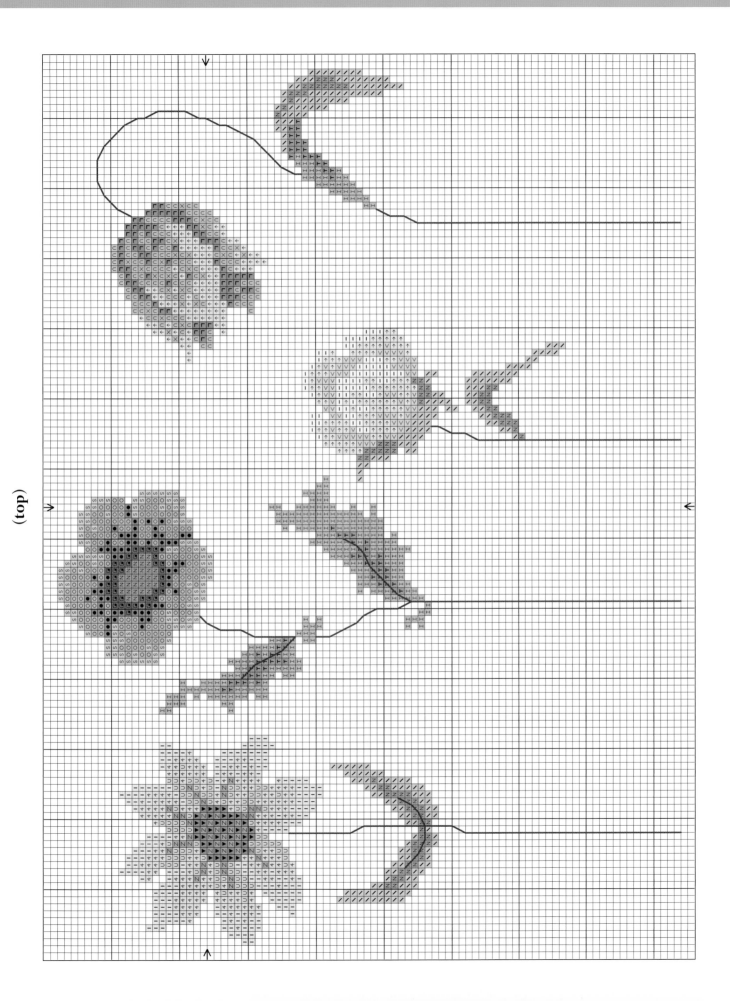

fuchsias

Worked in subtle shades of pink and cream, this popular garden flower makes a stylish motif.

stitching the design

1 Overcast the edges of the fabric to prevent fraying. Mark the midpoint of the fabric both vertically and horizontally with basting stitches; mount the fabric in an embroidery hoop (or stretcher frame) (see Getting Started, page 18).

2 Use the size guide below to calculate the size of motif A that will result from using different fabric counts (see How to Use This Book, page 13). Refer to the cross-stitch chart and thread key, and stitch from the middle outward.

3 Remove the finished design from the hoop and press gently on the wrong side.

size guide			
fabric count	number of threads/blocks	number of strands	size of design
14	1	2	4⅜ x 4⅞ in. (11 x 12.5 cm)
16	1	2	3⅞ x 4¼ in. (9.75 x 10.75 cm)
18	1	2	3⅜ x 3¾ in. (8.5 x 9.5 cm)
28	2	2	4⅜ x 4⅞ in. (11 x 12.5 cm)
28	3	3	6½ x 7¼ in. (16.5 x 18.5 cm)

materials

- The design shown here uses evenweave fabric, 28-count baby pink and white, and tapestry needle, size 26.

- Stranded cottons, one skein of each colour listed in key. Use two strands for cross-stitch and one for backstitch and straight stitch.

thread key

- ⊞ blanc
- ⊟ 165 pale lime
- Ⓢ 677 cold cream
- ◤ 704 pale lime green
- ⊡ 746 buttermilk
- ⊡ 819 ice pink
- ⊠ 963 cream pink
- ⊠ 3607 mid raspberry
- Ⓞ 3608 pale raspberry
- Ⓝ 3716 mid ice pink
- ◿ 3824 melon
- ◣ 3855 pale apricot

backstitch
- ◺ 316 pale old mauve
- ◺ 501 viridian green
- ◺ 915 cerise

straight stitch
- ◻ 963 cream pink

in detail

Once the flower is complete, work straight stitches over the top of the cross-stitch to add the stamens. Backstitch the tips to outline the pollen.

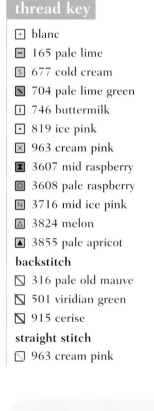

◀ This delicate design links different items of table linen—here, a place mat and napkin. To extend the theme, include a central motif on a tablecloth.

(A)

(B)

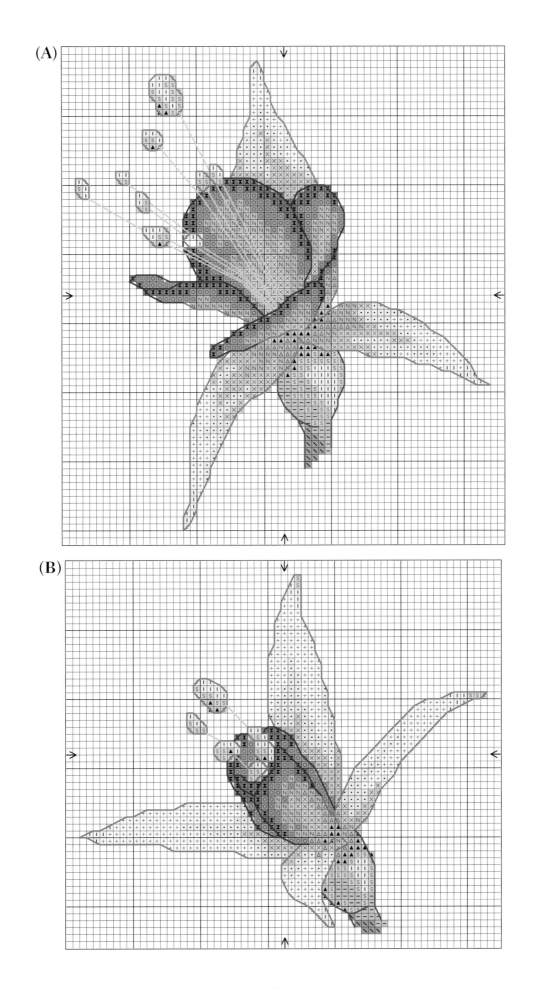

flower garden

Damask roses, tulips, and pinks are just some of the charming collection of motifs in this sampler.

stitching the design

1 Overcast the edges of the fabric to prevent fraying. Mark the midpoint of the fabric both vertically and horizontally with basting stitches; mount the fabric in an embroidery hoop (or stretcher frame) (see Getting Started, page 18).

2 Use the size guide below to calculate the size of design that will result from using different fabric counts (see How to Use This Book, page 13). Refer to the cross-stitch chart and thread key, and stitch from the middle outward.

3 Remove the finished design from the hoop and press gently on the wrong side.

size guide

fabric count	number of threads/blocks	number of strands	size of design
14	1	2	9⅝ x 7½ in. (24.5 x 19 cm)
16	1	2	8⅜ x 6⅝ in. (21.25 x 16.75 cm)
18	1	2	7½ x 5¾ in. (19 x 14.5 cm)
28	2	2	9⅝ x 7½ in. (24.5 x 19 cm)
28	3	3	14½ x 11¼ in. (36.75 x 28.5 cm)

materials

- The design shown here uses evenweave fabric, 28-count biscuit, and tapestry needle, size 26.

- Stranded cottons, one skein of each colour listed in key. Use two strands for cross-stitch and one for backstitch.

thread key

- ■ 209 pale lavender
- ▬ 327 dusty violet
- ◎ 352 salmon
- ▲ 353 peach
- ⊞ 355 dark terra cotta
- Ⓤ 356 mid terra cotta
- ▤ 469 dark avocado
- ⬆ 471 pale avocado
- ⊠ 728 bright gold
- ▽ 746 buttermilk
- Ⓢ 977 mid fudge
- ◲ 3855 pale apricot

backstitch

- ◳ 471 pale avocado
- ◳ 319 dark pistachio

◄ The colours used combine well to capture the vibrancy of flowers in full bloom. Samplers with a variety of motifs, such as this, are always a particular joy to stitch.

(top)

sunflower

An emblem of summer, the golden sunflower looks superb combined with warm colours, such as red.

stitching the design

1 Overcast the edges of the fabric to prevent fraying. Mark the midpoint of the fabric both vertically and horizontally with basting stitches; mount the fabric in an embroidery hoop (or stretcher frame) (see Getting Started, page 18).

2 Use the size guide below to calculate the size of motif A that will result from using different fabric counts (see How to Use This Book, page 13). Refer to the cross-stitch chart and thread key, and stitch from the middle outward.

3 Remove the finished design from the hoop and press gently on the wrong side.

size guide

fabric count	number of threads/blocks	number of strands	size of design
14	1	2	2⅞ in. (7.25 cm) square
16	1	2	2½ in. (6.25 cm) square
18	1	2	2¼ in. (5.75 cm) square
27	2	2	3 in. (7.5 cm) square
27	3	3	4½ in. (11.5 cm) square

materials

- The design shown here uses evenweave fabric, 27-count Christmas red, and tapestry needle, size 26.

- Stranded cottons, one skein of each colour listed in key. Use two strands for cross-stitch.

thread key

- ■ 728 bright gold
- ⊠ 743 buttercup yellow
- ⊟ 745 pale buttercup yellow

◀ The bold simplicity of this sunflower motif is ideal for decorating small accessories, such as a pincushion and needle case. The sunflower also works for items that will be folded in half, displaying a semicircle of petals on each side. Stylish tassels can be made to match the background fabric.

(A)

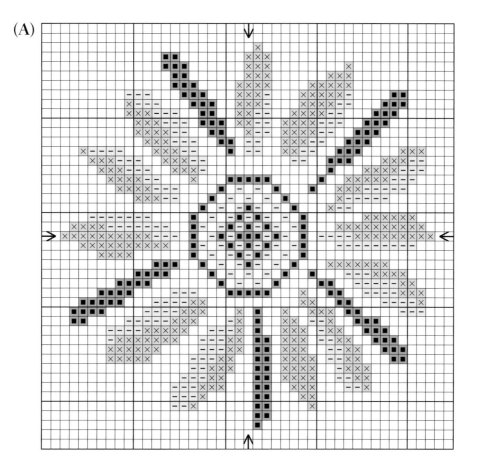

(B)

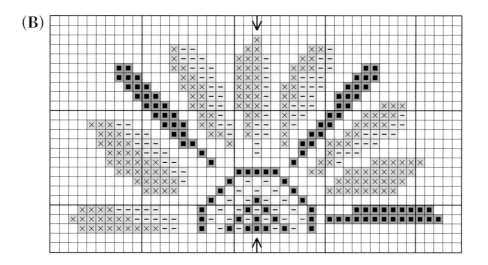

rose alphabet

A pretty pink-and-green sampler combines flowing letters with rosebuds for an old-fashioned look.

stitching the design

1 Overcast the edges of the fabric to prevent fraying. Mark the midpoint of the fabric both vertically and horizontally with basting stitches; mount the fabric in an embroidery hoop (or stretcher frame) (see Getting Started, page 18).

2 Use the size guide below to calculate the size of design that will result from using different fabric counts (see How to Use This Book, page 13). Refer to the cross-stitch chart and thread key, and stitch from the middle outward.

3 Remove the finished design from the hoop and press gently on the wrong side.

size guide

fabric count	number of threads/blocks	number of strands	size of design
14	1	2	10¾ x 11⅜ in. (27.25 x 29 cm)
16	1	2	9⅜ x 10 in. (23.75 x 25.5 cm)
18	1	2	8⅜ x 8⅞ in. (21.25 x 22.5 cm)
28	2	2	10¾ x 11⅜ in. (27.25 x 29 cm)
28	3	3	16⅛ x 17⅛ in. (41 x 43.5 cm)

materials

■ The design shown here uses evenweave fabric, 28-count antique white linen, and tapestry needle, size 26.

■ Stranded cottons, one skein of each colour listed in key. Use two strands for cross-stitch, backstitch, and French knots and one strand of 3687 for running stitch.

thread key

F 151 palest old pink
C 164 palest grass green
H 603 pink
I 605 pale pink
↑ 778 light old mauve
✓ 818 pale baby pink
■ 987 grass green
✗ 989 pale grass green
⊓ 3347 mid moss green
< 3348 pale moss green
▼ 3687 purple pink
S 3688 pink mauve
+ 3689 pale berry pink
Z 3731 dark old pink
U 3733 mid old pink
○ 3836 pale grape

backstitch and running stitch
◻ 987 grass green
◻ 989 pale grass green
◻ 3347 mid moss green
◻ 3687 purple pink

French knots
⊟ 605 pale pink
⊤ 3687 purple pink
N 3836 pale grape

◀ Inspired by the intricate floral designs of wallpaper produced in 18th-century Britain, this sampler is bordered by a combination of trellis and repeated rose motifs.

Repeat the left-hand panel as indicated by the finished design in the photograph.
Make sure you reorder the different rose sections accordingly.

passionflower

A central starburst of petals forms the focal point of this design featuring an exotic climbing plant.

stitching the design

1 Overcast the edges of the fabric to prevent fraying. Mark the midpoint of the fabric both vertically and horizontally with basting stitches; mount the fabric in an embroidery hoop (or stretcher frame) (see Getting Started, page 18).

2 Use the size guide below to calculate the size of design that will result from using different fabric counts (see How to Use This Book, page 13). Refer to the cross-stitch chart and thread key, and stitch from the middle outward.

3 Remove the finished design from the hoop and press gently on the wrong side.

size guide

fabric count	number of threads/blocks	number of strands	size of design
14	1	2	4⅛ x 7¾ in. (10.5 x 19.75 cm)
16	1	2	3⅝ x 6¾ in. (9.25 x 17.25 cm)
18	1	2	3¼ x 6 in. (8.25 x 15.25 cm)
27	2	2	4¼ x 8 in. (10.75 x 20.25 cm)
27	3	3	6⅜ x 12 in. (16.25 x 30.5 cm)

materials

- The design shown here uses evenweave fabric, 27-count white, and tapestry needle, size 26.

- Stranded cottons, one skein of each colour listed in key. Use four strands of 3348 for whipped straight stitch and two strands of 208 for lazy daisy stitch. Use two strands for cross-stitch and backstitch.

thread key

- ⬆ 208 lavender
- ▽ 211 pale lilac
- ▣ 500 dark green
- ▲ 581 moss green
- ☒ 745 pale buttercup yellow
- ⊡ 746 buttermilk
- ⊟ 772 pale leaf green
- ⊞ 987 grass green
- ◎ 3348 pale moss green
- ⊞ 3607 mid raspberry
- ⊟ 3826 golden brown

backstitch
- ◻ 208 lavender
- ◻ 581 moss green
- ◻ 987 grass green
- ◻ 3348 pale moss green

in detail

Make five whipped straight stitches radiating from the flower's middle; work a straight stitch across each end. Work two circles of lazy daisy stitches around the whipped stitches.

◄ Once framed, the passionflower can be displayed on a shelf or hung on a bedroom or sunroom wall.

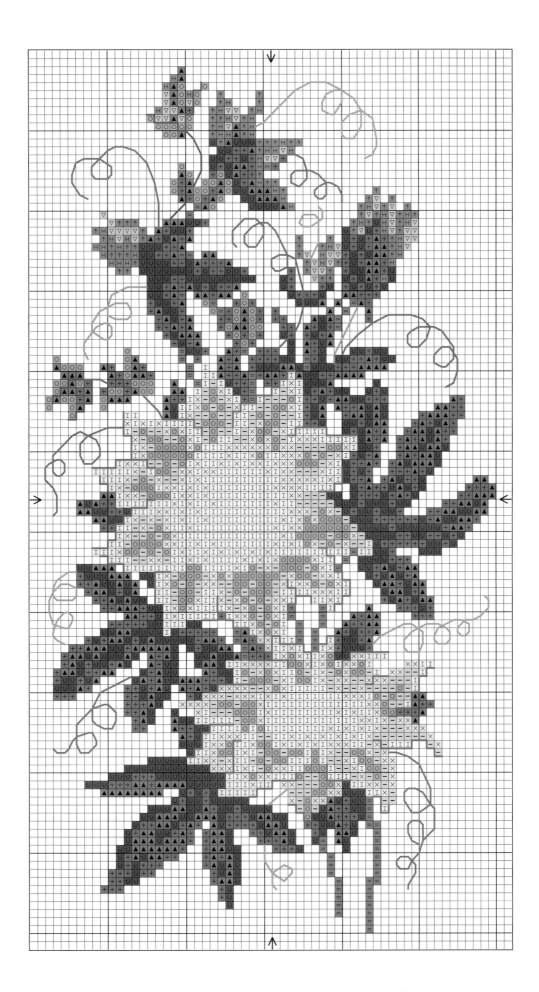

pink blossom

Asymmetrical design and trees in blossom are characteristic features of the Asian style.

stitching the design

1 Overcast the edges of the fabric to prevent fraying. Mark the midpoint of the fabric both vertically and horizontally with basting stitches; mount the fabric in an embroidery hoop (or stretcher frame) (see Getting Started, page 18).

2 Use the size guide below to calculate the size of design that will result from using different fabric counts (see How to Use This Book, page 13). Refer to the cross-stitch chart and thread key, and stitch from the middle outward.

3 Remove the finished design from the hoop and press gently on the wrong side.

size guide

fabric count	number of threads/blocks	number of strands	size of design
14	1	2	3⅜ x 4⅞ in. (8.5 x 12.5 cm)
16	1	2	3 x 4¼ in. (7.5 x 10.75 cm)
18	1	2	2⅝ x 3¾ in. (6.75 x 9.5 cm)
28	2	2	3⅜ x 4⅞ in. (8.5 x 12.5 cm)
28	3	3	5⅛ x 7¼ in. (13 x 18.5 cm)

materials

■ The design shown here uses evenweave fabric, 28-count antique white linen, and tapestry needle, size 26.

■ Stranded cottons, one skein of each colour listed in key. Use two strands for cross-stitch and one for backstitch and straight stitch. Stitch a seed bead in the middle of each flower.

thread key

- ☑ 327 dusty violet
- ☒ 601 cyclamen
- ◼ 718 raspberry
- ◉ 3608 pale raspberry

backstitch
- ◩ 166 mid lime

straight stitch
- ◧ 166 mid lime

seed beads
- ⊙ 3046 mid putty

◀ To enhance the Asian theme, the motif is repeated in a vertical line and bordered with fabric strips in toning shades of cerise and purple. For a minimalist effect, a single motif could be used on the central panel.

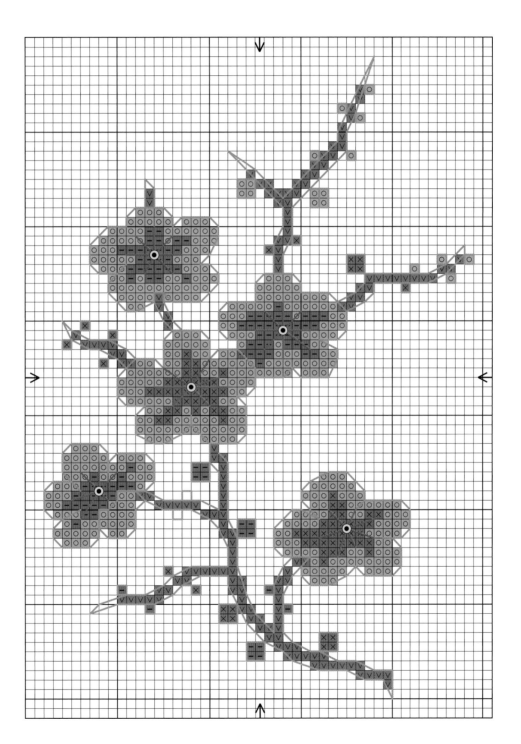

daffodils

A herald of spring, these trumpetlike golden yellow flowers show up well on fresh white fabric.

stitching the design

1 Overcast the edges of the fabric to prevent fraying. Mark the midpoint of the fabric both vertically and horizontally with basting stitches; mount the fabric in an embroidery hoop (or stretcher frame) (see Getting Started, page 18).

2 Use the size guide below to calculate the size of design that will result from using different fabric counts (see How to Use This Book, page 13). Refer to the cross-stitch chart and thread key, and stitch from the middle outward.

3 Remove the finished design from the hoop and press gently on the wrong side.

size guide

fabric count	number of threads/blocks	number of strands	size of design
14	1	2	8¼ x 5⅛ in. (21 x 13 cm)
16	1	2	7½ x 4½ in. (19 x 11.5 cm)
18	1	2	6⅝ x 4 in. (16.75 x 10.25 cm)
28	2	2	8¼ x 5⅛ in. (21 x 13 cm)
28	3	3	12¾ x 7⅝ in. (32.5 x 19.25 cm)

materials

- The design shown here uses evenweave fabric, 28-count white, and tapestry needle, size 26.

- Stranded cottons, one skein of each colour listed in key. Use two strands for cross-stitch and one for backstitch.

thread key

- ⊡ 703 lime green
- ◎ 726 daffodil yellow
- ⊠ 727 jonquil yellow
- ☑ 741 tangerine
- 🗍 742 pale sunshine yellow
- ⊟ 743 buttercup yellow
- 🇹 783 pale caramel
- ⊡ 3078 pale yellow
- ■ 3776 tan

backstitch

- ◺ 720 dark rust orange
- ◺ 783 pale caramel

in detail
The darker shades of yellow used for the daffodil trumpet bring it forward for a three-dimensional effect.

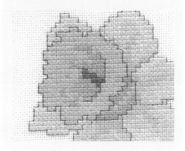

◀ Breakfast on a tray is even more welcome when presented on this cheerful tray cloth. The frilly edges of the flowers are emphasized by backstitching in dark rust orange and pale caramel threads. Each motif could also be worked individually.

(top)

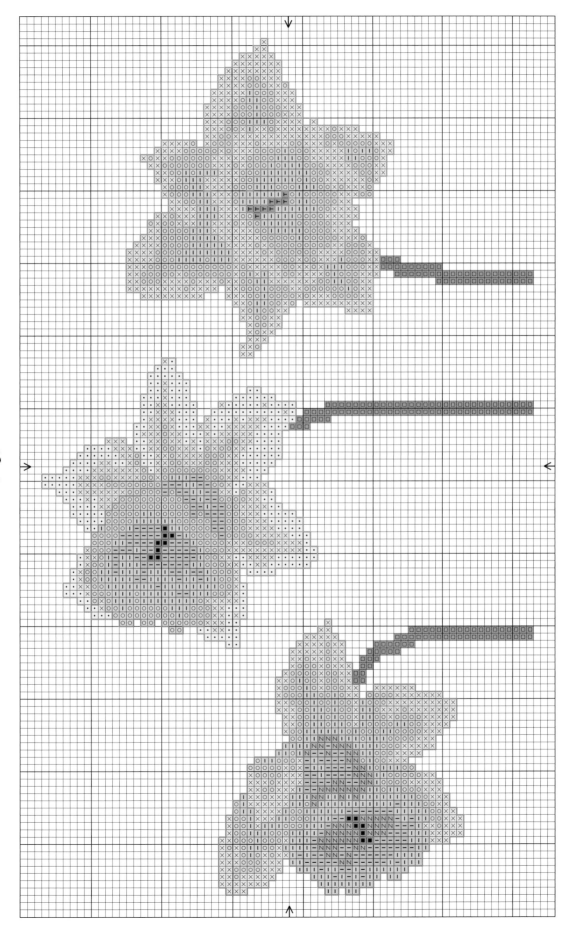

springtime

Try adorning samplers with buttons—here, flower-shaped ones add a fun element to the design.

stitching the design

1 Overcast the edges of the fabric to prevent fraying. Mark the midpoint of the fabric both vertically and horizontally with basting stitches; mount the fabric in an embroidery hoop (or stretcher frame) (see Getting Started, page 18).

2 Use the size guide below to calculate the size of design that will result from using different fabric counts (see How to Use This Book, page 13). Refer to the cross-stitch chart and thread key, and stitch from the middle outward.

3 Remove the finished design from the hoop and press gently on the wrong side.

size guide

fabric count	number of threads/blocks	number of strands	size of design
14	1	2	6¾ x 10⅜ in. (17.25 x 26.25 cm)
16	1	2	5⅞ x 9⅛ in. (15 x 23.25 cm)
18	1	2	5⅛ x 8⅛ in. (13 x 20.75 cm)
28	2	2	6¾ x 10⅜ in. (17.25 x 26.25 cm)
28	3	3	10⅛ x 15½ in. (25.75 x 39.25 cm)

materials

- The design shown here uses evenweave fabric, 28-count natural, and tapestry needle, size 26.

- Stranded cottons, one skein of each colour listed in key. Use two strands for cross-stitch and one for backstitch.

thread key

- → 166 mid lime
- ▲ 169 slate grey
- ✓ 301 mahogany
- ■ 310 black
- ▶ 333 deep lavender
- ⊞ 340 deep lilac
- U 349 rust
- ▤ 702 spring green
- ↑ 720 dark rust orange
- ▽ 726 daffodil yellow
- ▨ 728 bright gold
- ◀ 917 deep raspberry
- ◀ 922 gold copper
- ✳ 976 toffee
- ⌊ 3607 mid raspberry
- ⊤ 3609 ice raspberry
- ⊠ 3746 purple
- ● 3747 ice lilac
- ⊡ 3823 yellow cream
- ⊙ 3827 pale fudge
- ▣ 3837 dark lavender
- ◆ 3850 dark teal
- ⊞ 3852 dark gold

backstitch

- ◺ 300 dark mahogany
- ◺ 349 rust
- ◺ 3837 dark lavender
- ◺ 3850 dark teal

◀ This sampler is perfect for a nursery. It will give a child the pleasure of spotting all the letters of the alphabet, as well as animals and flowers in the countryside.

rambling rose

To give this delicate rose extra definition, the buds, flowers, and leaves are outlined in backstitch.

stitching the design

1 Overcast the edges of the fabric to prevent fraying. Mark the midpoint of the fabric both vertically and horizontally with basting stitches; mount the fabric in an embroidery hoop (or stretcher frame) (see Getting Started, page 18).

2 Use the size guide below to calculate the size of design that will result from using different fabric counts (see How to Use This Book, page 13). Refer to the cross-stitch chart and thread key, and stitch from the middle outward.

3 Remove the finished design from the hoop and press gently on the wrong side.

size guide

fabric count	number of threads/blocks	number of strands	size of design
14	1	2	10⅞ x 2⅞ in. (27.5 x 7.25 cm)
16	1	2	9½ x 2½ in. (24.25 x 6.25 cm)
18	1	2	8½ x 2¼ in. (21.5 x 5.75 cm)
28	2	2	10⅞ x 2⅞ in. (27.5 x 7.25 cm)
28	3	3	16¼ x 4¼ in. (41.25 x 10.75 cm)

materials

- The design shown here uses evenweave fabric, 14-count white Aida, and tapestry needle size 26.

- Stranded cottons, one skein of each colour listed in key. Use two strands for cross-stitch and three-quarter stitch and one for backstitch.

thread key

- · 746 buttermilk
- ☒ 772 pale leaf green
- ⊟ 818 pale baby pink
- ▲ 963 cream pink
- ◉ 988 mid grass green
- Ⓤ 3326 deep ice pink
- ▤ 3348 pale moss green
- ↑ 3821 pale gold
- ▽ 3823 yellow cream

backstitch
- ◺ 988 mid grass green
- ◹ 3326 deep ice pink

◀ Think of novel ways to use your cross-stitched pieces. These motifs can be wrapped around a notepad block, and you could use one or two roses to make a matching pen or pencil case.

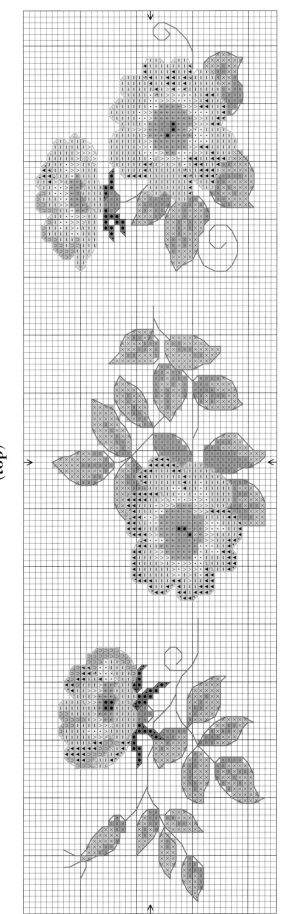

(top)

tulip

Botanical sketches of flowering plants are the inspiration for a tulip shown growing from its bulb.

stitching the design

1 Overcast the edges of the fabric to prevent fraying. Mark the midpoint of the fabric both vertically and horizontally with basting stitches; mount the fabric in an embroidery hoop (or stretcher frame) (see Getting Started, page 18).

2 Use the size guide below to calculate the size of design that will result from using different fabric counts (see How to Use This Book, page 13). Refer to the cross-stitch chart and thread key, and stitch from the middle outward.

3 Remove the finished design from the hoop and press gently on the wrong side.

	size guide		
fabric count	number of threads/blocks	number of strands	size of design
14	1	2	4½ x 10⅞ in. (11.5 x 27.5 cm)
16	1	2	3⅞ x 9½ in. (9.75 x 24.25 cm)
18	1	2	3½ x 8½ in. (9 x 21.5 cm)
26	2	2	4⅞ x 11¾ in. (12.5 x 30 cm)
28	2	2	4½ x 10⅞ in. (11.5 x 27.5 cm)

materials

- The design shown here uses evenweave fabric, 26-count ivory linen, and tapestry needle, size 26.

- Stranded cottons, one skein of each colour listed in key. Use two strands for cross-stitch and one for backstitch.

thread key

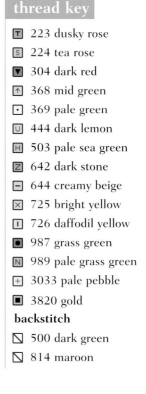

- T 223 dusky rose
- S 224 tea rose
- ▼ 304 dark red
- ↑ 368 mid green
- · 369 pale green
- U 444 dark lemon
- H 503 pale sea green
- Z 642 dark stone
- − 644 creamy beige
- X 725 bright yellow
- I 726 daffodil yellow
- ● 987 grass green
- N 989 pale grass green
- + 3033 pale pebble
- ■ 3820 gold

backstitch

- ◹ 500 dark green
- ◹ 814 maroon

◀ In 17th-century Holland, artists painted tulips in naturalistic still-life compositions. To give this design a look reminiscent of such still lifes, choose a dark blue or black fabric background instead.

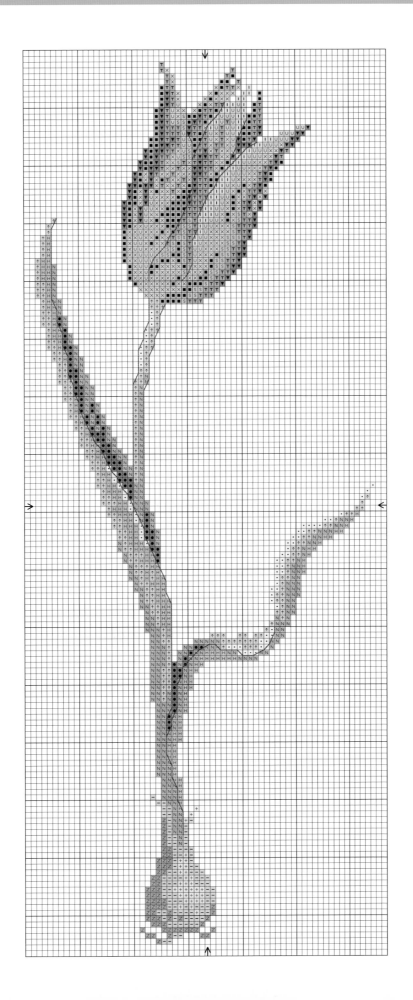

nasturtium

The bright orange flower of this annual plant forms a motif that is sure to suit many accessories.

stitching the design

1 Overcast the edges of the fabric to prevent fraying. Mark the midpoint of the fabric both vertically and horizontally with basting stitches; mount the fabric in an embroidery hoop (or stretcher frame) (see Getting Started, page 18).

2 Use the size guide below to calculate the size of design that will result from using different fabric counts (see How to Use This Book, page 13). Refer to the cross-stitch chart and thread key, and stitch from the middle outward.

3 Remove the finished design from the hoop and press gently on the wrong side.

size guide

fabric count	number of threads/blocks	number of strands	size of design
14	1	2	2 x 5 in. (5 x 12.75 cm)
16	1	2	1¾ x 4⅜ in. (4.5 x 11 cm)
18	1	2	1½ x 3¾ in. (4 x 9.5 cm)
28	2	2	2 x 5 in. (5 x 12.75 cm)
28	3	3	3 x 7½ in. (7.5 x 19 cm)

materials

- The design shown here uses evenweave fabric, 14-count white Aida, and tapestry needle, size 24.

- Stranded cottons, one skein of each colour listed in key. Use two strands for cross-stitch and French knots and one strand for backstitch.

thread key

- N 721 rusty orange
- X 722 tango
- − 728 bright gold
- ◉ 900 burnt orange
- ▲ 988 mid grass green
- ⊞ 3348 pale moss green
- U 3855 pale apricot

backstitch
- ⬚ 900 burnt orange

French knots
- S 721 rusty orange

in detail

A circle of French knots worked in 721 looks like the stamens in the middle of a real nasturtium.

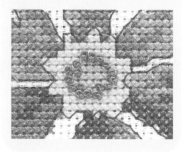

◄ A flower on a single upright stem is ideal for a bookmark—for a decorative finish fray the lower edge. To vary the design, look at nasturtium seed packets for inspiration. Different varieties include those with yellow, cream, and apricot flowers.

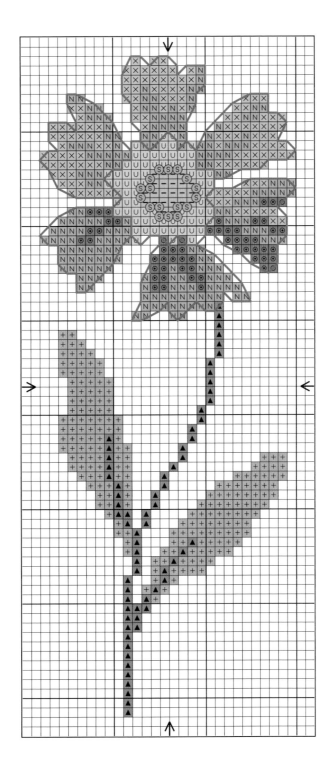

wildflowers

A design of daisies, clover, and buttercups is worked in pretty shades of sugar pink and yellow.

stitching the design

1 Overcast the edges of the fabric to prevent fraying. Mark the midpoint of the fabric both vertically and horizontally with basting stitches; mount the fabric in an embroidery hoop (or stretcher frame) (see Getting Started, page 18).

2 Use the size guide below to calculate the size of design that will result from using different fabric counts (see How to Use This Book, page 13). Refer to the cross-stitch chart and thread key, and stitch from the middle outward.

3 Remove the finished design from the hoop and press gently on the wrong side.

size guide			
fabric count	number of threads/blocks	number of strands	size of design
14	1	2	12⅝ x 4⅝ in. (32 x 11.75 cm)
16	1	2	11 x 4 in. (28 x 10.25 cm)
18	1	2	9¾ x 3½ in. (24.75 x 9 cm)
28	2	2	12⅝ x 4⅝ in. (32 x 11.75 cm)
28	3	3	18⅞ x 6⅞ in. (48 x 17.5 cm)

materials

- The design shown here uses evenweave fabric, 28-count antique white Quaker cloth, and tapestry needle, size 26.

- Stranded cottons, one skein of each colour listed in key. Use two strands for cross-stitch and one for backstitch.

thread key

- △ blanc
- ☒ 725 bright yellow
- ◉ 727 jonquil yellow
- ▽ 772 pale leaf green
- Ⓤ 3348 pale moss green
- ↑ 3708 pale strawberry
- Ⓗ 3712 mid salmon

backstitch

- ◹ 601 cyclamen
- ◹ 937 forest green

◀ The middle of this tablecloth is made by repeating the design to form a square. To complement the theme, stitch single flower motifs onto white, pink, or yellow napkins.

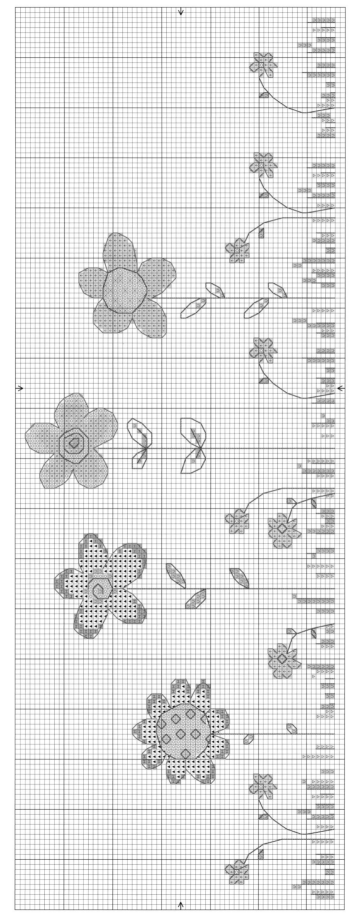

(top)

thistle

Clusters of blue squares at the corners give this design the look of a decorative tile.

stitching the design

1 Overcast the edges of the fabric to prevent fraying. Mark the midpoint of the fabric both vertically and horizontally with basting stitches; mount the fabric in an embroidery hoop (or stretcher frame) (see Getting Started, page 18).

2 Use the size guide below to calculate the size of design that will result from using different fabric counts (see How to Use This Book, page 13). Refer to the cross-stitch chart and thread key, and stitch from the middle outward.

3 Remove the finished design from the hoop and press gently on the wrong side.

materials

- The design shown here uses evenweave fabric, 14-count white Aida, and tapestry needle, size 26.

- Stranded cottons, one skein of each colour listed in key. Use two strands for cross-stitch and one for backstitch.

size guide			
fabric count	number of threads/blocks	number of strands	size of design
14	1	2	6 in. (15.25 cm) square
16	1	2	5¼ in. (13.25 cm) square
18	1	2	4¾ in. (12 cm) square
28	2	2	6 in. (15.25 cm) square
28	3	3	9 in. (22.75 cm) square

thread key

- ☒ 156 lavender blue
- ◨ 333 deep lavender
- ■ 791 purple blue
- ⊞ 993 pale green aqua
- ⊟ 3765 dark peacock
- ▲ 3808 deep green aqua
- ⊡ 3810 dark aqua
- ◎ 3849 teal

backstitch
- ◹ 791 purple blue
- ◺ 3808 deep green aqua

◄ Fabric strips sewn together make a geometric border, creating a wide frame for this bold image. The design could be repeated several times with the fabric border to form a patchwork.

summer trio

A poppy, a cornflower, and a yellow daisy, with buzzing insects, evoke a meadow on a sunny day.

stitching the design

1 Overcast the edges of the fabric to prevent fraying. Mark the midpoint of the fabric both vertically and horizontally with basting stitches; mount the fabric in an embroidery hoop (or stretcher frame) (see Getting Started, page 18).

2 Use the size guide below to calculate the size of design that will result from using different fabric counts (see How to Use This Book, page 13). Refer to the cross-stitch chart and thread key, and stitch from the middle outward.

3 Remove the finished design from the hoop and press gently on the wrong side.

size guide

fabric count	number of threads/blocks	number of strands	size of design
14	1	2	2¾ in. (7 cm) square
16	1	2	2⅜ in. (6 cm) square
18	1	2	2⅛ in. (5.5 cm) square
28	2	2	2¾ in. (7 cm) square
28	3	3	4⅛ in. (10.5 cm) square

materials

■ The design shown here uses evenweave fabric, 14-count white Aida, and tapestry needle, size 26.

■ Stranded cottons, one skein of each colour listed in key. Use two strands for cross-stitch and one for backstitch.

thread key

■ 349 rust
☒ 741 tangerine
⊟ 743 buttercup yellow
▨ 798 bright cornflower blue
▣ 906 apple green
backstitch
◹ 986 dark grass green

◀ The appeal of this design lies in its simplicity. Suited to a modern country interior, the design works well for coasters and could be stitched onto table linens as well.

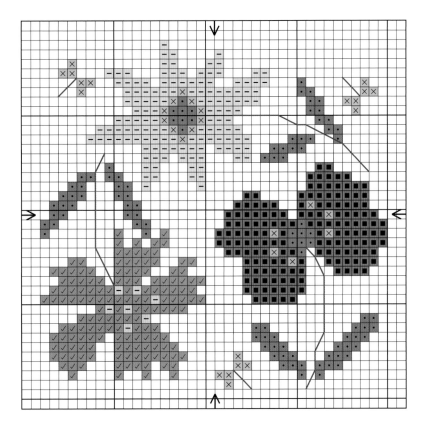

rose pattern

In full bloom, and with petals furled, roses repeat in vertical strips divided by striped and trellis borders.

stitching the design

1 Overcast the edges of the fabric to prevent fraying. Mark the midpoint of the fabric both vertically and horizontally with basting stitches; mount the fabric in an embroidery hoop (or stretcher frame) (see Getting Started, page 18).

2 Use the size guide below to calculate the size of design that will result from using different fabric counts (see How to Use This Book, page 13). Refer to the cross-stitch chart and thread key, and stitch from the middle outward.

3 Remove the finished design from the hoop and press gently on the wrong side.

size guide

fabric count	number of threads/blocks	number of strands	size of design
14	1	2	6⅝ x 3¼ in. (16.75 x 8.25 cm)
16	1	2	5¾ x 2⅞ in. (14.5 x 7.25 cm)
18	1	2	5⅛ x 2½ in. (13 x 6.25 cm)
28	2	2	6⅝ x 3¼ in. (16.75 x 8.25 cm)
28	3	3	9⅞ x 4¾ in. (25 x 12 cm)

materials

- The design shown here uses evenweave fabric, 14-count pale blue Aida, and tapestry needle, size 26.

- Stranded cottons, one skein of each colour listed in key. Use two strands for cross-stitch and one for backstitch.

thread key

- ⊟ 334 azure aqua
- ⊠ 666 flame red
- ▣ 3705 deep candy
- ⊠ 3708 pale strawberry
- ◉ 3755 azure blue
- ⊞ 3841 powder blue

backstitch
- ◣ 304 dark red
- ◣ 312 light navy blue
- ◣ 334 azure aqua
- ◣ 666 flame red

◀ The finished design has a vintage 1950s look, thanks to the red-and-white checked and polka-dot fabric borders. Yellow and pink is another combination worth exploring.

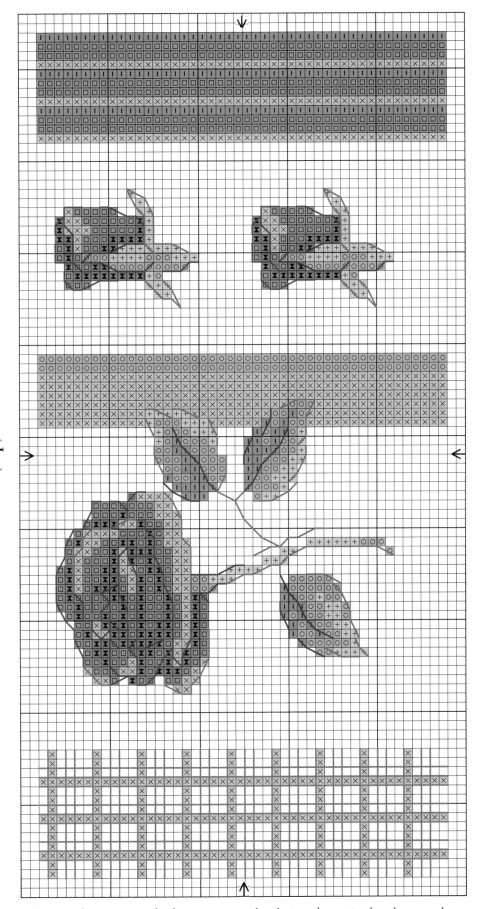

(top)

Repeat the cross-stitch chart to create the design shown in the photograph.

chapter four:

nature's bounty

vegetables

With their many and varied shapes, vegetables have long fascinated painters and embroiderers alike.

stitching the design

1 Overcast the edges of the fabric to prevent fraying. Mark the midpoint of the fabric both vertically and horizontally with basting stitches; mount the fabric in an embroidery hoop (or stretcher frame) (see Getting Started, page 18).

2 Use the size guide below to calculate the size of design that will result from using different fabric counts (see How to Use This Book, page 13). Refer to the cross-stitch chart and thread key, and stitch from the middle outward.

3 Remove the finished design from the hoop and press gently on the wrong side.

size guide

fabric count	number of threads/blocks	number of strands	size of design
14	1	2	6⅜ in. (16.25 cm) square
16	1	2	5⅝ in. (14.25 cm) square
18	1	2	5 in. (12.75 cm) square
25	2	2	7¼ in. (18.5 cm) square
28	2	2	6⅜ in. (16.25 cm) square

materials

- The design shown here uses evenweave fabric, 25-count raw linen, and tapestry needle, size 26.

- Stranded cottons, one skein of each colour listed in key. Use two strands for cross-stitch, three-quarter stitch, and running stitch; one strand for backstitch.

thread key

- ⊠ ecru
- ⊡ 164 palest grass green
- ▥ 407 maple sugar
- ⊟ 471 pale avocado
- ◎ 761 pale dusty rose
- ▲ 772 pale leaf green
- ⊞ 819 ice pink
- ▣ 895 dark hunter green
- ▤ 919 dark copper
- ▨ 921 brick orange
- ▽ 922 gold copper
- S 945 pink beige
- ✳ 951 pink cream
- ⌊ 976 toffee
- ⊤ 977 mid fudge
- ◥ 987 grass green
- ◁ 989 pale grass green
- ▮ 3350 deep old pink
- ◆ 3688 pink mauve
- ◉ 3827 pale fudge
- ◈ 3834 dark grape
- ⬆ 3835 grape
- N 3836 pale grape

backstitch
- ◥ 610 deep khaki

running stitch
- ◥ 987 grass green

◀ A patchwork design of popular vegetables looks attractive in the kitchen. The motifs can also be used individually to decorate kitchen towels, oven mitts, and aprons.

leaves

Stitch one or all of these horse chestnut leaves, which turn from green to gold, copper, and russet.

stitching the design

1 Overcast the edges of the fabric to prevent fraying. Mark the midpoint of the fabric both vertically and horizontally with basting stitches; mount the fabric in an embroidery hoop (or stretcher frame) (see Getting Started, page 18).

2 Use the size guide below to calculate the size of design that will result from using different fabric counts (see How to Use This Book, page 13). Refer to the cross-stitch chart and thread key, and stitch from the middle outward.

3 Remove the finished design from the hoop and press gently on the wrong side.

size guide

fabric count	number of threads/blocks	number of strands	size of design
14	1	2	10⅜ x 2⅛ in. (26.25 x 5.5 cm)
16	1	2	9⅛ x 1⅞ in. (23.25 x 4.75 cm)
18	1	2	8 x 1⅝ in. (20.25 x 4.25 cm)
28	2	2	10⅜ x 2⅛ in. (26.25 x 5.5 cm)
28	3	3	15½ x 3¼ in. (39.25 x 8.25 cm)

materials

- The design shown here uses evenweave fabric, 14-count white Aida, and tapestry needle, size 26.

- Stranded cottons, one skein of each colour listed in key. Use two strands for cross-stitch and one for backstitch.

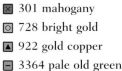

thread key

- ☒ 301 mahogany
- ◉ 728 bright gold
- ▲ 922 gold copper
- ▬ 3364 pale old green
- **backstitch**
- ◣ 300 dark mahogany

◄ These nature-inspired motifs complement outdoor living and add a decorative touch to a table in a garden or conservatory. The leaves can also be repeated to form a border.

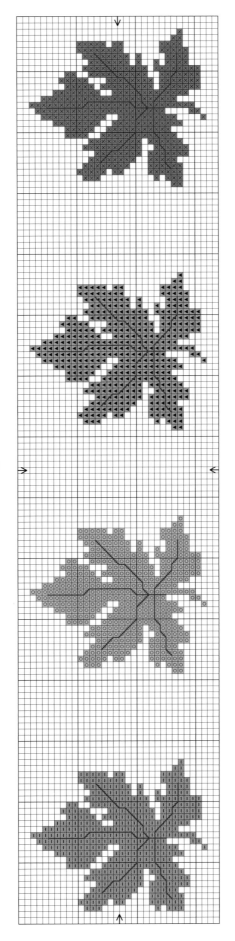

(top)

fruit garland

A ring of apples intertwined with blackberries
is reminiscent of late summer days.

stitching the design

1 Overcast the edges of the fabric to prevent fraying. Mark the midpoint of the
fabric both vertically and horizontally with basting stitches; mount the fabric
in an embroidery hoop (or stretcher frame) (see Getting Started, page 18).

2 Use the size guide below to calculate the size of design that will result from
using different fabric counts (see How to Use This Book, page 13). Refer to
the cross-stitch chart and thread key, and stitch from the middle outward.

3 Remove the finished design from the hoop and press gently on the wrong side.

size guide

fabric count	number of threads/blocks	number of strands	size of design
14	1	2	4¾ x 4⅞ in. (12 x 12.5 cm)
16	1	2	4⅛ x 4¼ in. (10.5 x 10.75 cm)
18	1	2	3⅝ x 3¾ in. (9.25 x 9.5 cm)
25	2	2	5¼ x 5½ in. (13.25 x 14 cm)
28	2	2	4¾ x 4⅞ in. (12 x 12.5 cm)

materials

- The design shown here uses
evenweave fabric, 25-count
white linen, and tapestry needle,
size 26.

- Stranded cottons, one skein of
each colour listed in key. Use
two strands for cross-stitch,
three-quarter stitch, and 839
backstitch. Use one strand for
890 backstitch.

thread key

- 320 poplar green
- 336 dark navy blue
- 368 mid green
- 471 pale avocado
- 472 light avocado
- 550 dark violet
- 772 pale leaf green
- 839 dark coffee
- 939 very dark blue
- 988 mid grass green

backstitch

- 839 dark coffee
- 890 bottle green

◀ Stitched onto a tablecloth,
this fruit garland makes a good
decoration for a summer picnic.
The circular design could also
be stitched onto round or square
seat pads, which would enhance
wicker or white-painted metal
chairs in a sunroom.

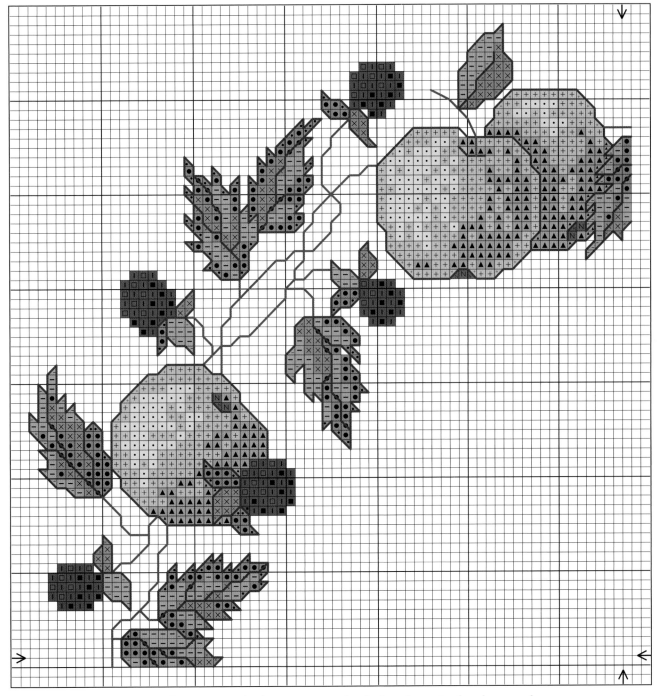

Repeat the cross-stitch chart to create the design shown in the photograph.

harvest corn

Ears of corn, framed by leafy stalks, complement a pared-down country-style interior.

stitching the design

1 Overcast the edges of the fabric to prevent fraying. Mark the midpoint of the fabric both vertically and horizontally with basting stitches; mount the fabric in an embroidery hoop (or stretcher frame) (see Getting Started, page 18).

2 Use the size guide below to calculate the size of design that will result from using different fabric counts (see How to Use This Book, page 13). Refer to the cross-stitch chart and thread key, and stitch from the middle outward.

3 Remove the finished design from the hoop and press gently on the wrong side.

size guide

fabric count	number of threads/blocks	number of strands	size of design
11	1	3	10 in. (25.5 cm) square
14	1	2	7⅞ in. (20 cm) square
16	1	2	6⅞ in. (17.5 cm) square
18	1	2	6⅛ in. (15.5 cm) square
28	2	2	7⅞ in. (20 cm) square

materials

- The design shown here uses evenweave fabric, 11-count cream Aida, and tapestry needle, size 26.

- Stranded cottons, one skein of each colour listed in key. Use three strands for cross-stitch and one for backstitch.

thread key

⊠ 676 pale old gold

backstitch

◻ 729 ochre

◀ Worked in shades of old gold and ochre, the corn motifs allow parts of the cream fabric to show through to create highlights. An ochre cord makes an excellent frame for the design.

bonsai trees

A perfect tree in miniature, the bonsai is a natural subject for the precision of cross-stitch.

stitching the design

1 Overcast the edges of the fabric to prevent fraying. Mark the midpoint of the fabric both vertically and horizontally with basting stitches; mount the fabric in an embroidery hoop (or stretcher frame) (see Getting Started, page 18).

2 Use the size guide below to calculate the size of motif B that will result from using different fabric counts (see How to Use This Book, page 13). Refer to the cross-stitch chart and thread key, and stitch from the middle outward.

3 Remove the finished design from the hoop and press gently on the wrong side.

size guide

fabric count	number of threads/blocks	number of strands	size of design
14	1	2	2¾ x 3⅝ in. (7 x 9.25 cm)
16	1	2	2⅜ x 3⅛ in. (6 x 8 cm)
18	1	2	2⅛ x 2¾ in. (5.5 x 7 cm)
28	2	2	2¾ x 3⅝ in. (7 x 9.25 cm)
28	3	3	4⅛ x 5⅜ in. (10.5 x 13.75 cm)

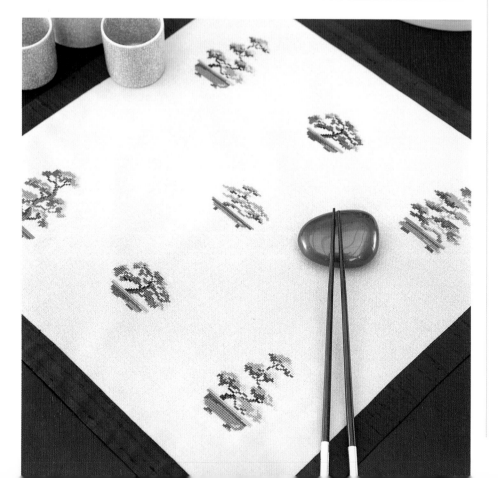

materials

- The design shown here uses evenweave fabric, 28-count dove grey, and tapestry needle, size 26.

- Stranded cottons, one skein of each colour listed in key. Use two strands for cross-stitch.

thread key

- ▣ 772 pale leaf green
- ☑ 869 hazel brown
- ⊞ 895 dark hunter green
- ☒ 898 chocolate
- ⬆ 937 forest green
- ⊠ 3347 mid moss green
- ⊡ 3348 pale moss green
- ⬛ 3371 dark chocolate
- Ⓤ 3685 dark mauve
- ▤ 3687 purple pink
- ⊙ 3688 pink mauve
- ✳ 3766 pale peacock
- Ⓛ 3808 deep green aqua
- Ⓣ 3810 dark aqua
- ◁ 3828 mid hazel

◀ To enhance a dinner table with a Japanese theme, stitch these bonsai trees onto a square piece of fabric to create a beautiful place mat. Arrange the motifs as you like and finish the edges of the fabric—perhaps by adding a fabric border.

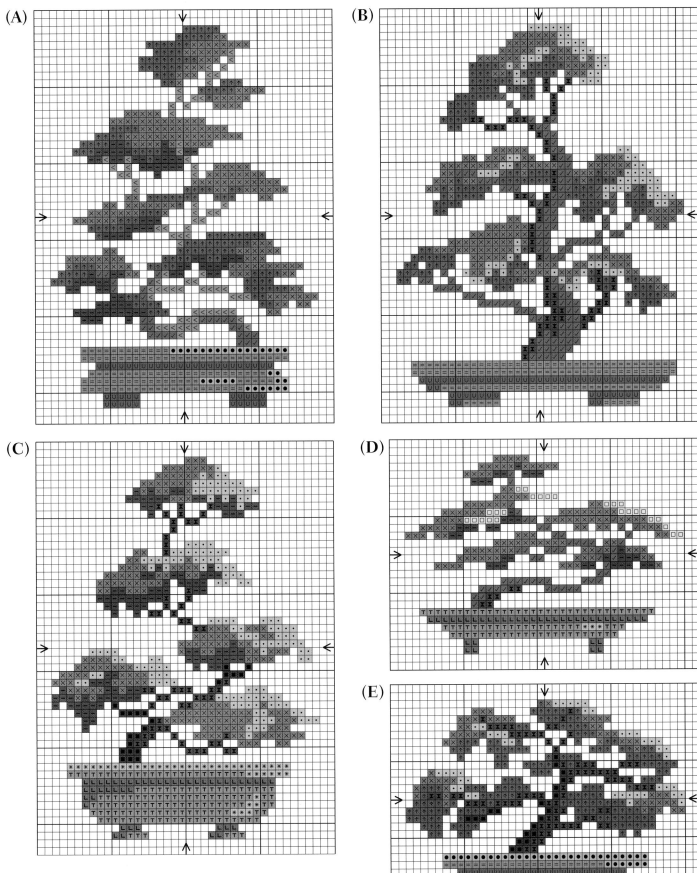

cherries

Both the bright red fruit and its fine green stalk stand out, thanks to the clarity of the design.

stitching the design

1 Overcast the edges of the fabric to prevent fraying. Mark the midpoint of the fabric both vertically and horizontally with basting stitches; mount the fabric in an embroidery hoop (or stretcher frame) (see Getting Started, page 18).

2 Use the size guide below to calculate the size of design that will result from using different fabric counts (see How to Use This Book, page 13). Refer to the cross-stitch chart and thread key, and stitch from the middle outward.

3 Remove the finished design from the hoop and press gently on the wrong side.

size guide

fabric count	number of threads/blocks	number of strands	size of design
14	1	2	3¾ x 2⅜ in. (9.5 x 6 cm)
16	1	2	3¼ x 2⅛ in. (8.25 x 5.5 cm)
18	1	2	3 x 1⅞ in. (7.5 x 4.75 cm)
28	2	2	3¾ x 2⅜ in. (9.5 x 6 cm)
28	3	3	5⅝ x 3½ in. (14.25 x 9 cm)

materials

- The design shown here uses evenweave fabric, 28-count white Quaker cloth, and tapestry needle, size 26.

- Stranded cottons, one skein of each colour listed in key. Use two strands for cross-stitch, half cross-stitch, and French knots. For whipped backstitch, use one strand for backstitch and two strands for completing the whipped stitches.

thread key

- ⊙ 347 berry red
- ⊠ 816 claret red
- ⊟ 3328 dark salmon
- ◉ 3685 dark mauve

half cross-stitch
- ⊘ 832 deep lime gold

whipped backstitch
- ⊠ 832 deep lime gold

French knots
- ▽ 819 ice pink

◁ Highlighting the cherries with a few pale-pink French knots suggests a shine. The three-dimensional effect is also enhanced by shading the cherries from dark salmon to claret red.

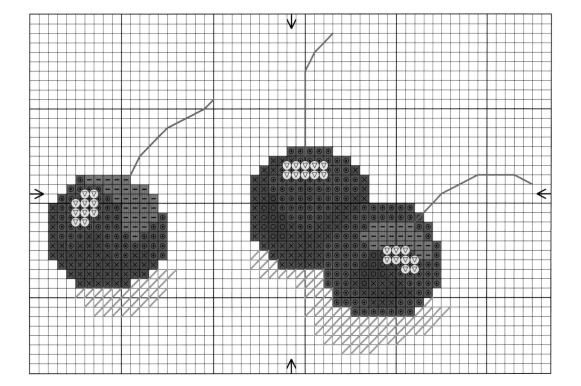

acorns

An oak leaf and acorns in golden brown make ideal embellishments when stitched onto squares of Aida.

stitching the design

1 Overcast the edges of the fabric to prevent fraying. Mark the midpoint of the fabric both vertically and horizontally with basting stitches; mount the fabric in an embroidery hoop (or stretcher frame) (see Getting Started, page 18).

2 Use the size guide below to calculate the size of motif C that will result from using different fabric counts (see How to Use This Book, page 13). Refer to the cross-stitch chart and thread key, and stitch from the middle outward.

3 Remove the finished design from the hoop and press gently on the wrong side.

size guide

fabric count	number of threads/blocks	number of strands	size of design
14	1	2	1⅜ in. (3.5 cm) square
16	1	2	1⅛ in. (2.75 cm) square
18	1	2	1 in. (2.5 cm) square
28	2	2	1⅜ in. (3.5 cm) square
28	3	3	2 in. (5 cm) square

materials

- The design shown here uses evenweave fabric, 18-count oatmeal Aida, and tapestry needle, size 26.

- Stranded cottons, one skein of each colour listed in key. Use two strands for cross-stitch and one for backstitch.

thread key

- ▲ 676 pale old gold
- ⊠ 680 mid old gold
- ⊞ 801 dark brown
- ⊙ 869 hazel brown
- **backstitch**
- ◩ 801 dark brown

◀ To decorate desk accessories, simply glue the square pieces of fabric in place. Here, the motifs add individuality to a leather notebook. They would look equally good on a plain diary, wallet, or portfolio.

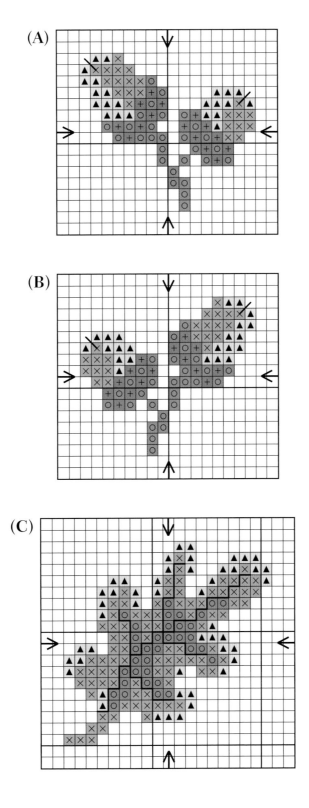

vegetable plot

This charming sampler features motifs that illustrate a well-tended herb and vegetable garden.

stitching the design

1 Overcast the edges of the fabric to prevent fraying. Mark the midpoint of the fabric both vertically and horizontally with basting stitches; mount the fabric in an embroidery hoop (or stretcher frame) (see Getting Started, page 18).

2 Use the size guide below to calculate the size of design that will result from using different fabric counts (see How to Use This Book, page 13). Refer to the cross-stitch chart and thread key, and stitch from the middle outward.

3 Remove the finished design from the hoop and press gently on the wrong side.

size guide

fabric count	number of threads/blocks	number of strands	size of design
14	1	2	7¾ x 11⅜ in. (19.75 x 29 cm)
16	1	2	6¾ x 9⅞ in. (17.25 x 25 cm)
18	1	2	6 x 8⅞ in. (15.25 x 22.5 cm)
25	2	2	8¾ x 12¾ in. (22.25 x 32.5)
28	2	2	7¾ x 11⅜ in. (19.75 x 29 cm)

materials

- The design shown here uses evenweave fabric, 25-count white, and tapestry needle, size 26.

- Stranded cottons, one skein of each colour listed in key. Use two strands for cross-stitch, backstitch, straight stitch, French knots, and lazy daisy stitch.

- Assorted doll's house garden tools and all-purpose adhesive.

thread key

- Ⓤ 209 pale lavender
- ✳ 356 mid terra cotta
- ■ 505 dusty green
- ↑ 554 pale violet
- ⊟ 704 pale lime green
- ▲ 722 tango
- ⊠ 739 dark cream
- ⊞ 741 tangerine
- ⊠ 954 mid spearmint
- ▽ 3045 yellow beige
- ⊟ 3609 ice raspberry
- Ⓞ 3819 lime moss green

backstitch and straight stitch

- ◻ 209 pale lavender
- ◻ 356 mid terra cotta
- ◻ 505 dusty green
- ◻ 554 pale violet
- ◻ 704 pale lime green
- ◻ 779 dark mink
- ◻ 954 mid spearmint
- ◻ 3045 yellow beige
- ◻ 3819 lime moss green

French knots

- Ⓢ 779 dark mink

◀ **To create the broom heads, use straight stitches, varying the lengths. For the apple and pear leaves, angle lazy daisy stitches across three fabric threads. In addition, attach toy garden tools. This sampler is a good example of how additional embroidery stitches add interest and texture.**

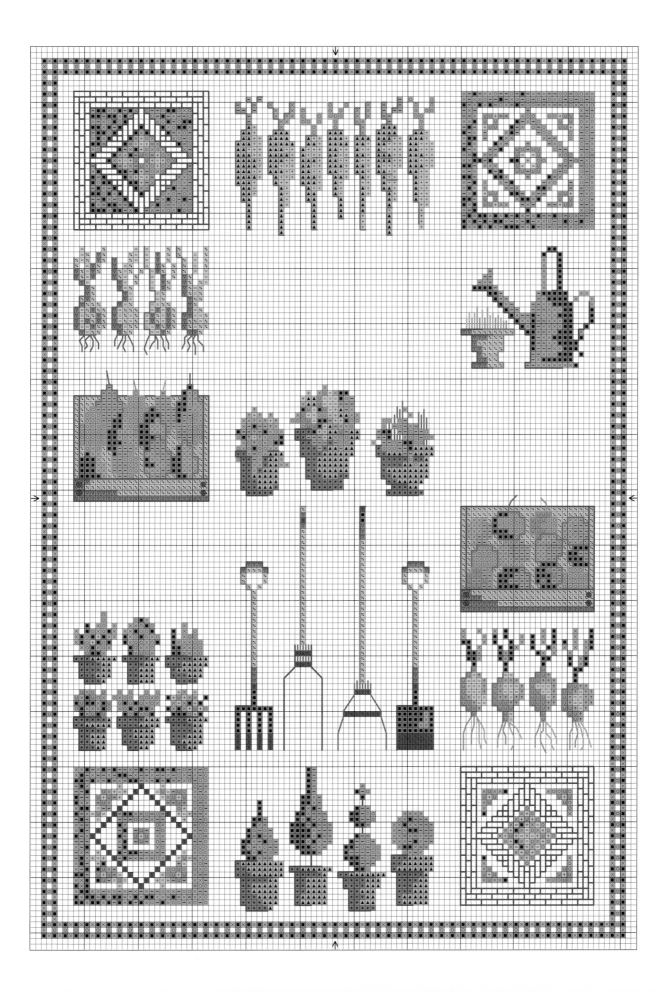

peas in a pod

A simple motif stitched in shades of green gains its appeal from subtle contrasts in shape.

stitching the design

1 Overcast the edges of the fabric to prevent fraying. Mark the midpoint of the fabric both vertically and horizontally with basting stitches; mount the fabric in an embroidery hoop (or stretcher frame) (see Getting Started, page 18).

2 Use the size guide below to calculate the size of design that will result from using different fabric counts (see How to Use This Book, page 13). Refer to the cross-stitch chart and thread key, and stitch from the middle outward.

3 Remove the finished design from the hoop and press gently on the wrong side.

size guide

fabric count	number of threads/blocks	number of strands	size of design
14	1	2	5⅝ in. (14.25 cm) square
16	1	2	4⅞ in. (12.5 cm) square
18	1	2	4⅜ in. (11 cm) square
28	2	2	5⅝ in. (14.25 cm) square
28	3	3	8⅜ in. (21.25 cm) square

materials

- The design shown here uses evenweave fabric, 14-count antique white Aida, and tapestry needle, size 26.

- Stranded cottons, one skein of each colour listed in key. Use two strands for cross-stitch and three-quarter stitch and one for backstitch.

thread key

- ☒ 164 palest grass green
- ⊞ 368 mid green
- ▣ 469 dark avocado
- ▲ 987 grass green
- ◎ 989 pale grass green

backstitch

- ◨ 986 dark grass green

◀ This design can be used to embellish purchased oven mitts. A variety of store-bought items—from napkins to canvas bags—can be transformed with the addition of cross-stitch.

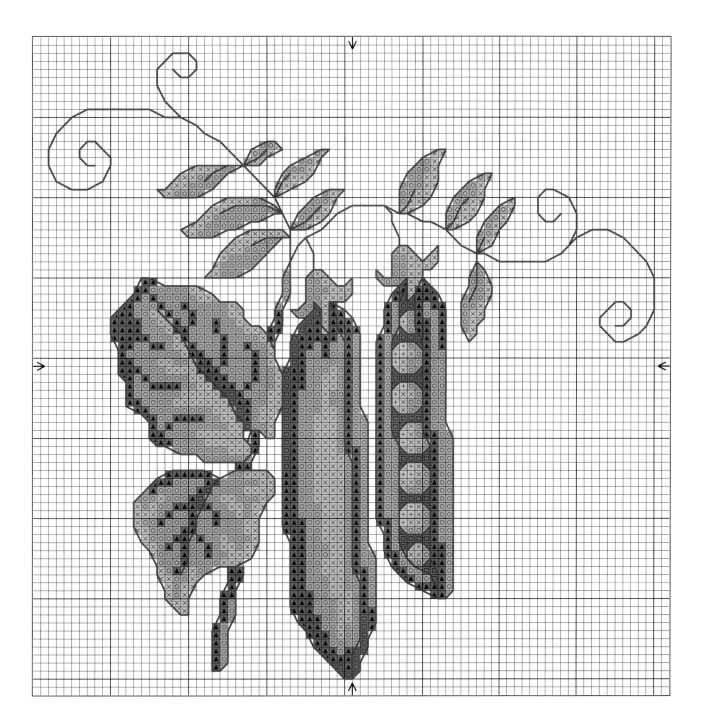

black grapes

A symbol of wine and plenty, a bunch of grapes has been a popular motif since Roman times.

stitching the design

1 Overcast the edges of the fabric to prevent fraying. Mark the midpoint of the fabric both vertically and horizontally with basting stitches; mount the fabric in an embroidery hoop (or stretcher frame) (see Getting Started, page 18).

2 Use the size guide below to calculate the size of design that will result from using different fabric counts (see How to Use This Book, page 13). Refer to the cross-stitch chart and thread key, and stitch from the middle outward.

3 Remove the finished design from the hoop and press gently on the wrong side.

size guide

fabric count	number of threads/blocks	number of strands	size of design
14	1	2	3⅛ x 3¼ in. (8 x 8.25 cm)
16	1	2	2⅝ x 2⅞ in. (6.75 x 7.25 cm)
18	1	2	2⅜ x 2½ in. (6 x 6.25 cm)
27	2	2	3⅛ x 3⅜ in. (8 x 8.5 cm)
27	3	3	4⅝ x 5⅛ in. (11.75 x 13 cm)

materials

■ The design shown here uses evenweave fabric, 27-count antique white, and tapestry needle, size 26.

■ Stranded cottons, one skein of each colour listed in key. Use two strands for cross-stitch and one for backstitch.

thread key

- ⊟ 316 pale old mauve
- ⊞ 503 pale sea green
- Ⓝ 926 mid grey blue
- ⊠ 3726 mid old mauve
- ▲ 3740 pale aubergine
- ◨ 3768 grey blue

backstitch

- ⬂ 924 dark grey blue
- ⬂ 926 mid grey blue

◁ The colours in the "black" grapes vary from aubergine to mauve. Such gradual shading conveys their roundness. The design, framed by bluish green stranded cotton that echoes the shade of the leaves, makes a decorative place mat.

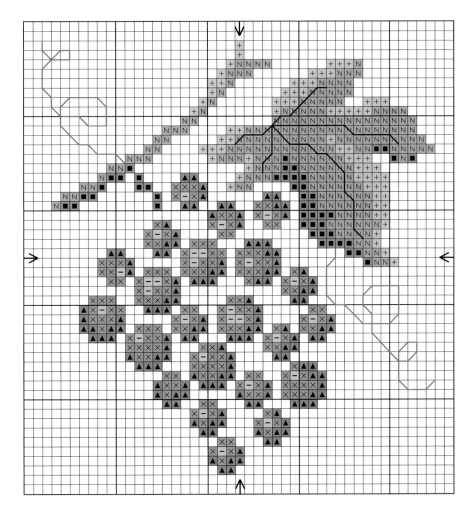

fruit medley

A varied combination of fruits—star fruit, kiwi, pomegranate, and apricot—makes a striking design.

stitching the design

1 Overcast the edges of the fabric to prevent fraying. Mark the midpoint of the fabric both vertically and horizontally with basting stitches; mount the fabric in an embroidery hoop (or stretcher frame) (see Getting Started, page 18).

2 Use the size guide below to calculate the size of motif A that will result from using different fabric counts (see How to Use This Book, page 13). Refer to the cross-stitch chart and thread key, and stitch from the middle outward.

3 Remove the finished design from the hoop and press gently on the wrong side.

size guide

fabric count	number of threads/blocks	number of strands	size of design
14	1	2	2⅜ in. (6 cm) square
16	1	2	2⅛ in. (5.5 cm) square
18	1	2	1⅞ in. (4.75 cm) square
28	2	2	2⅜ in. (6 cm) square
28	3	3	3½ in. (9 cm) square

materials

- The design shown here uses evenweave fabric, 28-count antique white linen, and tapestry needle, size 26.

- Stranded cottons, one skein of each colour listed in key. Use two strands for cross-stitch and one for backstitch.

thread key

- ⊟ 369 pale green
- ◰ 420 dark hazel
- Ⓤ 422 light hazel
- ◉ 783 pale caramel
- ↑ 822 light stone
- Ⓣ 830 mid green gold
- ☒ 907 pale apple green
- ☒ 988 mid grass green
- ◼ 3787 grey brown
- ◹ 3820 gold
- ◲ 3822 palest gold
- ⊞ 3823 yellow cream
- Ⓝ 3853 carrot orange
- Ⓢ 3854 pale carrot orange
- ◁ 3855 pale apricot

backstitch
- ☐ 369 pale green
- ◹ 3787 grey brown

◀ Each fruit is stitched onto a square of linen. These squares can be displayed together or used separately. A single fruit makes an eye-catching picture for the kitchen, or use one or all four motifs to make a set of coasters for the dining table.

(A)

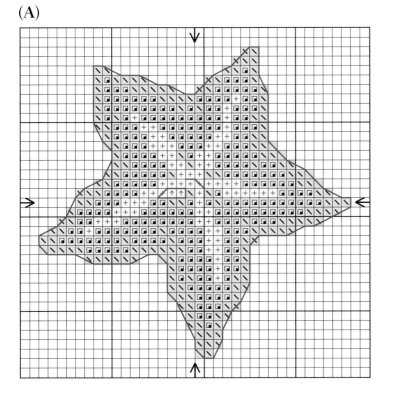

(B)

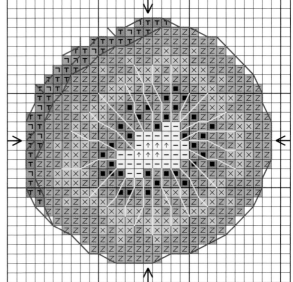

(C)

(D)

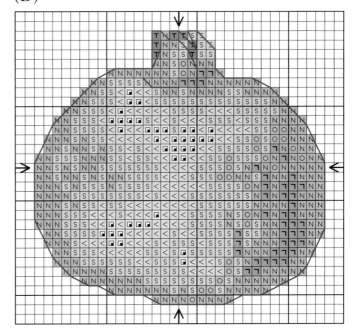

blackberries

For small repeating fruit or flower motifs, a trellis background provides a perfect framework.

stitching the design

1 Overcast the edges of the fabric to prevent fraying. Mark the midpoint of the fabric both vertically and horizontally with basting stitches; mount the fabric in an embroidery hoop (or stretcher frame) (see Getting Started, page 18).

2 Use the size guide below to calculate the size of design that will result from using different fabric counts (see How to Use This Book, page 13). Refer to the cross-stitch chart and thread key, and stitch from the middle outward.

3 Remove the finished design from the hoop and press gently on the wrong side.

size guide

fabric count	number of threads/blocks	number of strands	size of design
14	1	2	7 in. (17.75 cm) square
16	1	2	6⅛ in. (15.5 cm) square
18	1	2	5½ in. (14 cm) square
28	2	2	7 in. (17.75 cm) square
28	3	3	10½ in. (26.75 cm) square

materials

- The design shown here uses evenweave fabric, 28-count beige linen, and tapestry needle, size 26.

- Stranded cottons and metallic thread, one skein of each colour listed in key. Use two strands for cross-stitch and beaded cross-stitch and one for backstitch. Use two packs of 315 and 778 seed beads and one pack of each of the other colours listed.

thread key

cross-stitch

- ▲ 3345 hunter green
- N 3346 moss green
- ⊙ 3347 mid moss green
- ◧ 3348 pale moss green
- ⊟ 5279 copper

beaded cross-stitch

- ▨ 315 dark old mauve
- U 778 light old mauve
- ⊞ 818 pale baby pink
- ■ 823 deep navy blue
- ⊠ 950 rose beige

backstitch

- ◹ 315 dark old mauve
- ◺ 5279 copper

◀ Beaded cross-stitch, used for the blackberries and curvilinear pattern of the border, creates a glimmering, textural effect. This design would be attractive on a variety of home accessories, but it could also be folded in half to make an original evening bag.

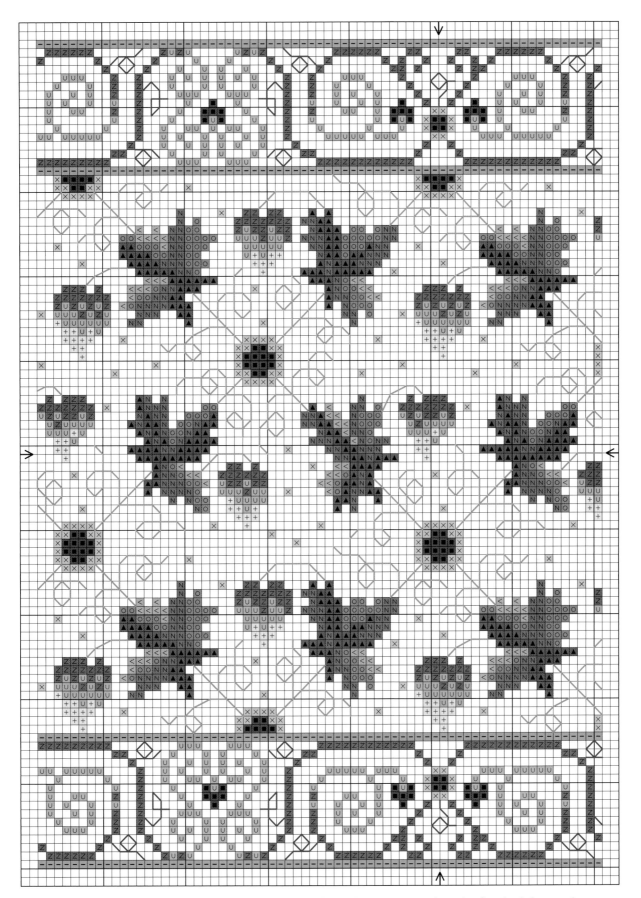

Only three-quarters of the cross-stitch chart is shown here. To complete the finished design shown in the photograph, repeat one column of grapes and leaves on the right-hand side.

rows of leaves

Nine leaves, arranged in rows of three, bestow
a Zen-like calm on a minimalist interior.

stitching the design

1 Overcast the edges of the fabric to prevent fraying. Mark the midpoint of the
fabric both vertically and horizontally with basting stitches; mount the fabric
in an embroidery hoop (or stretcher frame) (see Getting Started, page 18).

2 Use the size guide below to calculate the size of design that will result from
using different fabric counts (see How to Use This Book, page 13). Refer to
the cross-stitch chart and thread key, and stitch from the middle outward.

3 Remove the finished design from the hoop and press gently on the wrong side.

materials

■ The design shown here uses
evenweave fabric, 28-count
white linen, and tapestry needle,
size 26.

■ Stranded cottons, one skein of
each colour listed in key. Use
two strands for cross-stitch.

size guide

fabric count	number of threads/blocks	number of strands	size of design
14	1	2	2⅞ x 6¼ in. (7.25 x 16 cm)
16	1	2	2½ x 5⅜ in. (6.25 x 13.75 cm)
18	1	2	2¼ x 4⅞ in. (5.75 x 12.5 cm)
28	2	2	2⅞ x 6¼ in. (7.25 x 16 cm)
28	3	3	4¼ x 9⅜ in. (10.75 x 23.75 cm)

◀ A subtle change in the shade of
the central leaves adds interest
to this repeating motif. A white
fabric background complements
the simplicity of the design. Extend
the theme by stitching the motifs
onto plain pale curtains or shades.

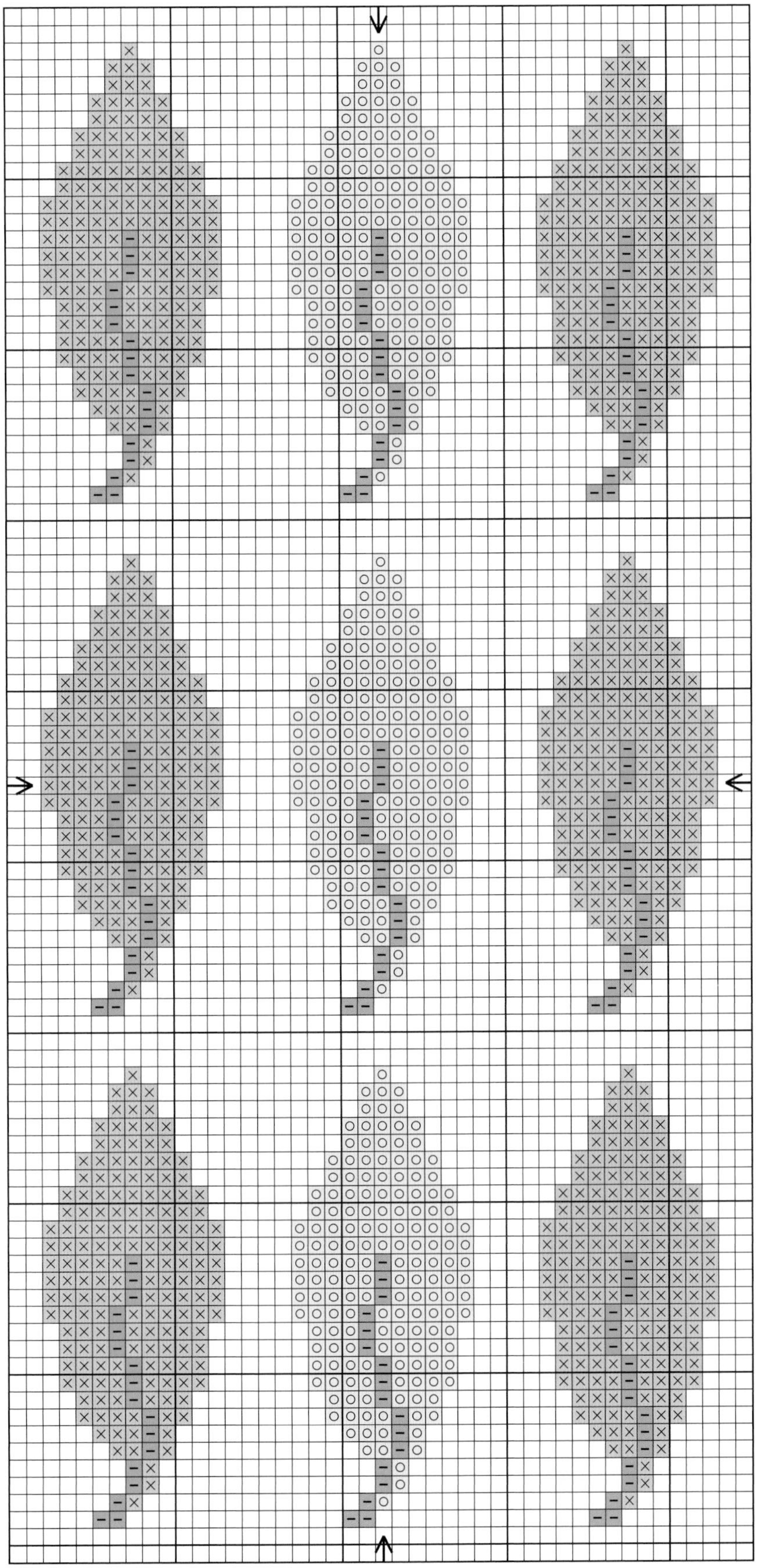

lemon

With clever shading and highlighting, this popular citrus fruit becomes a graphic motif.

stitching the design

1 Overcast the edges of the fabric to prevent fraying. Mark the midpoint of the fabric both vertically and horizontally with basting stitches; mount the fabric in an embroidery hoop (or stretcher frame) (see Getting Started, page 18).

2 Use the size guide below to calculate the size of design that will result from using different fabric counts (see How to Use This Book, page 13). Refer to the cross-stitch chart and thread key, and stitch from the middle outward.

3 Remove the finished design from the hoop and press gently on the wrong side.

size guide

fabric count	number of threads/blocks	number of strands	size of design
14	1	2	3⅞ x 4¼ in. (9.75 x 10.75 cm)
16	1	2	3⅜ x 3⅝ in. (8.5 x 9.25 cm)
18	1	2	3 x 3¼ in. (7.5 x 8.25 cm)
28	2	2	3⅞ x 4¼ in. (9.75 x 10.75 cm)
28	3	3	5¾ x 6⅜ in. (14.5 x 16.25 cm)

materials

- The design shown here uses evenweave fabric, 14-count antique white Aida, and tapestry needle, size 26.

- Stranded cottons, one skein of each colour listed in key. Use two strands for cross-stitch.

thread key

- ⊞ blanc
- ⊠ 444 dark lemon
- ⊟ 445 pale lemon
- ▲ 839 dark coffee
- ▣ 905 mid apple green
- ⊞ 907 pale apple green
- ◉ 972 sunshine yellow
- ◼ 986 dark grass green
- ⊤ 3041 dusty mauve
- ◉ 3853 carrot orange

◀ A cross-stitched patch decorates this kitchen container filled with lemons and limes. As a single motif, a lemon can brighten up a variety of storage holders. You could also repeat the design to create a border for kitchen towels and tablecloths.

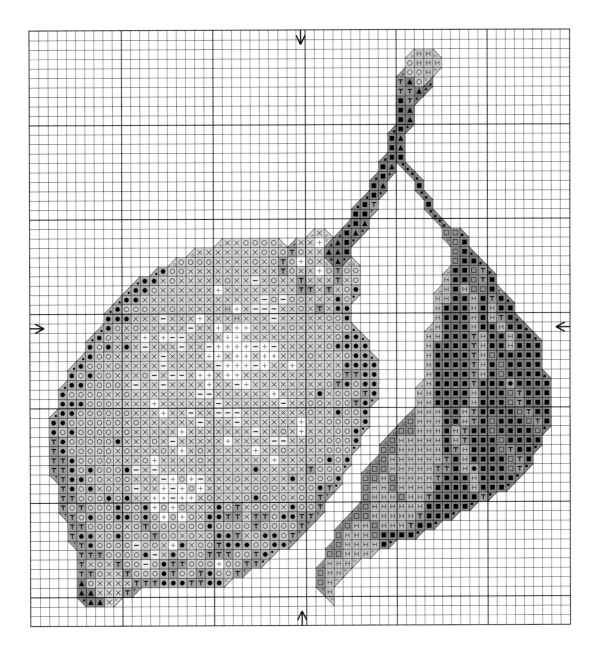

olives

The bold images and lettering on product labels can be interpreted creatively in a stitched design.

stitching the design

1 Overcast the edges of the fabric to prevent fraying. Mark the midpoint of the fabric both vertically and horizontally with basting stitches; mount the fabric in an embroidery hoop (or stretcher frame) (see Getting Started, page 18).

2 Use the size guide below to calculate the size of design that will result from using different fabric counts (see How to Use This Book, page 13). Refer to the cross-stitch chart and thread key, and stitch from the middle outward.

3 Remove the finished design from the hoop and press gently on the wrong side.

size guide

fabric count	number of threads/blocks	number of strands	size of design
14	1	2	3¼ x 4⅜ in. (8.25 x 11 cm)
16	1	2	2¾ x 3¾ in. (7 x 9.5 cm)
18	1	2	2½ x 3⅜ in. (6.25 x 8.5 cm)
28	2	2	3¼ x 4⅜ in. (8.25 x 11 cm)
28	3	3	4⅞ x 6½ in. (12.5 x 16.5 cm)

materials

- The design shown here uses evenweave fabric, 14-count natural Aida, and tapestry needle, size 26.
- Stranded cottons, one skein of each colour listed in key. Use two strands for cross-stitch and one for backstitch.

thread key

- 321 red
- 367 green
- 469 dark avocado
- 470 mid avocado
- 471 pale avocado
- 814 maroon
- 816 claret red
- 989 pale grass green
- 3371 dark chocolate
- 3820 gold
- 3822 palest gold

backstitch

- 3371 dark chocolate

Attached to a jar of fresh green olives, this design makes a decorative statement in any kitchen. Look at the labels on other food products for inspiration to create your own motifs.

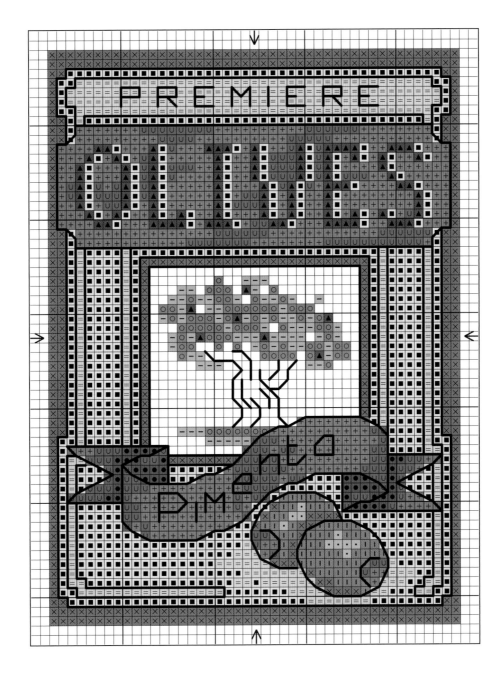

ivy leaves

With their ragged heart shapes and curling tendrils, ivy leaves make ideal decorations for accessories.

stitching the design

1 Overcast the edges of the fabric to prevent fraying. Mark the midpoint of the fabric both vertically and horizontally with basting stitches; mount the fabric in an embroidery hoop (or stretcher frame) (see Getting Started, page 18).

2 Use the size guide below to calculate the size of design that will result from using different fabric counts (see How to Use This Book, page 13). Refer to the cross-stitch chart and thread key, and stitch from the middle outward.

3 Remove the finished design from the hoop and press gently on the wrong side.

size guide

fabric count	number of threads/blocks	number of strands	size of design
14	1	2	4⅛ x 6⅝ in. (10.5 x 16.75 cm)
16	1	2	3⅝ x 5¾ in. (9.25 x 14.5 cm)
18	1	2	3¼ x 5⅛ in. (8.25 x 13 cm)
28	2	2	4⅛ x 6⅝ in. (10.5 x 16.75 cm)
28	3	3	6¼ x 9⅞ in. (16 x 25 cm)

materials

- The design shown here uses evenweave fabric, 28-count antique white Quaker cloth, and tapestry needle, size 26.

- Stranded cottons, one skein of each colour listed in key. Use two strands for cross-stitch, three-quarter stitch, and French knots; one strand for backstitch.

thread key

- ☑ 367 green
- ☒ 471 pale avocado
- ⊡ 677 cold cream

backstitch
- ◣ 895 dark hunter green
- ◣ 918 copper brown

French knots
- ◼ 3834 dark grape

in detail

French knots worked with two strands of 3834 look just like the seeds on a mature ivy plant.

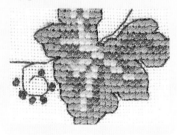

◀ A panel of twining ivy transforms the plain cover of a hardcover book. This design would also suit a diary or a book containing a collection of personal gardening tips.

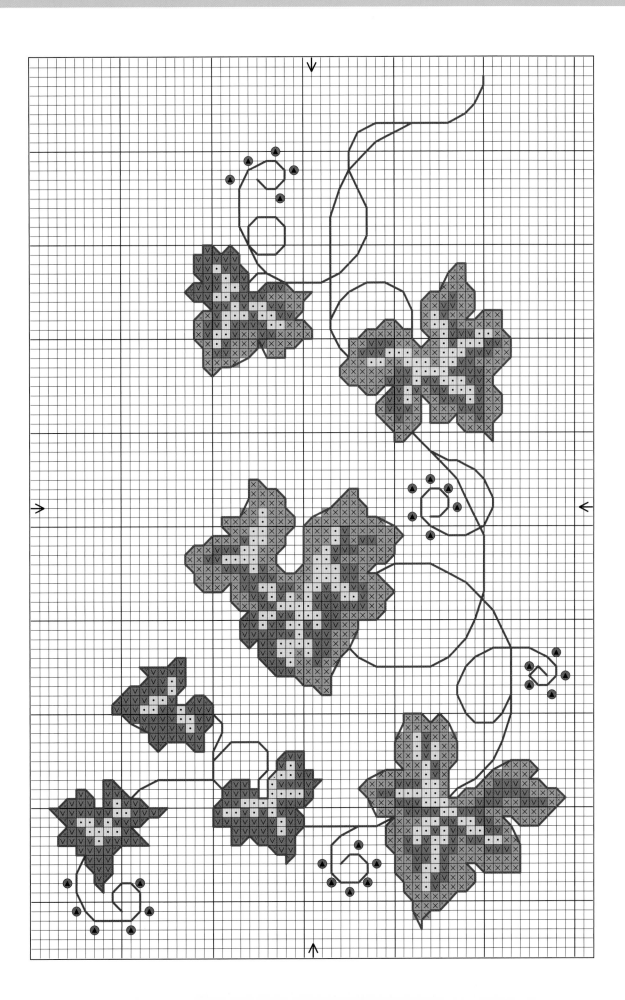

pumpkin

A vivid orange pumpkin with curved segments glows warmly against a patch of greenery.

stitching the design

1 Overcast the edges of the fabric to prevent fraying. Mark the midpoint of the fabric both vertically and horizontally with basting stitches; mount the fabric in an embroidery hoop (or stretcher frame) (see Getting Started, page 18).

2 Use the size guide below to calculate the size of design that will result from using different fabric counts (see How to Use This Book, page 13). Refer to the cross-stitch chart and thread key, and stitch from the middle outward.

3 Remove the finished design from the hoop and press gently on the wrong side.

size guide

fabric count	number of threads/blocks	number of strands	size of design
14	1	2	4⅛ x 2¼ in. (10.5 x 5.75 cm)
16	1	2	3⅝ x 2 in. (9.25 x 5 cm)
18	1	2	3¼ x 1¾ in. (8.25 x 4.5 cm)
28	2	2	4⅛ x 2¼ in. (10.5 x 5.75 cm)
28	3	3	6¼ x 3⅜ in. (16 x 8.5 cm)

materials

- The design shown here uses evenweave fabric, 14-count natural, and tapestry needle, size 26.

- Stranded cottons, one skein of each colour listed in key. Use two strands for cross-stitch and three-quarter stitch and one for backstitch.

thread key

- ⊟ 472 light avocado
- ⊡ 720 dark rust orange
- ▣ 721 rusty orange
- ⊠ 722 tango
- ▲ 987 grass green
- ⊞ 989 pale grass green
- ⊡ 3827 pale fudge

backstitch
- ◣ 898 chocolate
- ◺ 989 pale grass green

◄ To create a homespun look, this pumpkin is stitched onto a simple linen bag, and the edges of the fabric are left unfinished. For a party, wrap the design around a glass to form a decorative holder for a tea light. Shining through the orange motif, it will cast a cheerful pool of light.

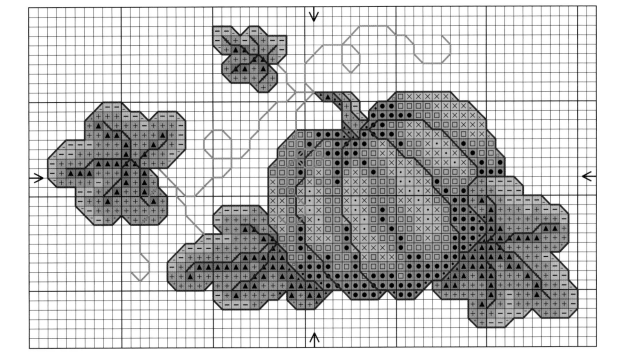

topiary

These bold motifs are inspired by topiary—the art of pruning trees and bushes into decorative shapes.

stitching the design

1 Overcast the edges of the fabric to prevent fraying. Mark the midpoint of the fabric both vertically and horizontally with basting stitches; mount the fabric in an embroidery hoop (or stretcher frame) (see Getting Started, page 18).

2 Use the size guide below to calculate the size of motif D that will result from using different fabric counts (see How to Use This Book, page 13). Refer to the cross-stitch chart and thread key, and stitch from the middle outward.

3 Remove the finished design from the hoop and press gently on the wrong side.

size guide

fabric count	number of threads/blocks	number of strands	size of design
14	1	2	2⅜ x 3½ in. (6 x 9 cm)
16	1	2	2 x 3 in. (5 x 7.5 cm)
18	1	2	1⅞ x 2¾ in. (4.75 x 7 cm)
28	2	2	2⅜ x 3½ in. (6 x 9 cm)
28	3	3	3½ x 5¼ in. (9 x 13.25 cm)

materials

■ The design shown here uses evenweave fabric, 28-count antique white linen, and tapestry needle, size 26.

■ Stranded cottons, one skein of each colour listed in key. Use two strands for cross-stitch and three-quarter stitch.

thread key

◎ 796 royal blue
▲ 797 French blue
⊡ 809 Delft blue
● 869 hazel brown
▤ 991 dark aqua
▣ 992 mid green aqua
▽ 993 pale green aqua

in detail

Three-quarter stitches create the angular shapes of the topiary bird's beak and forehead, as well as the crest on its head.

◄ Square patchwork complements the stylized shapes of the topiary motifs. A simple blue, green, and white colour scheme keeps the emphasis on the motifs, any of which could be used individually.

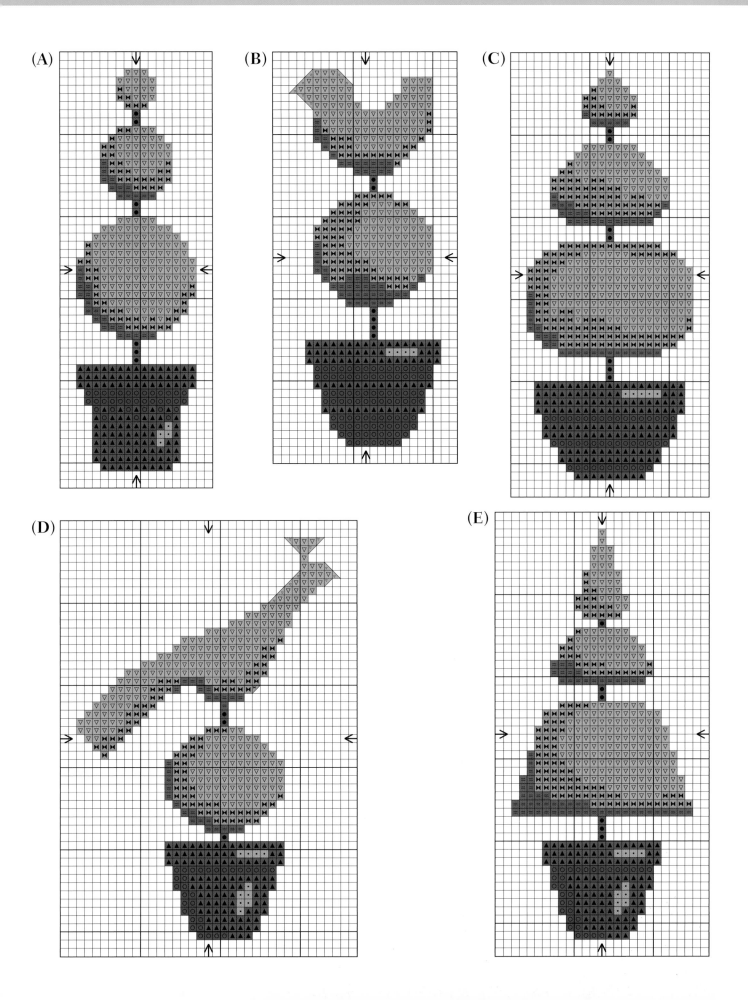

turning leaves

A warm mix of russet brown, golden yellow, and lime, this simple leaf design suits a country interior.

stitching the design

1 Overcast the edges of the fabric to prevent fraying. Mark the midpoint of the fabric both vertically and horizontally with basting stitches; mount the fabric in an embroidery hoop (or stretcher frame) (see Getting Started, page 18).

2 Use the size guide below to calculate the size of design that will result from using different fabric counts (see How to Use This Book, page 13). Refer to the cross-stitch chart and thread key, and stitch from the middle outward.

3 Remove the finished design from the hoop and press gently on the wrong side.

size guide

fabric count	number of threads/blocks	number of strands	size of design
14	1	2	3⅛ x 11¼ in. (8 x 28.5 cm)
16	1	2	2¾ x 9¾ in. (7 x 24.75 cm)
18	1	2	2½ x 8¾ in. (6.25 x 22.25 cm)
28	2	2	3⅛ x 11¼ in. (8 x 28.5 cm)
28	3	3	4⅝ x 16⅞ in. (11.75 x 42.75 cm)

materials

- The design shown here uses evenweave fabric, 28-count raw linen, and tapestry needle, size 26.

- Stranded cottons, one skein of each colour listed in key. Use two strands for cross-stitch and three-quarter stitch and one for backstitch.

thread key

- ◲ 470 mid avocado
- ☒ 471 pale avocado
- ⊞ 729 ochre
- ⊡ 734 gold lime
- ◉ 3012 mid dull green
- ⊟ 3776 tan
- ◢ 3830 terra cotta

backstitch

- ◩ 3362 dark old green
- ◩ 3830 terra cotta

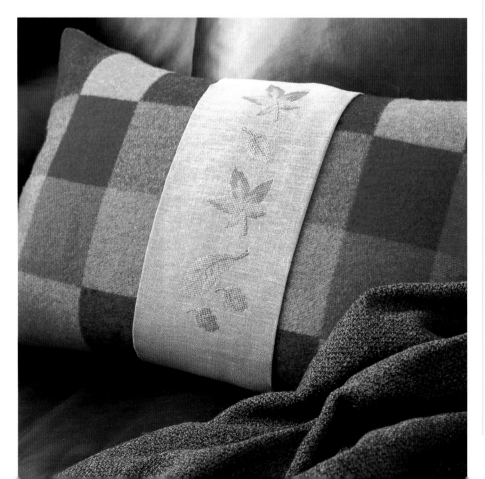

◀ Worked on raw linen, these leaves form an elegant band. The rich hues of the checked wool fabric echo those of the motifs. To make a matching curtain border, repeat the design to the desired length.

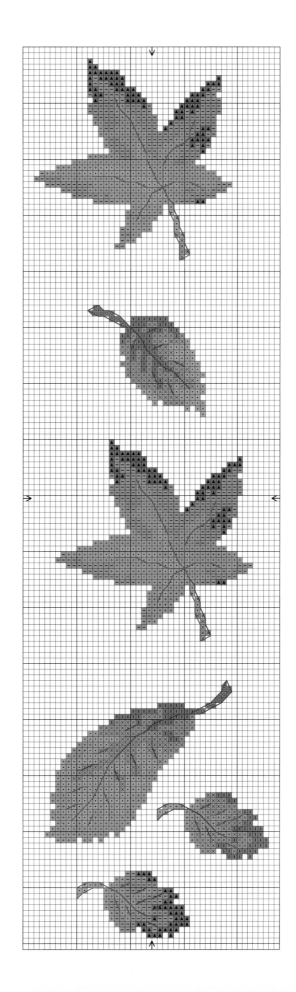

chapter five:

home comforts

swatches

Reminiscent of traditional patterned fabrics, this trio of floral and checked samples combines well.

stitching the design

1 Overcast the edges of the fabric to prevent fraying. Mark the midpoint of the fabric both vertically and horizontally with basting stitches; mount the fabric in an embroidery hoop (or stretcher frame) (see Getting Started, page 18).

2 Use the size guide below to calculate the size of design that will result from using different fabric counts (see How to Use This Book, page 13). Refer to the cross-stitch chart and thread key, and stitch from the middle outward.

3 Remove the finished design from the hoop and press gently on the wrong side.

size guide

fabric count	number of threads/blocks	number of strands	size of design
14	1	2	6¼ x 5¾ in. (16 x 14.5 cm)
16	1	2	5½ x 5 in. (14 x 12.75 cm)
18	1	2	4⅞ x 4½ in. (12.5 x 11.5 cm)
28	2	2	6¼ x 5¾ in. (16 x 14.5 cm)
28	3	3	9⅜ x 8⅝ in. (23.75 x 22 cm)

materials

■ The design shown here uses evenweave fabric, 14-count pale yellow, and tapestry needle, size 26.

■ Stranded cottons, one skein of each colour listed in key. Use two strands for cross-stitch and one for backstitch.

thread key

- ↑ 355 dark terra cotta
- ☒ 356 mid terra cotta
- ⊟ 470 mid avocado
- ◎ 471 pale avocado
- ▲ 472 light avocado
- ⊞ 758 mid rose brown
- Ⓤ 950 rose beige

backstitch

- ◩ 632 dark sugar

in detail

A pale yellow evenweave fabric gives the design a sepia tint, lending a slightly aged look to the fabric patterns.

◀ A fabric swatch is usually cut out with pinking shears to prevent the edges from fraying. In this case, backstitch is worked in slanting diagonals using a dark thread to reproduce the effect.

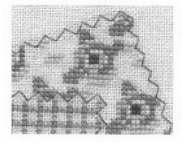

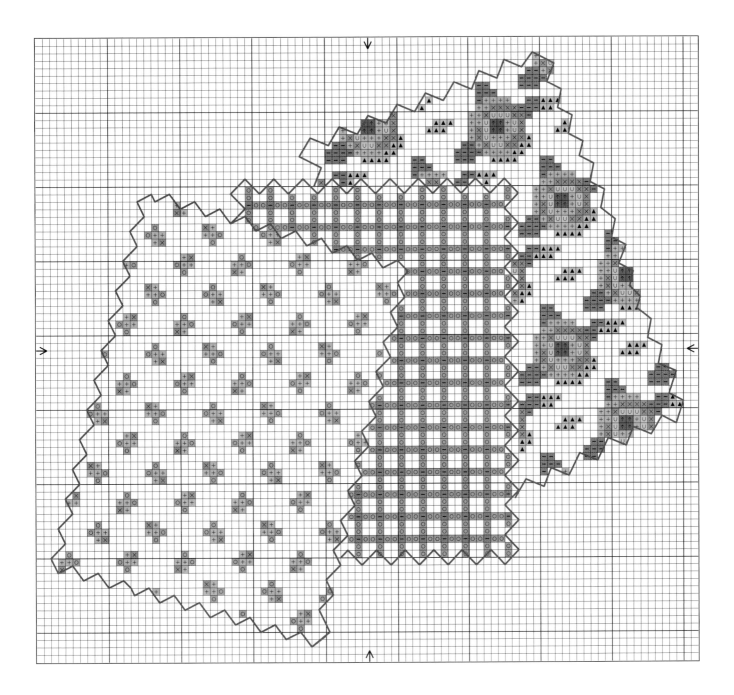

fragrant herbs

With leaves and flowers in shades of blue and green, lavender, chives, and rosemary offer a subtle charm.

stitching the design

1 Overcast the edges of the fabric to prevent fraying. Mark the midpoint of the fabric both vertically and horizontally with basting stitches; mount the fabric in an embroidery hoop (or stretcher frame) (see Getting Started, page 18).

2 Use the size guide below to calculate the size of motif B that will result from using different fabric counts (see How to Use This Book, page 13). Refer to the cross-stitch chart and thread key, and stitch from the middle outward.

3 Remove the finished design from the hoop and press gently on the wrong side.

size guide

fabric count	number of threads/blocks	number of strands	size of design
14	1	2	2⅛ x 4⅜ in. (5.5 x 11 cm)
16	1	2	1¾ x 3¾ in. (4.5 x 9.5 cm)
18	1	2	1⅝ x 3⅜ in. (4.25 x 8.5 cm)
28	2	2	2⅛ x 4⅜ in. (5.5 x 11 cm)
28	3	3	3¼ x 6½ in. (8.25 x 16.5 cm)

materials

- The design shown here uses evenweave fabric, 28-count white Quaker cloth, and tapestry needle, size 26.

- Stranded cottons, one skein of each colour listed in key. Use two strands for cross-stitch and one for backstitch.

◀ These small motifs make ideal labels for potted herbs. Attach them to purchased or handmade luggage labels, then thread raffia through the top so that you can tie them around the pots.

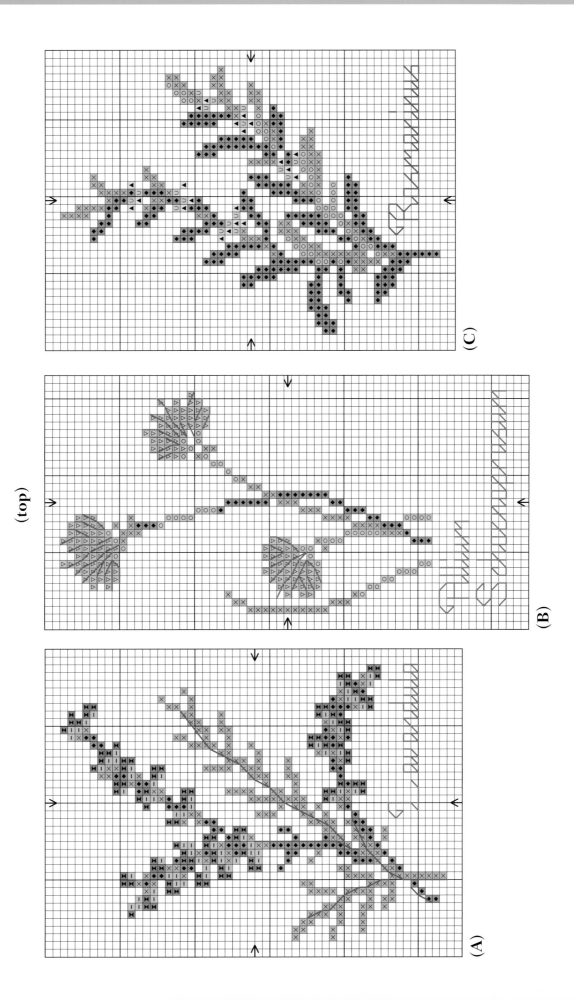

(top)

(A)

(B)

(C)

tiny houses

Variegated thread in shades of brick and sand is used to stitch these miniature houses.

stitching the design

1 Overcast the edges of the fabric to prevent fraying. Mark the midpoint of the fabric both vertically and horizontally with basting stitches; mount the fabric in an embroidery hoop (or stretcher frame) (see Getting Started, page 18).

2 Use the size guide below to calculate the size of design that will result from using different fabric counts (see How to Use This Book, page 13). Refer to the cross-stitch chart and thread key, and stitch from the middle outward.

3 Remove the finished design from the hoop and press gently on the wrong side.

size guide

fabric count	number of threads/blocks	number of strands	size of design
14	1	2	6⅛ x 1⅝ in. (15.5 x 4.25 cm)
16	1	2	5¼ x 1⅜ in. (13.25 x 3.5 cm)
18	1	2	4¾ x 1¼ in. (12 x 3.25 cm)
26	2	2	6½ x 1¾ in. (16.5 x 4.5 cm)
28	2	2	6⅛ x 1⅝ in. (15.5 x 4.25 cm)

materials

- The design shown here uses evenweave fabric, 26-count cream Aida band, and tapestry needle, size 26.

- Stranded cottons, one skein of each colour listed in key. Use two strands for cross-stitch.

thread key

 111 variegated gold

◀ You can make the row of houses in this design any length you choose. Using a fabric band with scalloped edging means that there are no raw edges to finish. Many other motifs can also be scaled down and repeated on Aida band.

(top)

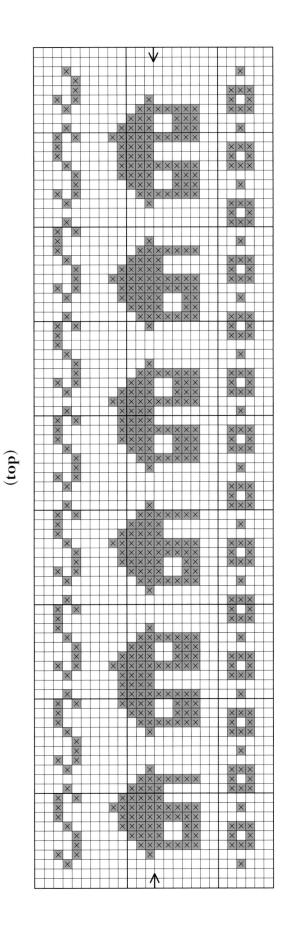

coffee bar

A reminder of life's simple pleasures, these motifs add style to everyday refreshments.

stitching the design

1 Overcast the edges of the fabric to prevent fraying. Mark the midpoint of the fabric both vertically and horizontally with basting stitches; mount the fabric in an embroidery hoop (or stretcher frame) (see Getting Started, page 18).

2 Use the size guide below to calculate the size of motif A that will result from using different fabric counts (see How to Use This Book, page 13). Refer to the cross-stitch chart and thread key, and stitch from the middle outward.

3 Remove the finished design from the hoop and press gently on the wrong side.

size guide

fabric count	number of threads/blocks	number of strands	size of design
14	1	2	2½ x 3⅛ in. (6.25 x 8 cm)
16	1	2	2¼ x 2⅝ in. (5.75 x 6.75 cm)
18	1	2	2 x 2⅜ in. (5 x 6 cm)
28	2	2	2½ x 3⅛ in. (6.25 x 8 cm)
28	3	3	3¾ x 4⅝ in. (9.5 x 11.75 cm)

materials

- The design shown here uses evenweave fabric, 14-count Aida, and tapestry needle, size 26.

- Stranded cottons, one skein of each colour listed in key. Use two strands for cross-stitch and one for backstitch and French knots.

◀ For this tray cloth, the mug and cup motifs have been stitched at opposite corners, and a polka-dot and floral border have been added for a bright, modern look. Both can be stitched individually to make coasters.

(A)

(B)

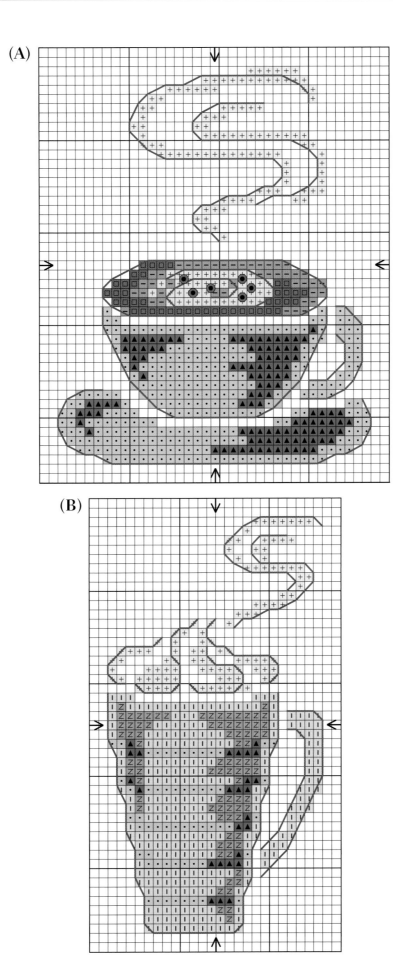

home baking

A striped jug and mixing bowl provide the necessary ingredients to brighten any kitchen decor.

stitching the design

1 Overcast the edges of the fabric to prevent fraying. Mark the midpoint of the fabric both vertically and horizontally with basting stitches; mount the fabric in an embroidery hoop (or stretcher frame) (see Getting Started, page 18).

2 Use the size guide below to calculate the size of design that will result from using different fabric counts (see How to Use This Book, page 13). Refer to the cross-stitch chart and thread key, and stitch from the middle outward.

3 Remove the finished design from the hoop and press gently on the wrong side.

size guide

fabric count	number of threads/blocks	number of strands	size of design
14	1	2	3¾ x 2¾ in. (9.5 x 7 cm)
16	1	2	3¼ x 2⅜ in. (8.25 x 6 cm)
18	1	2	3 x 2⅛ in. (7.5 x 5.5 cm)
28	2	2	3¾ x 2¾ in. (9.5 x 7 cm)
28	3	3	5⅝ x 4⅛ in. (14.25 x 10.5 cm)

materials

- The design shown here uses evenweave fabric, 14-count antique white Aida, and tapestry needle, size 26.

- Stranded cottons, one skein of each colour listed in key. Use two strands for cross-stitch and three-quarter stitch and one for backstitch.

thread key

- → blanc
- ☒ ecru
- ⊡ 164 palest grass green
- ◆ 437 old gold
- ▲ 772 pale leaf green
- Ⓢ 945 pink beige
- Ⓛ 976 toffee
- Ⓣ 977 mid fudge
- ◣ 987 grass green
- ◂ 989 pale grass green
- ◉ 3047 pale putty

backstitch

- ◼ 610 deep khaki

◀ Use fabric glue to attach the design to a fabric-bound recipe notebook. You could also stitch it onto a dish towel or the front pocket of an apron.

antique keys

Ornate keys provide the inspiration for this elegant design surrounded by a geometric border.

stitching the design

1 Overcast the edges of the fabric to prevent fraying. Mark the midpoint of the fabric both vertically and horizontally with basting stitches; mount the fabric in an embroidery hoop (or stretcher frame) (see Getting Started, page 18).

2 Use the size guide below to calculate the size of design that will result from using different fabric counts (see How to Use This Book, page 13). Refer to the cross-stitch chart and thread key, and stitch from the middle outward.

3 Remove the finished design from the hoop and press gently on the wrong side.

size guide

fabric count	number of threads/blocks	number of strands	size of design
14	1	2	3¾ x 6⅞ in. (9.5 x 17.5 cm)
16	1	2	3¼ x 6 in. (8.25 x 15.25 cm)
18	1	2	3 x 5⅜ in. (7.5 x 13.75 cm)
28	2	2	3¾ x 6⅞ in. (9.5 x 17.5 cm)
28	3	3	5⅝ x 10¼ in. (14.25 x 26 cm)

materials

- The design shown here uses evenweave fabric, 14-count antique white Aida, and tapestry needle, size 26.

- Stranded cottons, one skein of each colour listed in key. Use two strands for cross-stitch and three-quarter stitch and one for backstitch.

thread key

- ⊟ 318 dark pearl grey
- ■ 414 light pewter
- ⊠ 415 steel grey
- **backstitch**
- ◻ 317 mid pewter

◀ A pair of keys is ideal for decorating the front panel of a key cupboard. The border is taken from a motif typically painted on classical Greek vases. For the curvilinear shape of each key, three-quarter stitch is used to create a smooth outline. Either the key or the border could be used alone.

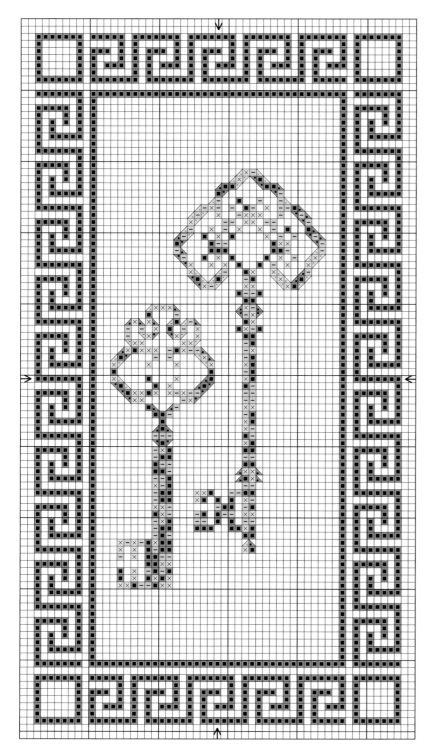

This chart indicates where backstitch should be worked on the keys.

salon chair

Covered with *toile de Jouy* fabric, this chair motif evokes the look of an 18th-century French salon.

stitching the design

1 Overcast the edges of the fabric to prevent fraying. Mark the midpoint of the fabric both vertically and horizontally with basting stitches; mount the fabric in an embroidery hoop (or stretcher frame) (see Getting Started, page 18).

2 Use the size guide below to calculate the size of design that will result from using different fabric counts (see How to Use This Book, page 13). Refer to the cross-stitch chart and thread key, and stitch from the middle outward.

3 Remove the finished design from the hoop and press gently on the wrong side.

size guide

fabric count	number of threads/blocks	number of strands	size of design
14	1	2	5 x 7⅝ in. (12.75 x 19.25 cm)
16	1	2	4⅜ x 6⅜ in. (11 x 16.25 cm)
18	1	2	3⅞ x 5⅞ in. (9.25 x 15 cm)
27	2	2	5⅛ x 7⅞ in. (13 x 20 cm)
27	3	3	7⅝ x 11¾ in. (19.25 x 30 cm)

materials

■ The design shown here uses evenweave fabric, 27-count antique white, and tapestry needle, size 26.

■ Stranded cottons, one skein of each colour listed in key. Use two strands for cross-stitch and three-quarter stitch and one for backstitch.

thread key

■ 347 berry red
⊠ 414 light pewter
⊟ 415 steel grey
⊞ 3078 pale yellow
◎ 3328 dark salmon
▲ 3822 palest gold

backstitch

◺ 347 berry red
◺ 414 light pewter
◺ 3822 palest gold

in detail

Toile de Jouy fabrics typically feature scenes from the countryside. A close look at the design reveals a shepherdess with her flock.

◀ The soft red of the surrounding fabric and tassels complements the *toile de Jouy* design on the chair. Other interesting colour combinations include substituting moss green or royal blue for the red fabric.

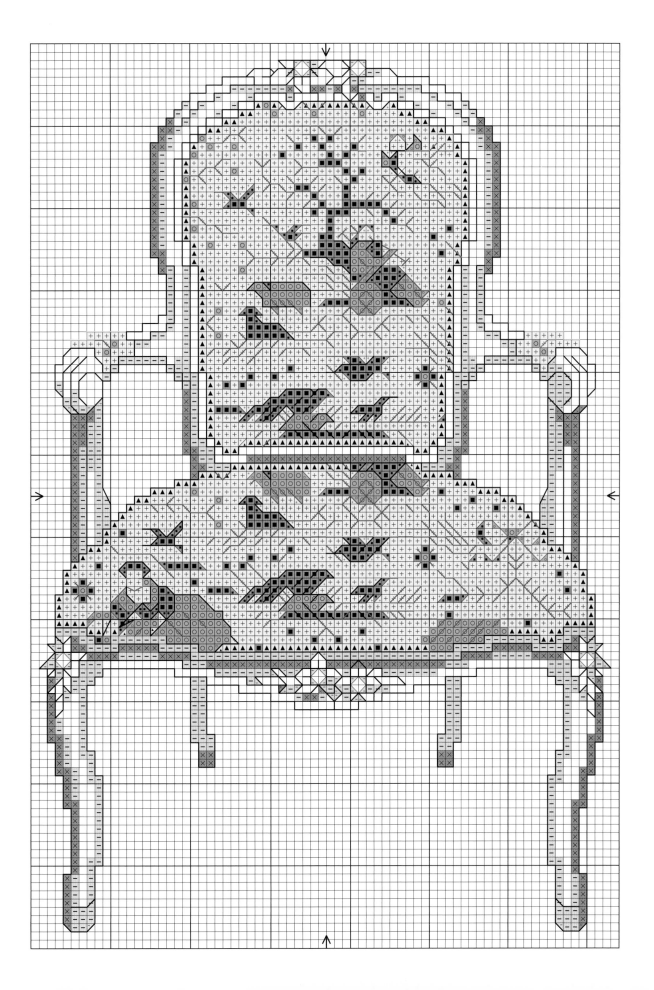

kitchen kit

This sampler features a range of decorative kitchen motifs, using toy utensils to add texture.

stitching the design

1 Overcast the edges of the fabric to prevent fraying. Mark the midpoint of the fabric both vertically and horizontally with basting stitches; mount the fabric in an embroidery hoop (or stretcher frame) (see Getting Started, page 18).

2 Use the size guide below to calculate the size of design that will result from using different fabric counts (see How to Use This Book, page 13). Refer to the cross-stitch chart and thread key, and stitch from the middle outward.

3 Remove the finished design from the hoop and press gently on the wrong side.

size guide

fabric count	number of threads/blocks	number of strands	size of design
14	1	2	7¾ x 11⅜ in. (19.75 x 29 cm)
16	1	2	6¾ x 9⅞ in. (17.25 x 25 cm)
18	1	2	6 x 8⅞ in. (15.25 x 22.5 cm)
25	2	2	8¾ x 12¾ in. (22.25 x 32.5 cm)
28	2	2	7¾ x 11⅜ in. (19.75 x 29 cm)

materials

- The design shown here uses evenweave fabric, 25-count white, and tapestry needle, size 26.

- Stranded cottons, one skein of each colour listed in key. Use two strands for cross-stitch, backstitch, and lazy daisy stitch.

- Assorted doll's house kitchen utensils and all-purpose adhesive.

thread key

- **S** 505 dusty green
- **✳** 553 violet
- **L** 554 pale violet
- **%** 704 pale lime green
- **⊟** 744 primrose yellow
- **U** 746 buttermilk
- **◎** 779 dark mink
- **■** 791 purple blue
- **✕** 793 pale cornflower blue
- **▲** 841 coffee
- **▽** 954 mid spearmint
- **T** 3609 ice raspberry
- **▣** 3747 ice lilac
- **↑** 3819 lime moss green
- **+** 3827 pale fudge

backstitch

- ◣ 505 dusty green
- ◥ 553 violet
- ◰ 554 pale violet
- ◢ 704 pale lime green
- ◩ 779 dark mink
- ◪ 791 purple blue
- ◿ 793 pale cornflower blue
- ◣ 841 coffee
- ◻ 954 mid spearmint
- ◹ 3827 pale fudge

◀ **To enhance the three-dimensional effect of the sampler, glue toy kitchen equipment in neat rows, as shown. Work the tiny leaves of the plums and apples with single lazy daisy stitches over three fabric threads.**

garden tools

With the simplicity characteristic of children's pictures, this design evokes the joy of practical tasks.

stitching the design

1 Overcast the edges of the fabric to prevent fraying. Mark the midpoint of the fabric both vertically and horizontally with basting stitches; mount the fabric in an embroidery hoop (or stretcher frame) (see Getting Started, page 18).

2 Use the size guide below to calculate the size of design that will result from using different fabric counts (see How to Use This Book, page 13). Refer to the cross-stitch chart and thread key, and stitch from the middle outward.

3 Remove the finished design from the hoop and press gently on the wrong side.

size guide

fabric count	number of threads/blocks	number of strands	size of design
14	1	2	8½ x 6⅞ in. (21.5 x 17.5 cm)
16	1	2	7⅜ x 6 in. (18.75 x 15.25 cm)
18	1	2	6⅝ x 5⅜ in. (16.75 x 13.75 cm)
28	2	2	8½ x 6⅞ in. (21.5 x 17.5 cm)
28	3	3	12¾ x 10¼ in. (32.5 x 26 cm)

materials

- The design shown here uses evenweave fabric, 14-count natural linen Aida, and tapestry needle, size 26.

- Stranded cottons, one skein of each colour listed in key. Use two strands for cross-stitch and one for backstitch.

thread key

- ▲ 156 lavender blue
- ◉ 317 mid pewter
- ⊠ 318 dark pearl grey
- ■ 920 light brick
- ⊞ 921 brick orange
- ⊟ 987 grass green

backstitch

- ◲ 317 mid pewter
- ◲ 318 dark pearl grey
- ◲ 920 light brick
- ◲ 987 grass green

◀ A canvas bag is a good place to store gardening gloves and other useful items so that they can be carried outdoors easily. One or more of the motifs could be stitched onto a pair of gloves or a gardener's sun hat.

(top)

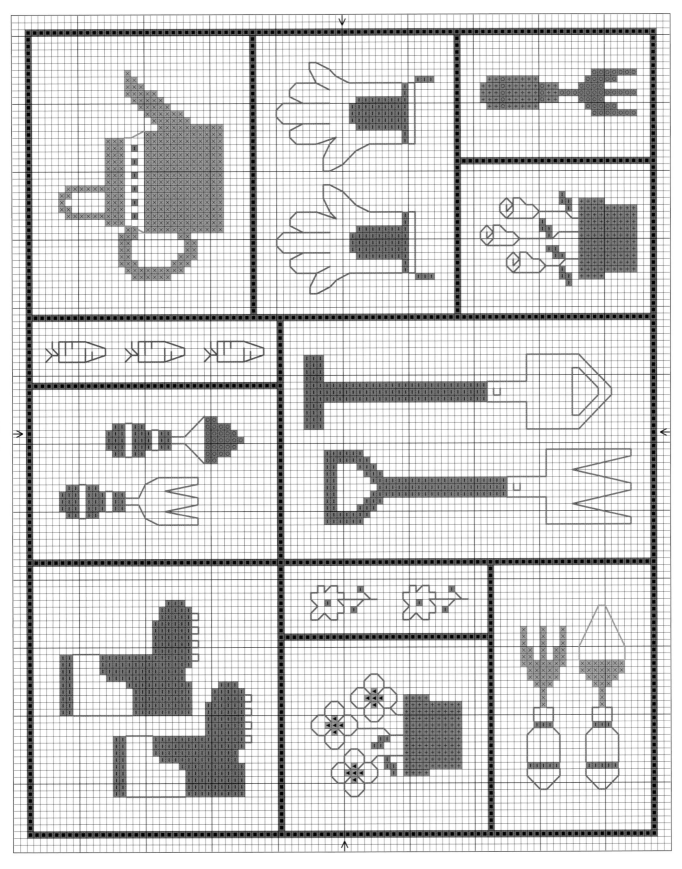

toolbox

The intriguing shapes of household tools make them decorative, if unusual, motifs.

stitching the design

1 Overcast the edges of the fabric to prevent fraying. Mark the midpoint of the fabric both vertically and horizontally with basting stitches; mount the fabric in an embroidery hoop (or stretcher frame) (see Getting Started, page 18).

2 Use the size guide below to calculate the size of design that will result from using different fabric counts (see How to Use This Book, page 13). Refer to the cross-stitch chart and thread key, and stitch from the middle outward.

3 Remove the finished design from the hoop and press gently on the wrong side.

size guide

fabric count	number of threads/blocks	number of strands	size of design
14	1	1	7¾ x 11⅜ in. (19.75 x 29 cm)
16	1	1	6¾ x 9⅞ in. (17.25 x 25 cm)
18	1	1	6 x 8⅞ in. (15.25 x 22.5 cm)
25	2	2	8¾ x 12¾ in. (22.25 x 32.5 cm)
28	2	2	7¾ x 11⅜ in. (19.75 x 29 cm)

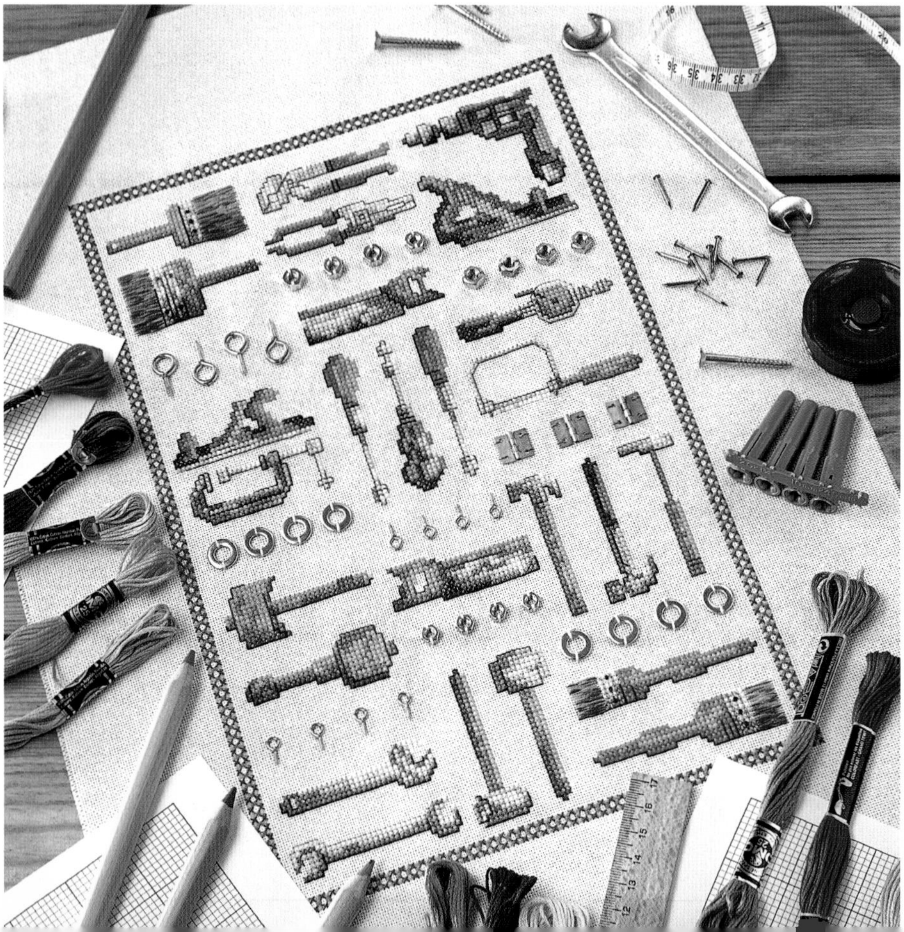

materials

- The design shown here uses evenweave fabric, 25-count white, and tapestry needle, size 26.
- Stranded cottons, one skein of each colour listed in key. Use two strands for cross-stitch, backstitch, straight stitch, and French knots.
- Small metal nuts, screw hooks, washers, and hinges. All-purpose adhesive.

thread key

- 154 aubergine
- 309 mid rose
- 340 deep lilac
- 351 deep coral
- 402 pale tan
- 414 light pewter
- 648 pale mud green
- 704 pale lime green
- 762 pale pearl grey
- 791 purple blue
- 899 rich ice pink
- 918 copper brown
- 991 dark aqua
- 3747 ice lilac
- 3815 deep jade
- 3817 pale jade
- 3829 dark old gold

backstitch

- 154 aubergine
- 309 mid rose
- 414 light pewter
- 648 pale mud green
- 704 pale lime green
- 791 purple blue
- 918 copper brown

French knots

- 154 aubergine
- 414 light pewter

◄ For the bristles of the brushes, work straight stitches in 402, 918, and 3829, mixing them freely. Attach small nuts and screws.

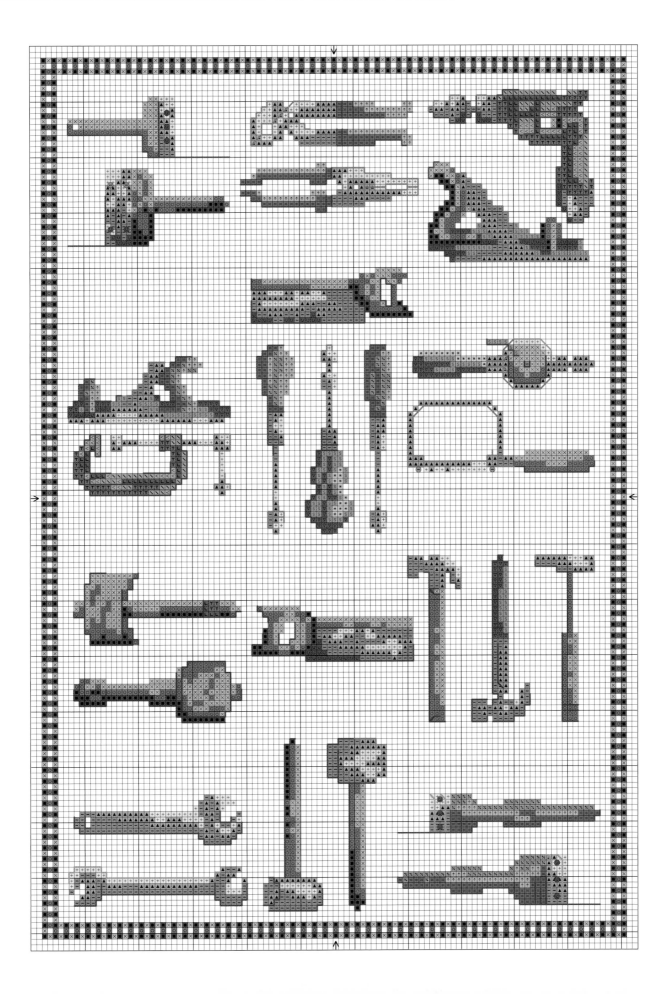

landscape

Poplar trees add a focal point to a patchwork landscape in shades of aqua, blue, and green.

stitching the design

1 Overcast the edges of the fabric to prevent fraying. Mark the midpoint of the fabric both vertically and horizontally with basting stitches; mount the fabric in an embroidery hoop (or stretcher frame) (see Getting Started, page 18).

2 Use the size guide below to calculate the size of design that will result from using different fabric counts (see How to Use This Book, page 13). Refer to the cross-stitch chart and thread key, and stitch from the middle outward.

3 Remove the finished design from the hoop and press gently on the wrong side.

size guide

fabric count	number of threads/blocks	number of strands	size of design
14	1	2	4 x 3⅛ in. (10.25 x 8 cm)
16	1	2	3½ x 2⅝ in. (9 x 6.75 cm)
18	1	2	3⅛ x 2⅜ in. (8 x 6 cm)
28	2	2	4 x 3⅛ in. (10.25 x 8 cm)
28	3	3	6 x 4⅝ in. (15.25 x 11.75 cm)

materials

- The design shown here uses evenweave fabric, 14-count antique white Aida, and tapestry needle, size 26.

- Stranded cottons, one skein of each colour listed in key. Use two strands for cross-stitch.

thread key

- ☒ 699 dark pine green
- Ⓝ 700 pine green
- Ⓞ 702 spring green
- ■ 796 royal blue
- ⬒ 797 French blue
- ◩ 799 deep blue
- ◁ 958 aqua
- ⊞ 959 mid aqua
- ⊡ 964 ice aqua
- ▲ 991 dark aqua
- Ⓤ 992 mid green aqua
- ⊟ 993 pale green aqua
- ☒ 3814 aquamarine

◀ Complemented by a blue frame that echoes the sky, this design achieves its serenity by using a restricted palette of cool colours. The shape of the landscape design also makes it suitable for a wallet or purse.

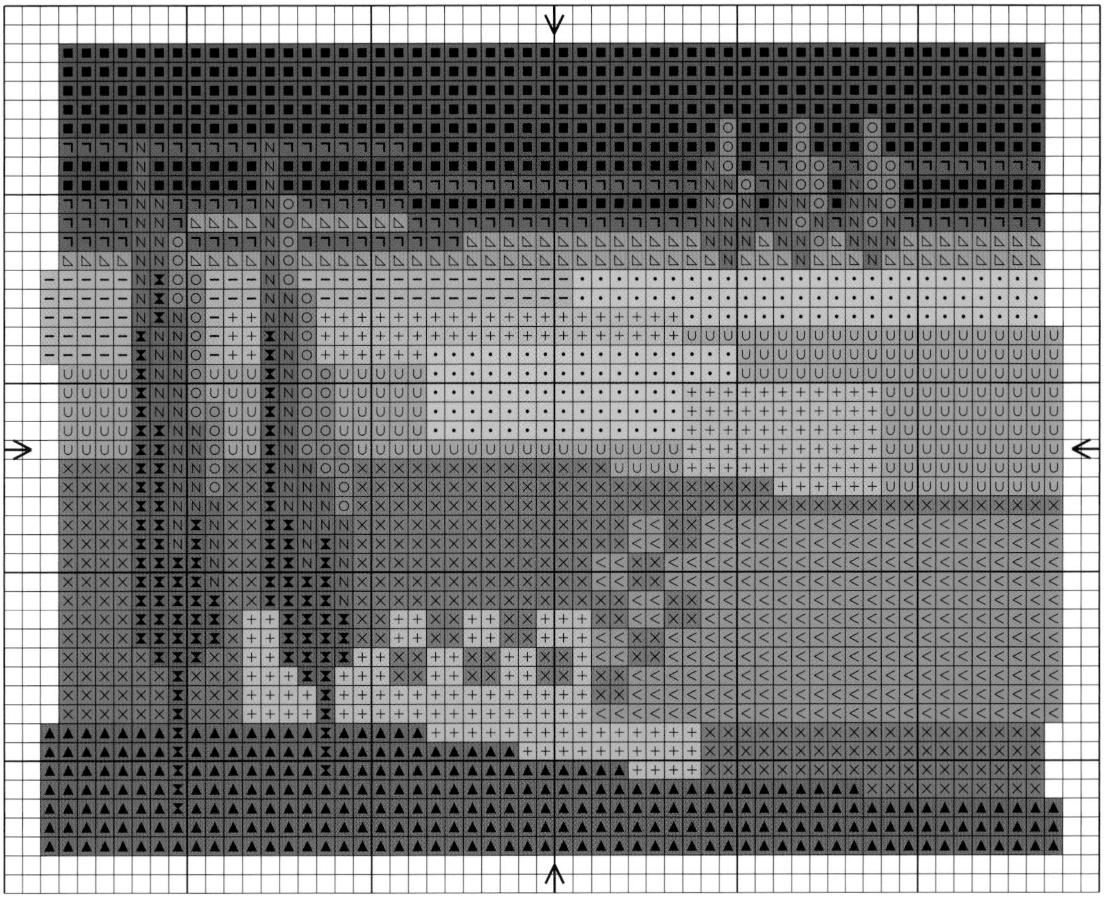

cakes

Topped with flowers and candles, cake motifs make perfect decorations for celebratory events.

stitching the design

1 Overcast the edges of the fabric to prevent fraying. Mark the midpoint of the fabric both vertically and horizontally with basting stitches; mount the fabric in an embroidery hoop (or stretcher frame) (see Getting Started, page 18).

2 Use the size guide below to calculate the size of motif A that will result from using different fabric counts (see How to Use This Book, page 13). Refer to the cross-stitch chart and thread key, and stitch from the middle outward.

3 Remove the finished design from the hoop and press gently on the wrong side.

materials

■ The design shown here uses evenweave fabric, 14-count antique white Aida, and tapestry needle, size 26.

■ Stranded cottons, one skein of each colour listed in key. Use two strands for cross-stitch and one for backstitch.

size guide

fabric count	number of threads/blocks	number of strands	size of design
14	1	2	2⅜ x 3⅝ in. (6 x 9.25 cm)
16	1	2	2⅛ x 3¼ in. (5.5 x 8.25 cm)
18	1	2	1⅞ x 2⅞ in. (4.75 x 7.25 cm)
28	2	2	2⅜ x 3⅝ in. (6 x 9.25 cm)
28	3	3	3½ x 5⅜ in. (9 x 13.75 cm)

thread key

▣ 340 deep lilac
▪ 437 old gold
☒ 744 primrose yellow
◉ 3747 ice lilac
⊞ 3823 yellow cream
⊟ 3855 pale apricot
▲ 3862 dark suede
backstitch
◼ 413 dark pewter

◀ A chocolate cake makes an attractive motif for a birthday card or a reusable cake band. Try different colours to suit other special occasions. For a wedding, stitch the larger cake in pastel peach or pink, with the detailing in cream or yellow. Adapt the smaller cakes to match, and use them on place cards or wedding menus.

(A)

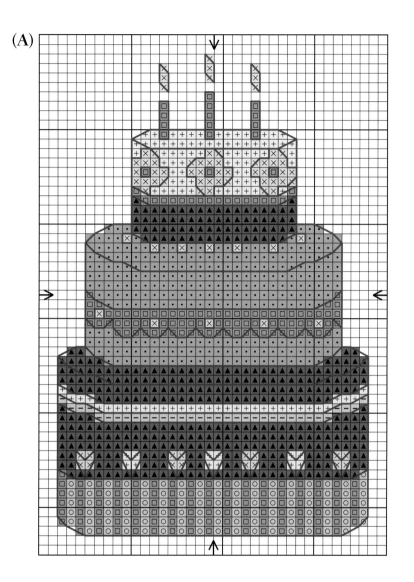

(B)

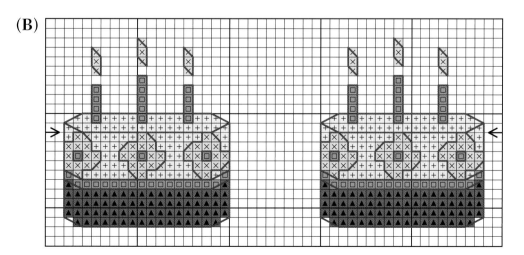

child's house

Inspired by children's paintings, this simple motif will brighten up any nursery.

stitching the design

1 Overcast the edges of the fabric to prevent fraying. Mark the midpoint of the fabric both vertically and horizontally with basting stitches; mount the fabric in an embroidery hoop (or stretcher frame) (see Getting Started, page 18).

2 Use the size guide below to calculate the size of design that will result from using different fabric counts (see How to Use This Book, page 13). Refer to the cross-stitch chart and thread key, and stitch from the middle outward.

3 Remove the finished design from the hoop and press gently on the wrong side.

size guide

fabric count	number of threads/blocks	number of strands	size of design
11	1	3	3¾ x 4¼ in. (9.5 x 10.75 cm)
14	1	2	3 x 3⅜ in. (7.5 x 8.5 cm)
16	1	2	2⅝ x 2⅞ in. (6.75 x 7.25 cm)
18	1	2	2⅜ x 2⅝ in. (6 x 6.75 cm)
28	2	2	3 x 3⅜ in. (7.5 x 8.5 cm)

materials

- The design shown here uses evenweave fabric, 11-count antique white Aida, and tapestry needle, size 26.

- Stranded cottons, one skein of each colour listed in key. Use three strands for cross-stitch.

thread key

- 355 dark terra cotta
- S 729 ochre
- ⊠ 3812 bright aqua

◀ Large red running stitches around the edge of the motif form an effective border. Mount the motif on a striped fabric that highlights the red and white elements in the house—a checked fabric would also work well.

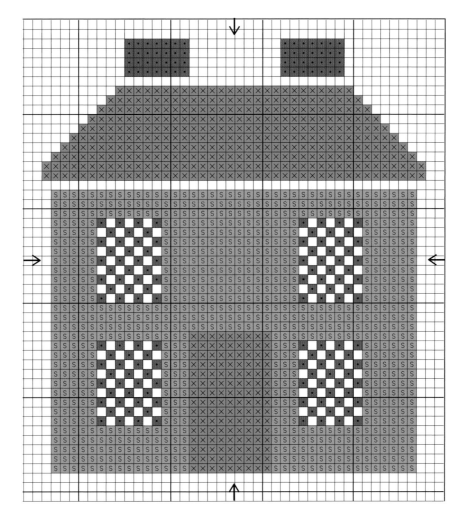

cocktails

These lively 1950s-style motifs make fun embellishments for many party accessories.

stitching the design

1 Overcast the edges of the fabric to prevent fraying. Mark the midpoint of the fabric both vertically and horizontally with basting stitches; mount the fabric in an embroidery hoop (or stretcher frame) (see Getting Started, page 18).

2 Use the size guide below to calculate the size of design that will result from using different fabric counts (see How to Use This Book, page 13). Refer to the cross-stitch chart and thread key, and stitch from the middle outward.

3 Remove the finished design from the hoop and press gently on the wrong side.

size guide

fabric count	number of threads/blocks	number of strands	size of design
11	1	3	11⅛ x 4 in. (28.25 x 10.25 cm)
14	1	2	8¾ x 3⅛ in. (22.25 x 8 cm)
16	1	2	7⅝ x 2¾ in. (19.25 x 7 cm)
18	1	2	6⅞ x 2½ in. (17.5 x 6.25 cm)
28	2	2	8¾ x 3⅛ in. (22.25 x 8 cm)

materials

- The design shown here uses evenweave fabric, 11-count white Aida, and tapestry needle, size 26.

- Stranded cottons, one skein of each colour listed in key. Use three strands for cross-stitch and one for backstitch.

thread key

- ☒ 321 red
- ↑ 601 cyclamen
- ⊟ 741 tangerine
- ⊟ 775 pale ice blue
- ⊚ 907 pale apple green
- ⊞ 973 yellow
- ⊍ 3845 bold turquoise

backstitch

- ◺ 775 pale ice blue
- ◹ 783 pale caramel

◀ To bring style and a sense of occasion to a cocktail party, decorate a tray cloth with a vodka martini, a margarita, a blue martini, a buck's fizz, and a pink cocktail shaker. Each one can easily be stitched onto coasters, napkins, or other accessories in the home cocktail bar.

(top)

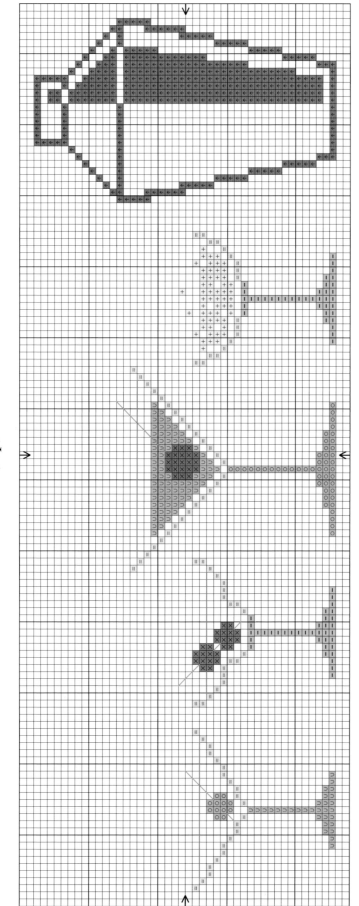

fancy teapots

In sugared almond shades, traditionally patterned teapots on a lace-edged shelf are a visual treat.

stitching the design

1 Overcast the edges of the fabric to prevent fraying. Mark the midpoint of the fabric both vertically and horizontally with basting stitches; mount the fabric in an embroidery hoop (or stretcher frame) (see Getting Started, page 18).

2 Use the size guide below to calculate the size of design that will result from using different fabric counts (see How to Use This Book, page 13). Refer to the cross-stitch chart and thread key, and stitch from the middle outward.

3 Remove the finished design from the hoop and press gently on the wrong side.

size guide

fabric count	number of threads/blocks	number of strands	size of design
14	1	2	7¼ x 8 in. (18.5 x 20.25 cm)
16	1	2	6⅜ x 7 in. (16.25 x 17.75 cm)
18	1	2	5⅝ x 6¼ in. (14.25 x 16 cm)
25	2	2	8⅛ x 9 in. (20.75 x 22.75 cm)
28	2	2	7¼ x 8 in. (18.5 x 20.25 cm)

materials

- The design shown here uses evenweave fabric, 25-count white, and tapestry needle size 26.

- Stranded cottons, one skein of each colour listed in key. Use two strands for cross-stitch and one for backstitch.

thread key

- ⊡ ecru
- ⊠ 164 palest grass green
- ⊟ 320 poplar green
- ◎ 368 mid green
- ▲ 420 dark hazel
- Ⓤ 518 mid sky blue
- ⊟ 519 sky blue
- ↟ 535 ash grey
- ⊠ 772 pale leaf green
- ▽ 775 pale ice blue
- Ⓢ 834 lime gold
- ✳ 963 cream pink
- Ⓛ 3046 mid putty
- Ⓣ 3047 pale putty
- ◿ 3354 pale old pink
- ◁ 3687 purple pink
- ➔ 3688 pink mauve

backstitch

- ◿ 420 dark hazel

◀ Flowers, dots, checks, stripes, and heart motifs are used to decorate rows of assorted teapots. Variety contributes to the charm of this design—notice how the lids and handles differ from one to the next.

mini house

Hardly larger than a postage stamp, this tiny gabled house is ideal for cards or gift tags.

stitching the design

1 Overcast the edges of the fabric to prevent fraying. Mark the midpoint of the fabric both vertically and horizontally with basting stitches; mount the fabric in an embroidery hoop (or stretcher frame) (see Getting Started, page 18).

2 Use the size guide below to calculate the size of design that will result from using different fabric counts (see How to Use This Book, page 13). Refer to the cross-stitch chart and thread key, and stitch from the middle outward.

3 Remove the finished design from the hoop and press gently on the wrong side.

size guide

fabric count	number of threads/blocks	number of strands	size of design
14	1	2	1½ x 1⅞ in. (4 x 4.75 cm)
16	1	2	1¼ x 1⅝ in. (3.25 x 4.25 cm)
18	1	2	1⅛ x 1½ in. (2.75 x 4 cm)
28	2	2	1½ x 1⅞ in. (4 x 4.75 cm)
28	3	3	2¼ x 2¾ in. (5.75 x 7 cm)

materials

- The design shown here uses evenweave fabric, 14-count white Aida, and tapestry needle, size 24.

- Stranded cottons, one skein of each colour listed in key. Use two strands for cross-stitch and one for backstitch.

thread key

- ▨ 310 black
- ☑ 728 bright gold
- ⊚ 799 deep blue
- ☒ 3328 dark salmon
- ⊟ 3849 teal

backstitch

- ◣ 310 black

◀ Quick and easy to stitch, this vivid design is used here to add a personal touch to a postcard. It could also decorate a small gift box or key ring. Think about individual preferences of friends and family—some may prefer cool or pastel shades, others these warm, bright colours.

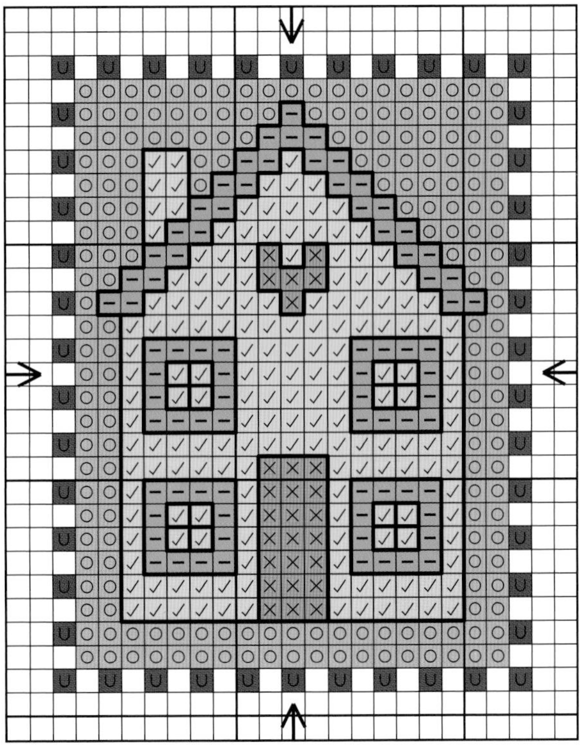

packages

Perk up even the plainest household item with this cheerful band of gift-wrapped packages.

stitching the design

1 Overcast the edges of the fabric to prevent fraying. Mark the midpoint of the fabric both vertically and horizontally with basting stitches; mount the fabric in an embroidery hoop (or stretcher frame) (see Getting Started, page 18).

2 Use the size guide below to calculate the size of design that will result from using different fabric counts (see How to Use This Book, page 13). Refer to the cross-stitch chart and thread key, and stitch from the middle outward.

3 Remove the finished design from the hoop and press gently on the wrong side.

size guide

fabric count	number of threads/blocks	number of strands	size of design
14	1	2	6⅜ x 1⅝ in. (16.25 x 4.25 cm)
16	1	2	5⅝ x 1⅜ in. (14.25 x 3.5 cm)
18	1	2	5 x 2⅞ in. (12.75 x 7.25 cm)
28	2	2	6⅜ x 1⅝ in. (16.25 x 4.25 cm)
28	3	3	9½ x 2⅜ in. (24.25 x 6 cm)

materials

- The design shown here uses evenweave fabric, 16-count white Aida band, and tapestry needle, size 26.

- Stranded cottons, one skein of each colour listed in key. Use two strands for cross-stitch and one for backstitch.

thread key

- Z 471 pale avocado
- U 472 light avocado
- X 743 buttercup yellow
- E 744 primrose yellow
- ● 3854 pale carrot orange
- H 3855 pale apricot

backstitch

- ◣ 469 dark avocado
- ◣ 3772 dark maple sugar

◀ Stitch as many motifs as you need, varying the length of Aida band accordingly. For a greeting card, stitch just one of the motifs on a single fabric square.

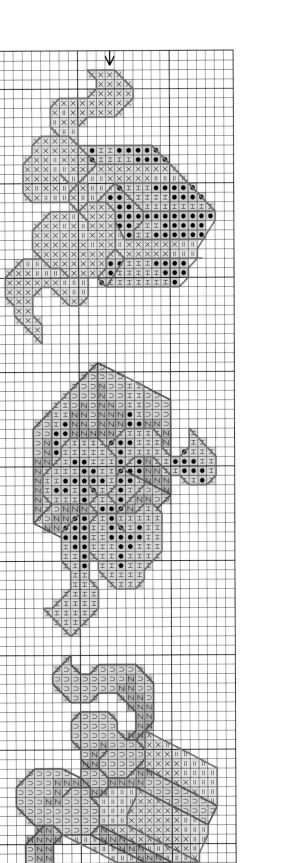

(top)

grand house

Celebrate a move to a new place by personalizing this stylish hearth and home sampler.

stitching the design

1 Overcast the edges of the fabric to prevent fraying. Mark the midpoint of the fabric both vertically and horizontally with basting stitches; mount the fabric in an embroidery hoop (or stretcher frame) (see Getting Started, page 18).

2 Use the size guide below to calculate the size of design that will result from using different fabric counts (see How to Use This Book, page 13). Refer to the cross-stitch chart and thread key, and stitch from the middle outward.

3 Remove the finished design from the hoop and press gently on the wrong side.

size guide

fabric count	number of threads/blocks	number of strands	size of design
14	1	2	11⅜ x 7¾ in. (29 x 19.75 cm)
16	1	2	9⅞ x 6¾ in. (25 x 17.25 cm)
18	1	2	8⅞ x 6 in. (22.5 x 15.25 cm)
28	2	2	11⅜ x 7¾ in. (29 x 19.75 cm)
28	3	3	17⅛ x 11⅝ in. (43.5 x 29.5 cm)

materials

- The design shown here uses evenweave fabric, 28-count biscuit linen, and tapestry needle, size 26.

- Stranded cottons, one skein of each colour listed in key. Use two strands for cross-stitch and one for backstitch.

thread key

- 315 dark old mauve
- 316 pale old mauve
- 318 dark pearl grey
- 414 light pewter
- 500 dark green
- 502 sea green
- 676 pale old gold
- 712 cream
- 948 peach cream
- 987 grass green
- 3041 dusty mauve
- 3052 mid thyme
- 3053 pale thyme
- 3348 pale moss green
- 3778 light terra cotta
- 3813 light jade
- 3828 mid hazel
- 3863 suede
- 3864 pale suede

backstitch

- 3348 pale moss green

◀ Framed by a rose-patterned border, this sampler has all the elements of a traditional sampler style. In the foreground, pheasants strut and hounds leap playfully between clipped trees and shrubs. Use letters from any of the alphabet samplers in this book to stitch your own name and, if you wish, the date.

(top)

tea party

Decorated cakes and pretty china make ideal motifs for a child's birthday party.

stitching the design

1 Overcast the edges of the fabric to prevent fraying. Mark the midpoint of the fabric both vertically and horizontally with basting stitches; mount the fabric in an embroidery hoop (or stretcher frame) (see Getting Started, page 18).

2 Use the size guide below to calculate the size of motif A that will result from using different fabric counts (see How to Use This Book, page 13). Refer to the cross-stitch chart and thread key, and stitch from the middle outward.

3 Remove the finished design from the hoop and press gently on the wrong side.

size guide

fabric count	number of threads/blocks	number of strands	size of design
11	1	3	1¾ x 2⅝ in. (4.5 x 6.75 cm)
14	1	2	1⅜ x 2⅛ in. (3.5 x 5.5 cm)
16	1	2	1¼ x 1¾ in. (3.25 x 4.5 cm)
18	1	2	1⅛ x 1⅝ in. (2.75 x 4.25 cm)
28	2	2	1⅜ x 2⅛ in. (3.5 x 5.5 cm)

materials

- The design shown here uses evenweave fabric, 11- and 14-count white Aida, and tapestry needle, size 26.

- Stranded cottons, one skein of each colour listed in key. Use two strands for cross-stitch on 14-count Aida and three strands on 11-count Aida. Use one strand for backstitch.

thread key

- ⊡ blanc
- ☑ 340 deep lilac
- ◬ 437 old gold
- ⊟ 739 dark cream
- ⛊ 744 primrose yellow
- ◎ 913 spearmint
- ↑ 955 pale spearmint
- ⊤ 956 geranium
- ⊍ 957 mid geranium
- → 963 cream pink
- ◁ 3747 ice lilac
- ⊞ 3823 yellow cream
- ⊠ 3855 pale apricot
- ▣ 3862 dark suede
- ⬤ 3864 pale suede

backstitch
- ◹ 413 dark pewter

◀ **The great thing about these little motifs is that you can stitch them with almost any combination of threads. Bright yellows and greens, for example, give a fresh springlike look, while creams and peaches create a more sophisticated effect.**

(A)

(B)

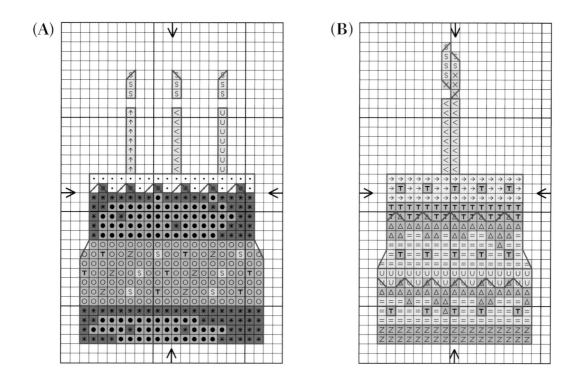

(C)

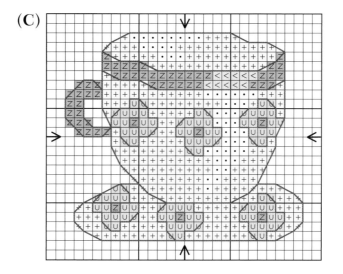

chapter six:

animal magic

farm animals

This lively sampler makes good use of traditional farmyard animals and equipment.

stitching the design

1 Overcast the edges of the fabric to prevent fraying. Mark the midpoint of the fabric both vertically and horizontally with basting stitches; mount the fabric in an embroidery hoop (or stretcher frame) (see Getting Started, page 18).

2 Use the size guide below to calculate the size of design that will result from using different fabric counts (see How to Use This Book, page 13). Refer to the cross-stitch chart and thread key, and stitch from the middle outward.

3 Remove the finished design from the hoop and press gently on the wrong side.

size guide

fabric count	number of threads/blocks	number of strands	whole design
14	1	2	6½ x 11¼ in. (16.5 x 28.5 cm)
16	1	2	5⅝ x 9⅞ in. (14.25 x 25 cm)
18	1	2	5 x 8¾ in. (12.75 x 22.25 cm)
28	2	2	6½ x 11¼ in. (16.5 x 28.5 cm)
28	3	3	9¾ x 16⅞ in. (24.75 x 42.75 cm)

materials

- The design shown here uses evenweave fabric, 28-count white Quaker cloth, and tapestry needle, size 26.

- Stranded cottons, one skein of each colour listed in key. Use two strands for cross-stitch and three-quarter stitch and one for backstitch.

thread key

- U 169 slate grey
- ▲ 517 deep sky blue
- V 519 sky blue
- + 676 pale old gold
- ⋈ 729 ochre
- ✳ 920 light brick
- ▽ 922 gold copper
- ▣ 924 dark grey blue
- T 928 silver grey
- ⊟ 951 pink cream
- ● 976 toffee
- S 977 mid fudge
- ↑ 988 mid grass green
- ⊠ 3779 rose beige
- ◆ 3814 aquamarine
- ▫ 3865 soft white

backstitch

- ◺ 801 dark brown

◀ Stitching the motifs in rows gives this design a playful appeal. In a child's bedroom, this sampler could even serve as a fun learning tool. A single motif could be used as a small gift for someone who collects, say, items with a pig theme.

swallow

Outlined in backstitch, this elegant bird complements home interiors that have a blue-and-white decor.

stitching the design

1 Overcast the edges of the fabric to prevent fraying. Mark the midpoint of the fabric both vertically and horizontally with basting stitches; mount the fabric in an embroidery hoop (or stretcher frame) (see Getting Started, page 18).

2 Use the size guide below to calculate the size of design that will result from using different fabric counts (see How to Use This Book, page 13). Refer to the cross-stitch chart and thread key, and stitch from the middle outward.

3 Remove the finished design from the hoop and press gently on the wrong side.

materials

- The design shown here uses evenweave fabric, 28-count white Quaker cloth, and tapestry needle, size 26.

- Stranded cottons, one skein of each colour listed in key. Use two strands for cross-stitch and one for backstitch.

size guide

fabric count	number of threads/blocks	number of strands	size of design
14	1	2	4½ x 3⅜ in. (11.5 x 8.5 cm)
16	1	2	3⅞ x 2⅞ in. (9.75 x 7.25 cm)
18	1	2	3½ x 2⅝ in. (9 x 6.75 cm)
28	2	2	4½ x 3⅜ in. (11.5 x 8.5 cm)
28	3	3	6¾ x 5⅛ in. (17.25 x 13 cm)

thread key

- ⊟ blanc
- ■ 336 dark navy blue
- ⊞ 712 cream
- ▲ 744 primrose yellow
- ⊠ 824 rich blue
- ◎ 826 light rich blue
- Ⓤ 951 pink cream

backstitch

- ◲ 823 deep navy blue

◀ Here, the swallow decorates a white wash bag tied at the top with a matching blue cord.

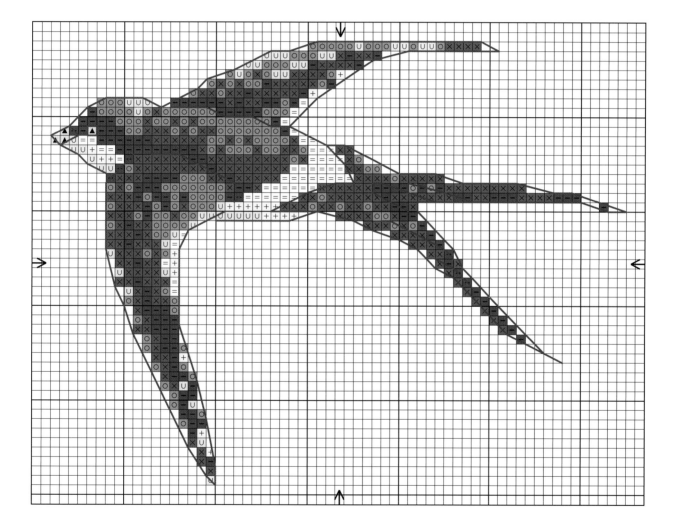

animal shapes

Worked in solid colours, these graphic duck, cat, dog, and rabbit motifs can be put to many uses.

stitching the design

1 Overcast the edges of the fabric to prevent fraying. Mark the midpoint of the fabric both vertically and horizontally with basting stitches; mount the fabric in an embroidery hoop (or stretcher frame) (see Getting Started, page 18).

2 Use the size guide below to calculate the size of motif D that will result from using different fabric counts (see How to Use This Book, page 13). Refer to the cross-stitch chart and thread key, and stitch from the middle outward.

3 Remove the finished design from the hoop and press gently on the wrong side.

materials

- The design shown here uses evenweave fabric, 11-count white Aida, and tapestry needle, size 26.

- Stranded cottons, one skein of each colour listed in key. Use three strands for cross-stitch.

size guide

fabric count	number of threads/blocks	number of strands	size of design
11	1	3	2½ x 3⅜ in. (6.25 x 8.5 cm)
14	1	2	2 x 2⅝ in. (5 x 6.75 cm)
16	1	2	1¾ x 2¼ in. (4.5 x 5.75 cm)
18	1	2	1½ x 2 in. (4 x 5 cm)
28	2	2	2 x 2⅝ in. (5 x 6.75 cm)

thread key

- ▲ 340 deep lilac
- ◉ 907 pale apple green
- ⊠ 3806 pale fuchsia
- ⊟ 3846 light turquoise

◀ These animals can be arranged in a vertical strip or used to form a clever patchwork. Any combination can be stitched onto children's bedroom accessories and nursery equipment.

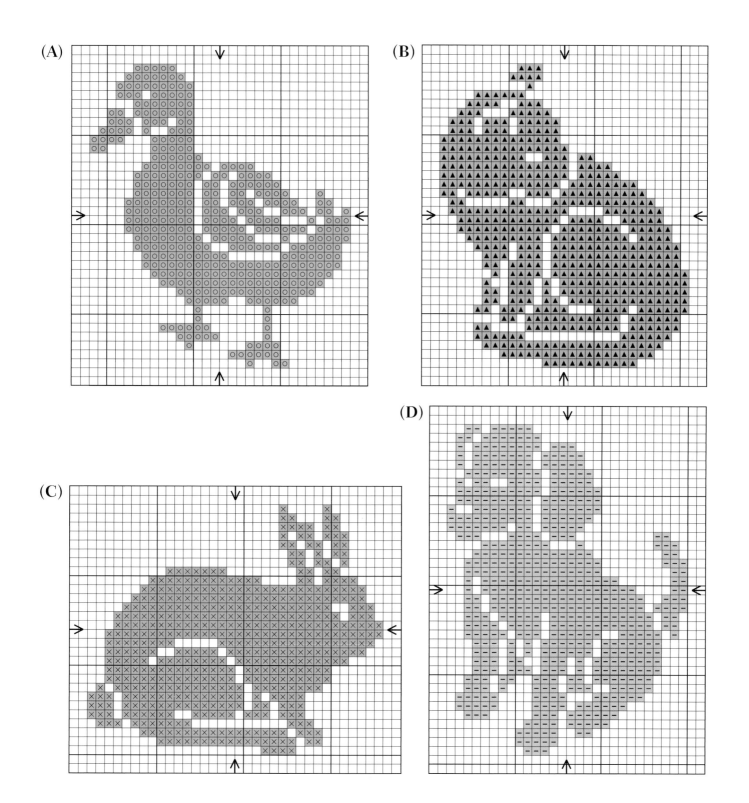

(A)

(B)

(C)

(D)

cow cartoon

Bright cartoon images, such as this smiling cow, are ideal for cross-stitching and sure to delight any child.

stitching the design

1 Overcast the edges of the fabric to prevent fraying. Mark the midpoint of the fabric both vertically and horizontally with basting stitches; mount the fabric in an embroidery hoop (or stretcher frame) (see Getting Started, page 18).

2 Use the size guide below to calculate the size of design that will result from using different fabric counts (see How to Use This Book, page 13). Refer to the cross-stitch chart and thread key, and stitch from the middle outward.

3 Remove the finished design from the hoop and press gently on the wrong side.

materials

- The design shown here uses evenweave fabric, 14-count white Aida, and tapestry needle, size 26.

- Stranded cottons, one skein of each colour listed in key. Use two strands for cross-stitch and one for backstitch.

size guide

fabric count	number of threads/blocks	number of strands	size of design
14	1	2	4⅜ x 3⅞ in. (11 x 9.75 cm)
16	1	2	3¾ x 3⅜ in. (9.5 x 8.5 cm)
18	1	2	3⅜ x 3 in. (8.5 x 7.5 cm)
28	2	2	4⅜ x 3⅞ in. (11 x 9.75 cm)
28	3	3	6½ x 5¾ in. (16.5 x 14.5 cm)

thread key

- ■ 310 black
- ⊟ 604 mid rose
- ⊞ 645 dark mud grey
- ⊠ 725 bright yellow
- ⊙ 996 mid turquoise

backstitch

- ◇ 310 black

◄ A single motif makes a good greeting card or could be sewn onto a child's T-shirt. A row of these cows stitched onto Aida band could be used to decorate curtains in a nursery.

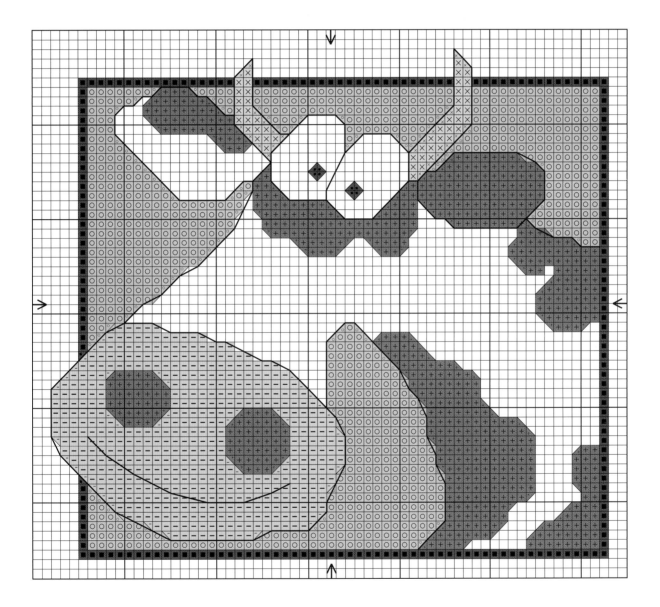

sea horses

In shades of green and aqua, this family of sea horses is ideal for bathroom accessories.

stitching the design

1 Overcast the edges of the fabric to prevent fraying. Mark the midpoint of the fabric both vertically and horizontally with basting stitches; mount the fabric in an embroidery hoop (or stretcher frame) (see Getting Started, page 18).

2 Use the size guide below to calculate the size of design that will result from using different fabric counts (see How to Use This Book, page 13). Refer to the cross-stitch chart and thread key, and stitch from the middle outward.

3 Remove the finished design from the hoop and press gently on the wrong side.

size guide

fabric count	number of threads/blocks	number of strands	size of design
14	1	2	4⅞ x 5¾ in. (12.5 x 14.5 cm)
16	1	2	4¼ x 5 in. (10.75 x 12.75 cm)
18	1	2	3¾ x 4½ in. (9.5 x 11.5 cm)
28	2	2	4⅞ x 5¾ in. (12.5 x 14.5 cm)
28	3	3	7¼ x 8⅝ in. (18.5 x 22 cm)

materials

- The design shown here uses evenweave fabric, 14-count white Aida, and tapestry needle, size 26.

- Stranded cottons, one skein of each colour listed in key. Use two strands for cross-stitch. Stitch an aqua glass seed bead over the smallest sea horse's eye and a beaded aqua sequin over the other sea horses' eyes. Add aqua or lilac sequins to the bubbles.

thread key

- ⊞ 415 steel grey
- Ⓤ 563 mid leaf
- Ⓢ 597 aqua
- ◎ 598 mid aqua
- ▲ 3809 green aqua

◄ Many cabinets and other objects with inset panels can be decorated with cross-stitch. To extend the sea horse theme throughout a bathroom, stitch the design onto laundry bags, fabric slippers, robes, or towels.

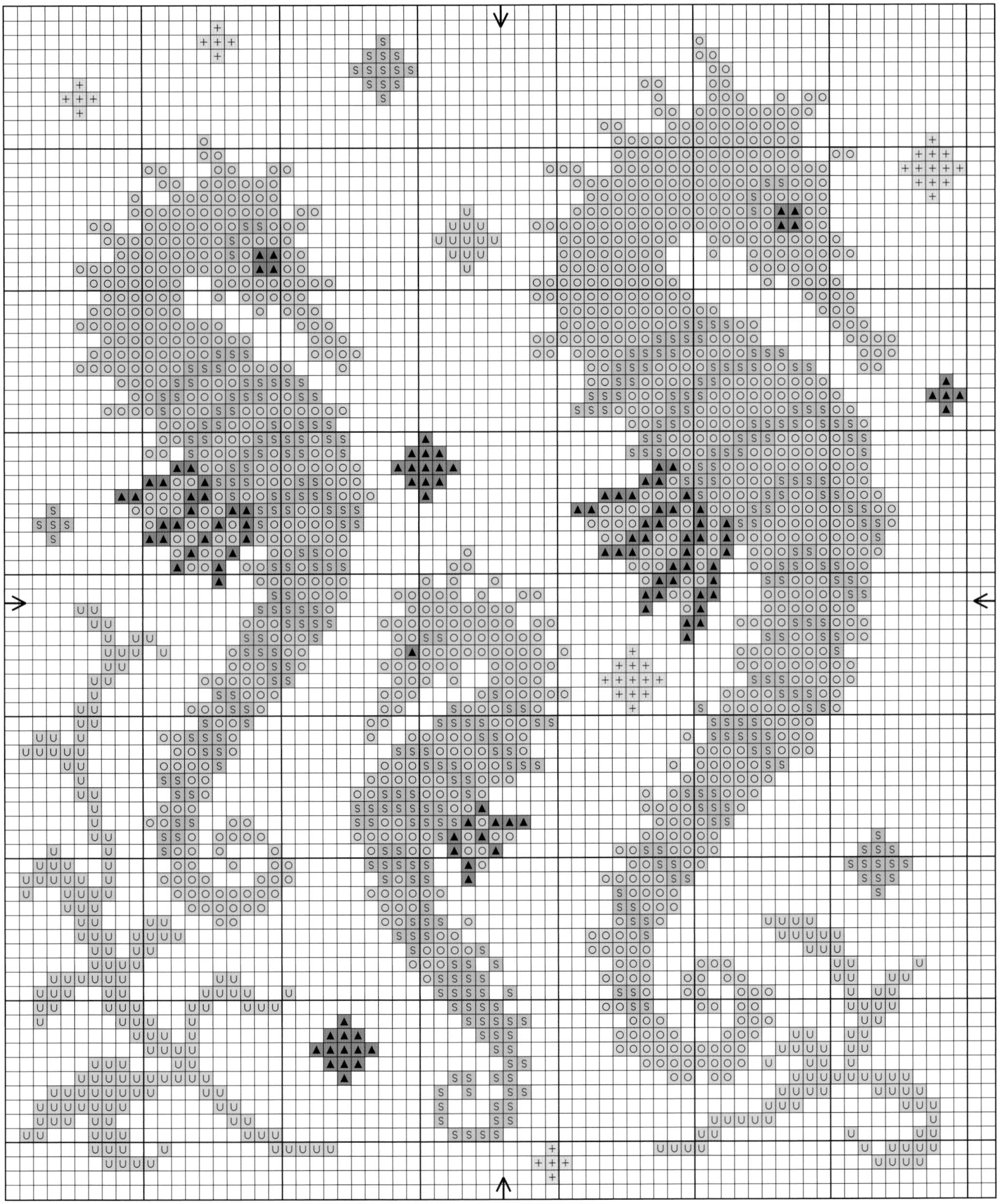

cats

Pen-and-wash illustrations inspire this group of cats, with backstitch imitating bold strokes of the pen.

stitching the design

1 Overcast the edges of the fabric to prevent fraying. Mark the midpoint of the fabric both vertically and horizontally with basting stitches; mount the fabric in an embroidery hoop (or stretcher frame) (see Getting Started, page 18).

2 Use the size guide below to calculate the size of design that will result from using different fabric counts (see How to Use This Book, page 13). Refer to the cross-stitch chart and thread key, and stitch from the middle outward.

3 Remove the finished design from the hoop and press gently on the wrong side.

size guide

fabric count	number of threads/blocks	number of strands	size of design
14	1	2	4⅜ x 6¼ in. (11 x 16 cm)
16	1	2	3⅞ x 5½ in. (9.75 x 14 cm)
18	1	2	3½ x 4⅞ in. (9 x 12.5 cm)
28	2	2	4⅜ x 6¼ in. (11 x 16 cm)
28	3	3	6½ x 9⅜ in. (16.5 x 23.75 cm)

materials

- The design shown here uses evenweave fabric, 28-count antique white linen, and tapestry needle, size 26.

- Stranded cottons, one skein of each colour listed in key. Use two strands for cross-stitch. Use one strand for backstitch and two strands for backstitch on the ball of yarn.

thread key

- 231 pale shell grey
- 233 grey putty
- 235 dark steel grey
- 236 charcoal
- 352 salmon
- 362 light camel
- 366 tan beige
- 858 pale spearmint
- 860 grey green
- 918 copper brown
- 1048 tan
- 3326 deep ice pink

backstitch

- 310 black
- 860 grey green

◀ The slightly textured evenweave linen on which the design is worked suggests artist's paper. A pale or white background is essential because parts of the motifs have been left bare to represent the white markings on the cats.

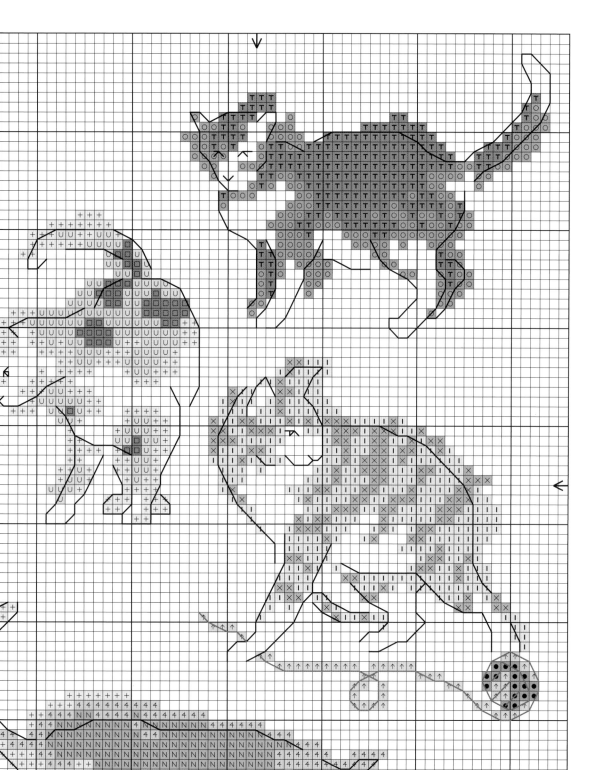

fishing flies

Vividly depicted fishing flies make a thoughtful gift for an avid angler.

stitching the design

1 Overcast the edges of the fabric to prevent fraying. Mark the midpoint of the fabric both vertically and horizontally with basting stitches; mount the fabric in an embroidery hoop (or stretcher frame) (see Getting Started, page 18).

2 Use the size guide below to calculate the size of design that will result from using different fabric counts (see How to Use This Book, page 13). Refer to the cross-stitch chart and thread key, and stitch from the middle outward.

3 Remove the finished design from the hoop and press gently on the wrong side.

size guide

fabric count	number of threads/blocks	number of strands	size of design
14	1	2	5¾ in. (14.5 cm) square
16	1	2	5 in. (12.75 cm) square
18	1	2	4½ in. (11.5 cm) square
28	2	2	5¾ in. (14.5 cm) square
28	3	3	8⅝ in. (22 cm) square

materials

- The design shown here uses evenweave fabric, 28-count natural linen, and tapestry needle, size 26.

- Stranded cottons and metallic threads, one skein or reel of each colour listed in key. Use two strands for cross-stitch and backstitch and one strand for backstitch in Art 273.

thread key

- ■ Art 273 black gold
- ◎ 743 buttercup yellow
- ⊟ 746 buttermilk
- ⊞ 920 light brick
- ◙ 3808 deep green aqua
- ⊠ 3827 pale fudge
- ▲ 3852 dark gold
- ✳ 3853 carrot orange
- ⊡ 3855 pale apricot
- Ⅱ 5282 metallic gold
- ◆ 5283 metallic silver

backstitch

- ◣ Art 273 black gold
- ◣ 920 light brick
- ◺ 5282 metallic gold

◀ Inspired by an illustration in a book, this design features different types of fishing flies, numbered for easy reference. A combination of cross-stitch and backstitch is used to indicate the fishhook attached to each fly. One or more flies would also look effective on a wallet or a bookmark.

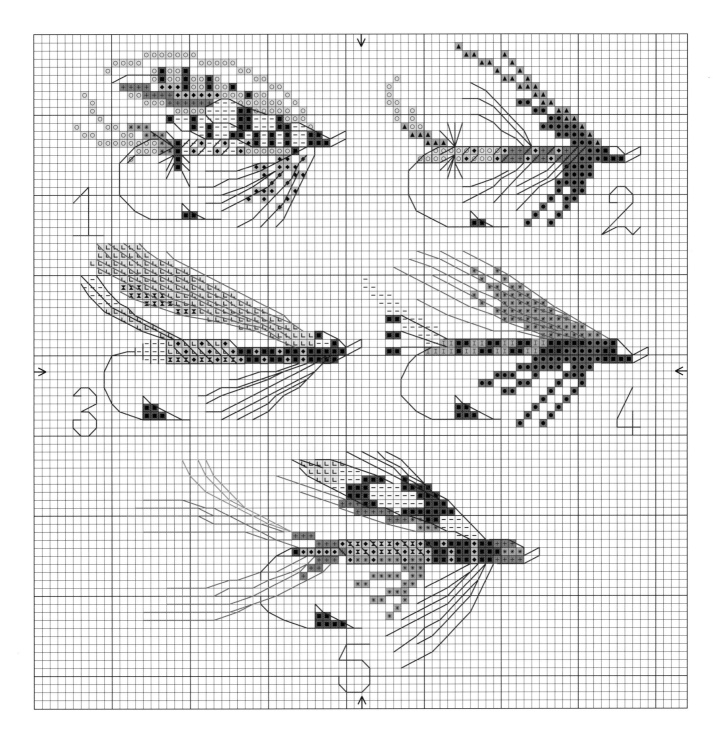

lovebirds

Based on a ceramic tile, this symmetrical design is worked solely in blue on antique white fabric.

stitching the design

1 Overcast the edges of the fabric to prevent fraying. Mark the midpoint of the fabric both vertically and horizontally with basting stitches; mount the fabric in an embroidery hoop (or stretcher frame) (see Getting Started, page 18).

2 Use the size guide below to calculate the size of design that will result from using different fabric counts (see How to Use This Book, page 13). Refer to the cross-stitch chart and thread key, and stitch from the middle outward.

3 Remove the finished design from the hoop and press gently on the wrong side.

size guide

fabric count	number of threads/blocks	number of strands	size of design
14	1	2	3¼ in. (8.25 cm) square
16	1	2	2¾ in. (7 cm) square
18	1	2	2½ in. (6.25 cm) square
28	2	2	3¼ in. (8.25 cm) square
28	3	3	4⅞ in. (12.5 cm) square

materials

■ The design shown here uses evenweave fabric, 18-count antique white Aida, and tapestry needle, size 26.

■ Stranded cottons, one skein of each colour listed in key. Use two strands for cross-stitch.

thread key

⊠ 798 bright cornflower blue

in detail

Parts of the design are left unstitched to create details such as the lovebirds' eyes and wings.

◄ Framed to form a greeting card, this design would complement any blue-and-white interior. The lovebirds could be stitched onto larger accessories or repeated to form a square patchwork.

Scottie dogs

A tartan background perfectly complements these little Scottie dogs in their red collars.

stitching the design

1 Overcast the edges of the fabric to prevent fraying. Mark the midpoint of the fabric both vertically and horizontally with basting stitches; mount the fabric in an embroidery hoop (or stretcher frame) (see Getting Started, page 18).

2 Use the size guide below to calculate the size of motif A that will result from using different fabric counts (see How to Use This Book, page 13). Refer to the cross-stitch chart and thread key, and stitch from the middle outward.

3 Remove the finished design from the hoop and press gently on the wrong side.

size guide

fabric count	number of threads/blocks	number of strands	size of design
14	1	2	3⅜ in. (8.5 cm) square
16	1	2	3 in. (7.5 cm) square
18	1	2	2⅝ in. (6.75 cm) square
28	2	2	3⅜ in. (8.5 cm) square
28	3	3	5⅛ in. (13 cm) square

materials

- The design shown here uses evenweave fabric, 14-count white Aida, and tapestry needle, size 26.

- Stranded cottons, one skein of each colour listed in key. Use two strands for cross-stitch and one for backstitch and straight stitch.

thread key

- ◉ 169 slate grey
- ■ 310 black
- ☑ 349 rust
- ☒ 535 ash grey
- ⊟ 3799 charcoal

backstitch and straight stitch

- ◻ 169 slate grey
- ◻ 310 black
- ◻ 701 light pine green

◀ Working straight stitches over the top of the cross-stitches suggests the Scottie's shaggy coat. The two motifs show different views of the dog. These could also be used, together or separately, for a little picture or greeting card.

(A)

(B)

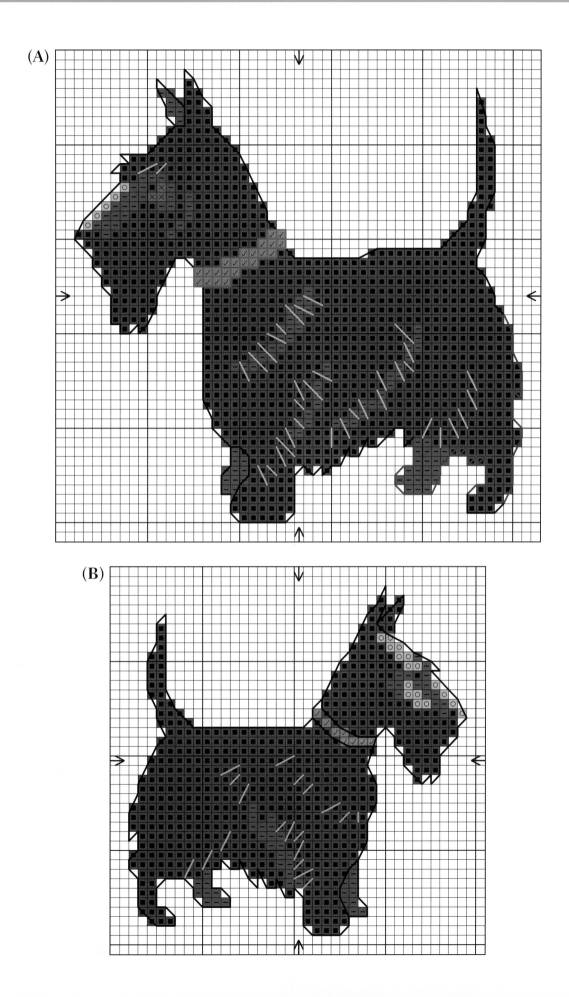

leopard print

Enduringly popular, fur prints can be re-created in cross-stitch for chic contemporary designs.

stitching the design

1 Overcast the edges of the fabric to prevent fraying. Mark the midpoint of the fabric both vertically and horizontally with basting stitches; mount the fabric in an embroidery hoop (or stretcher frame) (see Getting Started, page 18).

2 Use the size guide below to calculate the size of design that will result from using different fabric counts (see How to Use This Book, page 13). Refer to the cross-stitch chart and thread key, and stitch from the middle outward.

3 Remove the finished design from the hoop and press gently on the wrong side.

size guide

fabric count	number of threads/blocks	number of strands	size of design
14	1	2	5¾ x 3⅝ in. (14.5 x 9.25 cm)
16	1	2	5 x 3⅛ in. (12.75 x 8 cm)
18	1	2	4½ x 2¾ in. (11.5 x 7 cm)
25	2	2	6⅜ x 4 in. (16.25 x 10.25 cm)
28	2	2	5¾ x 3⅝ in. (14.5 x 9.25 cm)

materials

- The design shown here uses evenweave fabric, 25-count pale yellow, and tapestry needle, size 26.

- Stranded cottons, one skein of each colour listed in key. Use two strands for cross-stitch.

thread key

- ⊠ 434 mid brown
- ■ 3371 dark chocolate

in detail

The unstitched areas form part of the design; the spots are worked in two shades of brown.

◄ The leopard print design is stitched onto a pale yellow background. A warm beige fabric would also work well, but avoid white, because it would create an unnatural contrast.

(top)

tropical bird

A brightly coloured bird perched amid exotic plants makes a vibrant motif for a modern interior.

stitching the design

1 Overcast the edges of the fabric to prevent fraying. Mark the midpoint of the fabric both vertically and horizontally with basting stitches; mount the fabric in an embroidery hoop (or stretcher frame) (see Getting Started, page 18).

2 Use the size guide below to calculate the size of design that will result from using different fabric counts (see How to Use This Book, page 13). Refer to the cross-stitch chart and thread key, and stitch from the middle outward.

3 Remove the finished design from the hoop and press gently on the wrong side.

size guide

fabric count	number of threads/blocks	number of strands	size of design
14	1	2	5 in. (12.75 cm) square
16	1	2	4⅜ in. (11 cm) square
18	1	2	3⅞ in. (9.75 cm) square
28	2	2	5 in. (12.75 cm) square
28	3	3	7½ in. (19 cm) square

materials

- The design shown here uses evenweave fabric, 14-count antique white Aida, and tapestry needle, size 26.

- Stranded cottons, one skein of each colour listed in key. Use two strands for cross-stitch and one for backstitch and straight stitch.

thread key

- ☑ blanc
- Ⓤ 726 daffodil yellow
- Ⓣ 797 French blue
- Ⓗ 799 deep blue
- → 800 pale blue
- ▼ 817 poppy red
- Ⓘ 907 pale apple green
- Ⓝ 970 orange

backstitch and straight stitch

- ◻ 797 French blue
- ◻ 817 poppy red
- ◻ 904 dark apple green

◀ Mounted in a cherry red frame, the design makes a whimsical picture. It could also be used as a decoration for a tablecloth or tray cloth.

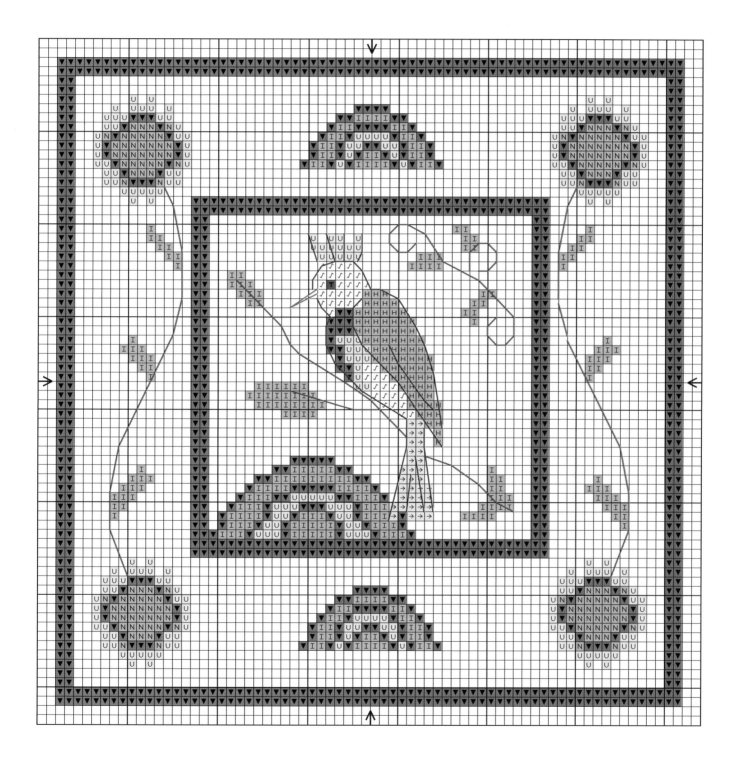

zebra

This composition features simple, bold shapes that give the design a naïve charm.

stitching the design

1 Overcast the edges of the fabric to prevent fraying. Mark the midpoint of the fabric both vertically and horizontally with basting stitches; mount the fabric in an embroidery hoop (or stretcher frame) (see Getting Started, page 18).

2 Use the size guide below to calculate the size of design that will result from using different fabric counts (see How to Use This Book, page 13). Refer to the cross-stitch chart and thread key, and stitch from the middle outward.

3 Remove the finished design from the hoop and press gently on the wrong side.

size guide

fabric count	number of threads/blocks	number of strands	size of design
14	1	2	5¾ in. (14.5 cm) square
16	1	2	5 in. (12.75 cm) square
18	1	2	4½ in. (11.5 cm) square
28	2	2	5¾ in. (14.5 cm) square
28	3	3	8⅝ in. (22 cm) square

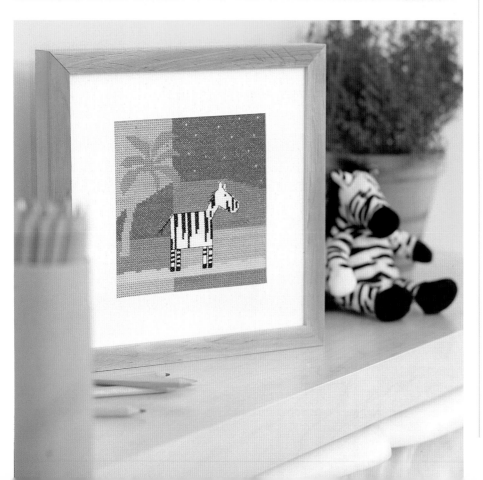

materials

- The design shown here uses evenweave fabric, 14-count white Aida, and tapestry needle, size 26.

- Stranded cottons, one skein of each colour listed in key. Use two strands for cross-stitch and one for backstitch and straight stitch.

thread key

- ▽ blanc
- ■ 310 black
- ▣ 718 raspberry
- ⊟ 906 apple green
- ◉ 971 mid pumpkin
- ⊞ 972 sunshine yellow
- ▦ 3607 mid raspberry
- ↑ 3608 pale raspberry

backstitch and straight stitch

- ◩ 310 black

◄ Filling in the background with shades of raspberry pink helps the main motif to stand out. Black thread is used to define the zebra's outline in backstitch and its stripes in cross-stitch.

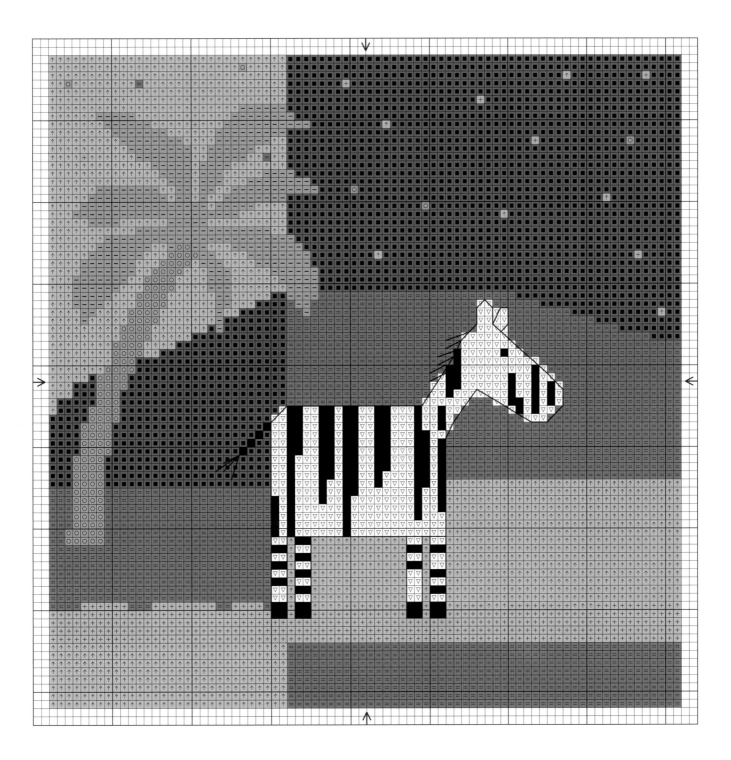

exotic bird

A simple border worked in backstitch defines this bird of paradise atop a climbing plant in bloom.

stitching the design

1 Overcast the edges of the fabric to prevent fraying. Mark the midpoint of the fabric both vertically and horizontally with basting stitches; mount the fabric in an embroidery hoop (or stretcher frame) (see Getting Started, page 18).

2 Use the size guide below to calculate the size of design that will result from using different fabric counts (see How to Use This Book, page 13). Refer to the cross-stitch chart and thread key, and stitch from the middle outward.

3 Remove the finished design from the hoop and press gently on the wrong side.

size guide

fabric count	number of threads/blocks	number of strands	size of design
14	1	2	2¼ x 5⅞ in. (5.75 x 15 cm)
16	1	2	1⅞ x 5¼ in. (4.75 x 13.25 cm)
18	1	2	1¾ x 4⅝ in. (4.5 x 11.75 cm)
28	2	2	2¼ x 5⅞ in. (5.75 x 15 cm)
28	3	3	3⅜ x 8⅞ in. (8.5 x 22.5 cm)

materials

- The design shown here uses evenweave fabric, 14-count white Aida, and tapestry needle, size 24.

- Stranded cottons, one skein of each colour listed in key. Use two strands for cross-stitch and one for backstitch.

thread key

- S 602 bright pink
- X 604 mid rose
- ▬ 718 raspberry
- ☑ 964 ice aqua
- ▪ 3812 bright aqua

backstitch
- ◸ 3765 dark peacock

◀ Clear, bright shades of pink and aqua form a feminine palette. For a more masculine look, experiment with burgundies, greens, and browns.

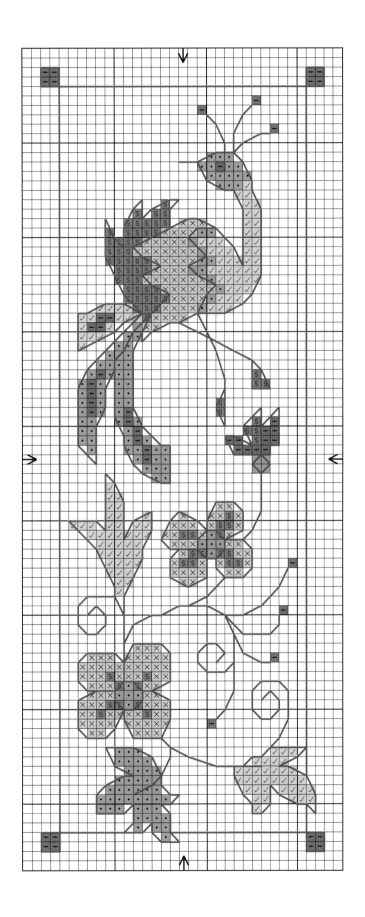

cat silhouette

The outline of this motif is created in part by letting the background fabric show through.

stitching the design

1 Overcast the edges of the fabric to prevent fraying. Mark the midpoint of the fabric both vertically and horizontally with basting stitches; mount the fabric in an embroidery hoop (or stretcher frame) (see Getting Started, page 18).

2 Use the size guide below to calculate the size of design that will result from using different fabric counts (see How to Use This Book, page 13). Refer to the cross-stitch chart and thread key, and stitch from the middle outward.

3 Remove the finished design from the hoop and press gently on the wrong side.

size guide

fabric count	number of threads/blocks	number of strands	size of design
14	1	2	5⅝ x 3¼ in. (14.25 x 8.25 cm)
16	1	2	4⅞ x 2¾ in. (12.5 x 7 cm)
18	1	2	4⅜ x 2½ in. (11 x 6.25 cm)
28	2	2	5⅝ x 3¼ in. (14.25 x 8.25 cm)
28	3	3	8⅜ x 4⅞ in. (21.25 x 12.5 cm)

materials

- The design shown here uses evenweave fabric, 28-count white, and tapestry needle, size 26.

- Stranded cottons, one skein of each colour listed in key. Use two strands for cross-stitch.

thread key

- ☒ 3740 pale aubergine

◀ White fabric has been dyed magenta to make a bold background for this design. Cat lovers can use this adaptable design on a wide assortment of items, from desk accessories to a bath or cosmetics bag.

(top)

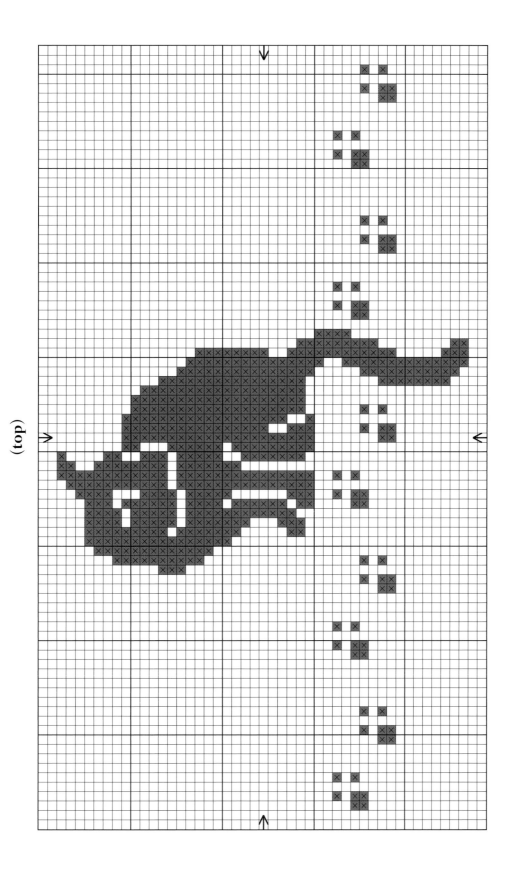

ocean waves

This fanciful design presents a view of a sailing ship tossed on the waves above a coral reef.

stitching the design

1 Overcast the edges of the fabric to prevent fraying. Mark the midpoint of the fabric both vertically and horizontally with basting stitches; mount the fabric in an embroidery hoop (or stretcher frame) (see Getting Started, page 18).

2 Use the size guide below to calculate the size of design that will result from using different fabric counts (see How to Use This Book, page 13). Refer to the cross-stitch chart and thread key, and stitch from the middle outward.

3 Remove the finished design from the hoop and press gently on the wrong side.

size guide

fabric count	number of threads/blocks	number of strands	size of design
14	1	2	4⅝ x 10⅛ in. (11.75 x 25.75 cm)
16	1	2	4 x 8⅞ in. (10.25 x 22.5 cm)
18	1	2	3½ x 7⅞ in. (9 x 20 cm)
28	2	2	4⅝ x 10⅛ in. (11.75 x 25.75 cm)
28	3	3	6⅞ x 15¼ in. (17.5 x 38.75 cm)

materials

- The design shown here uses evenweave fabric, 14-count antique white Aida, and tapestry needle, size 26.

- Stranded cottons, one skein of each colour listed in key. Use two strands for cross-stitch and one for backstitch.

thread key

- ⊡ blanc
- ⊠ 347 berry red
- ◙ 349 rust
- ▲ 413 dark pewter
- ⊞ 436 light camel
- ■ 500 dark green
- ▼ 501 viridian green
- ⊟ 564 pale dusty green
- ◎ 597 aqua
- ◁ 598 mid aqua
- ⋔ 742 pale sunshine yellow
- 4 744 primrose yellow
- ⊕ 745 pale buttercup yellow
- ⊟ 775 pale ice blue
- ▽ 782 mid mustard
- ⬚ 819 ice pink
- ⊍ 924 dark grey blue
- ⊠ 962 dusty pink
- → 963 cream pink
- ⬚ 976 toffee
- ★ 991 dark green aqua
- ⬚ 993 pale green aqua
- ⬚ 3752 antique blue
- ⬚ 3777 brick brown
- ✳ 3808 deep green aqua
- ⊤ 3809 green aqua
- ⬚ 3810 dark aqua
- ↑ 3811 pale aqua
- ⬚ 3814 aquamarine

backstitch
- ◣ 413 dark pewter
- ◣ 414 light pewter

◀ This design could also form a central panel on a window shade to create a focal point in a bathroom.

wildlife

Animals, birds, and insects, as well as the alphabet, create a mix of decorative shapes on this sampler.

stitching the design

1 Overcast the edges of the fabric to prevent fraying. Mark the midpoint of the fabric both vertically and horizontally with basting stitches; mount the fabric in an embroidery hoop (or stretcher frame) (see Getting Started, page 18).

2 Use the size guide below to calculate the size of design that will result from using different fabric counts (see How to Use This Book, page 13). Refer to the cross-stitch chart and thread key, and stitch from the middle outward.

3 Remove the finished design from the hoop and press gently on the wrong side.

size guide

fabric count	number of threads/blocks	number of strands	size of design
14	1	2	8½ x 11⅛ in. (21.5 x 28.25 cm)
16	1	2	7⅜ x 9⅝ in. (18.75 x 24.5 cm)
18	1	2	6⅝ x 8⅝ in. (16.75 x 22 cm)
27	2	2	8⅞ x 11½ in. (22.5 x 29.25 cm)
27	3	3	13¼ x 17¼ in. (33.75 x 43.75 cm)

materials

- The design shown here uses evenweave fabric, 27-count ivory, and tapestry needle, size 26.

- Stranded cottons, one skein of each colour listed in key. Use two strands for cross-stitch and backstitch.

thread key

- ▨ 436 light camel
- ⊡ 738 tan beige
- ⊠ 758 mid rose brown
- ◎ 931 metal blue
- ◙ 3777 brick brown
- ▽ 3778 light terra cotta
- ▣ 3830 terra cotta
- **backstitch**
- ◹ 931 metal blue

in detail

The backstitches are worked with two strands of thread, so they have the same visual "weight" as the cross-stitch. This creates a light inner border to frame the motifs.

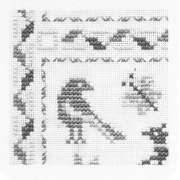

◀ This design will be particularly enjoyed by wildlife enthusiasts. It is also ideal for children, who will have fun guessing the names of the different creatures.

blue whales

Surfacing blue whales, with jets of water spurting from their blowholes, make a fun border.

materials

- The design shown here uses evenweave fabric, 16-count white Aida band, and tapestry needle size 26.

- Stranded cottons, one skein of each colour listed in key. Use two strands for cross-stitch and one for backstitch.

stitching the design

1 Overcast the edges of the fabric to prevent fraying. Mark the midpoint of the fabric both vertically and horizontally with basting stitches; mount the fabric in an embroidery hoop (or stretcher frame) (see Getting Started, page 18).

2 Use the size guide below to calculate the size of design that will result from using different fabric counts (see How to Use This Book, page 13). Refer to the cross-stitch chart and thread key, and stitch from the middle outward.

3 Remove the finished design from the hoop and press gently on the wrong side.

thread key

○	blanc
▲	676 pale old gold
⊠	3756 pale duck egg
✳	3838 Delft blue
S	3839 pale Delft blue
H	3840 palest Delft blue
⊟	3841 powder blue
backstitch	
◲	3799 charcoal

size guide

fabric count	number of threads/blocks	number of strands	size of design
14	1	2	5⅞ x 1¾ in. (15 x 4.5 cm)
16	1	2	5⅛ x 1½ in. (13 x 4 cm)
18	1	2	4½ x 1⅜ in. (11.5 x 3.5 cm)
28	2	2	5⅞ x 1¾ in. (15 x 4.5 cm)
28	3	3	8¾ x 2⅝ in. (22.25 x 6.75 cm)

in detail
All of the outlines in this design, including those of the spurts of water, are worked in backstitch.

◀ **By stitching several of the whale motifs in a row, you can create a border for a towel or washcloth.**

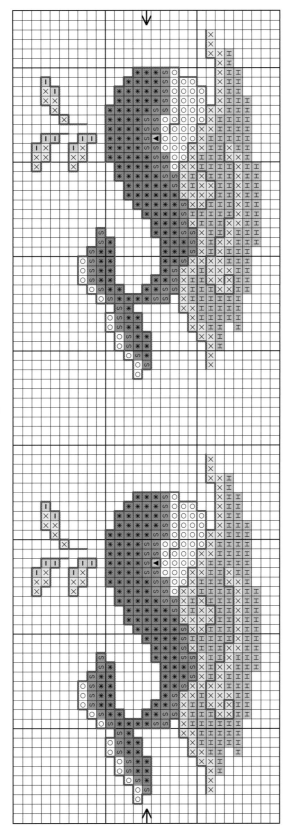

(top)

zebra stripes

Stitching covers all of the fabric to convey the texture, as well as the markings, of a zebra's coat.

stitching the design

1 Overcast the edges of the fabric to prevent fraying. Mark the midpoint of the fabric both vertically and horizontally with basting stitches; mount the fabric in an embroidery hoop (or stretcher frame) (see Getting Started, page 18).

2 Use the size guide below to calculate the size of design that will result from using different fabric counts (see How to Use This Book, page 13). Refer to the cross-stitch chart and thread key, and stitch from the middle outward.

3 Remove the finished design from the hoop and press gently on the wrong side.

size guide

fabric count	number of threads/blocks	number of strands	size of design
14	1	2	8 in. (20.25 cm) square
16	1	2	7 in. (17.75 cm) square
18	1	2	6¼ in. (16 cm) square
28	2	2	8 in. (20.25 cm) square
28	3	3	12 in. (30.5 cm) square

materials

- The design shown here uses evenweave fabric, 14-count white Aida, and tapestry needle, size 24.

- Stranded cottons—three skeins of 310, two skeins of blanc and 712, and one skein of 3799. Use two strands for cross-stitch.

thread key

- ⊡ blanc
- ◣ 310 black
- ⊟ 712 cream
- ⊠ 3799 charcoal

◀ Zebra stripes look striking on a tote bag, and can also be used to make purses and evening bags. Try stitching the design with dark brown threads for variety.

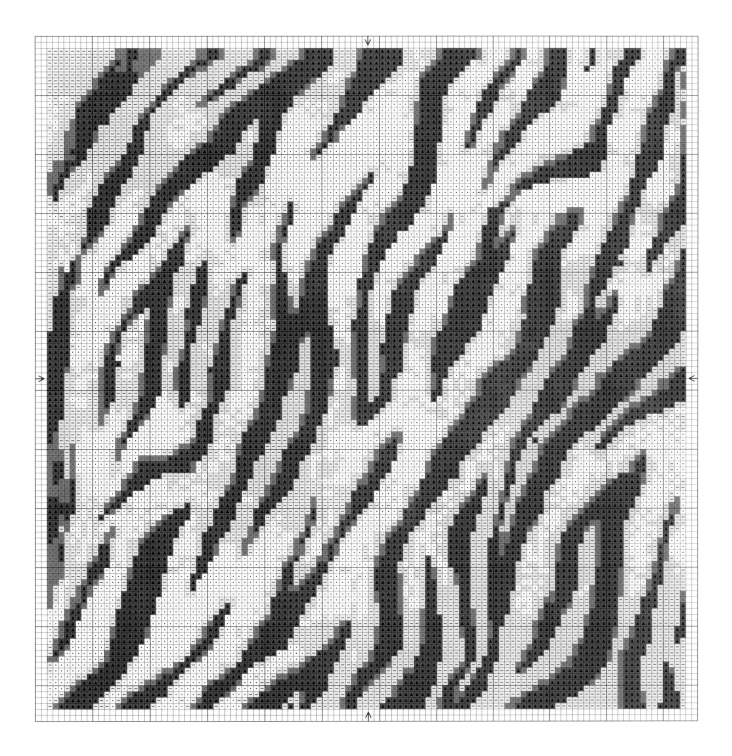

tropical fish

With vivid markings and in a variety of colours, these fish make bright, bold bathroom accessories.

stitching the design

1 Overcast the edges of the fabric to prevent fraying. Mark the midpoint of the fabric both vertically and horizontally with basting stitches; mount the fabric in an embroidery hoop (or stretcher frame) (see Getting Started, page 18).

2 Use the size guide below to calculate the size of motif A that will result from using different fabric counts (see How to Use This Book, page 13). Refer to the cross-stitch chart and thread key, and stitch from the middle outward.

3 Remove the finished design from the hoop and press gently on the wrong side.

size guide			
fabric count	number of threads/blocks	number of strands	size of design
14	1	2	10⅛ x 2 in. (25.75 x 5 cm)
16	1	2	8⅞ x 1¾ in. (22.5 x 4.5 cm)
18	1	2	7⅞ x 1½ in. (20 x 4 cm)
28	2	2	10⅛ x 2 in. (25.75 x 5 cm)
28	3	3	15¼ x 3 in. (38.75 x 7.5 cm)

materials

■ The design shown here uses evenweave fabric, 16-count white Aida band, and tapestry needle, size 26.

■ Stranded cottons, one skein of each colour listed in key. Use two strands for cross-stitch and one for backstitch.

thread key

⊡ blanc
⊞ 210 lilac
■ 310 black
▲ 333 deep lavender
▣ 350 orange red
◉ 519 sky blue
▨ 562 mid dusty green
⊟ 743 buttercup yellow
◙ 817 poppy red
⊠ 3348 pale moss green

backstitch
◩ 310 black

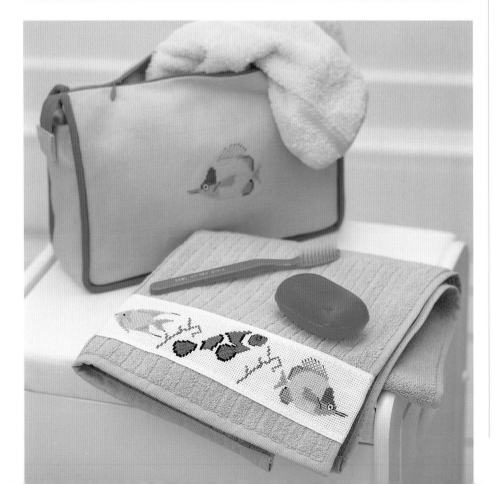

◀ Stitch the fish individually to add a decorative accent to a toiletry bag. In a row, they form a fun border for a towel. The motifs suit zesty tropical shades, such as lime green, yellow, and purple.

(A)

(B)

(top)

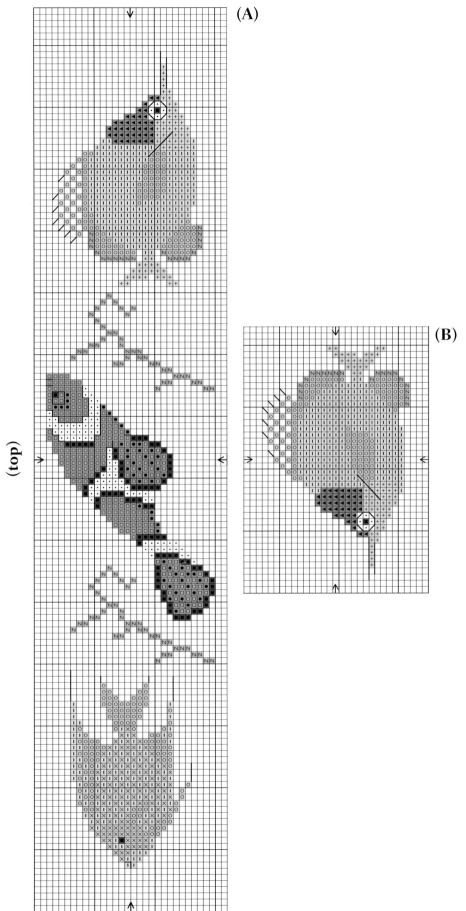

chicken

Based on the simple shapes of folk art, this long-legged chicken makes a charming decoration.

stitching the design

1 Overcast the edges of the fabric to prevent fraying. Mark the midpoint of the fabric both vertically and horizontally with basting stitches; mount the fabric in an embroidery hoop (or stretcher frame) (see Getting Started, page 18).

2 Use the size guide below to calculate the size of design that will result from using different fabric counts (see How to Use This Book, page 13). Refer to the cross-stitch chart and thread key, and stitch from the middle outward.

3 Remove the finished design from the hoop and press gently on the wrong side.

size guide

fabric count	number of threads/blocks	number of strands	size of design
14	1	2	5⅜ x 6⅝ in. (13.75 x 16.75 cm)
16	1	2	4⅝ x 5¾ in. (11.75 x 14.5 cm)
18	1	2	4⅛ x 5⅛ in. (10.5 x 13 cm)
28	2	2	5⅜ x 6⅝ in. (13.75 x 16.75 cm)
28	3	3	8⅛ x 9⅞ in. (20.75 x 25 cm)

materials

- The design shown here uses evenweave fabric, 14-count natural Aida, and tapestry needle, size 26.

- Stranded cottons, one skein of each colour listed in key. Use two strands for cross-stitch. Use one strand for the chicken's legs and feet in backstitch. Or use six strands for the legs, knotted at the knees, and heart-shaped buttons for the feet.

thread key

- 347 berry red
- ⊠ 703 lime green
- ⊟ 922 gold copper
- ▨ 996 mid turquoise
- ▪ 3850 dark teal

backstitch

- ◩ 3850 dark teal

◀ Heart motifs that sprout like plants from the ground are echoed in the buttons used for the chicken's feet. Bordered by simple running stitches, this design makes a cheerful tray cloth for a Shaker-style interior.

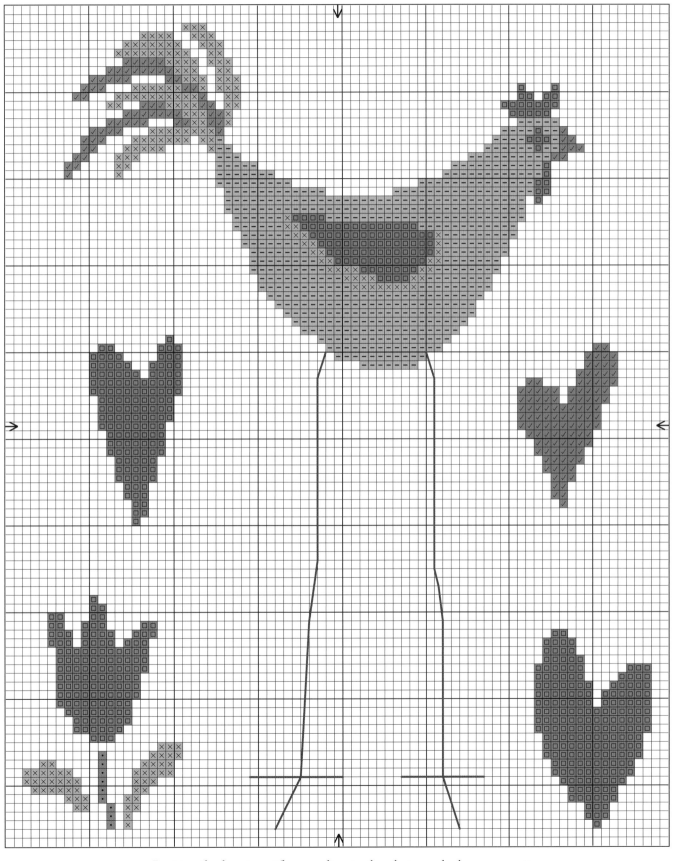

Position the heart motifs according to the photograph shown opposite.

sleeping cat

This design is reminiscent of a painting in a sketchbook, and its stitches mimic tiny brushstrokes.

stitching the design

1 Overcast the edges of the fabric to prevent fraying. Mark the midpoint of the fabric both vertically and horizontally with basting stitches; mount the fabric in an embroidery hoop (or stretcher frame) (see Getting Started, page 18).

2 Use the size guide below to calculate the size of design that will result from using different fabric counts (see How to Use This Book, page 13). Refer to the cross-stitch chart and thread key, and stitch from the middle outward.

3 Remove the finished design from the hoop and press gently on the wrong side.

materials

- The design shown here uses evenweave fabric, 14-count antique white Aida, and tapestry needle, size 24.
- Stranded cottons, one skein of each colour listed in key. Use two strands for cross-stitch and one for backstitch.

size guide

fabric count	number of threads/blocks	number of strands	size of design
14	1	2	2⅝ x 2¼ in. (6.75 x 5.75 cm)
16	1	2	2¼ x 1⅞ in. (5.75 x 4.75 cm)
18	1	2	2 x 1¾ in. (5 x 4.5 cm)
28	2	2	2⅝ x 2¼ in. (6.75 x 5.75 cm)
28	3	3	3⅞ x 3⅜ in. (9.75 x 6 cm)

thread key

- ☒ B5200 bright white
- ◼ 310 black
- Ⓤ 402 pale tan
- ▤ 3776 tan

backstitch
- ◹ 3781 brown

◀ The outline of the cat is worked in backstitch to give it sketchy definition. The design is shown mounted on a greeting card, but it could also be used as a bookmark or on a photo album devoted to a pet cat.

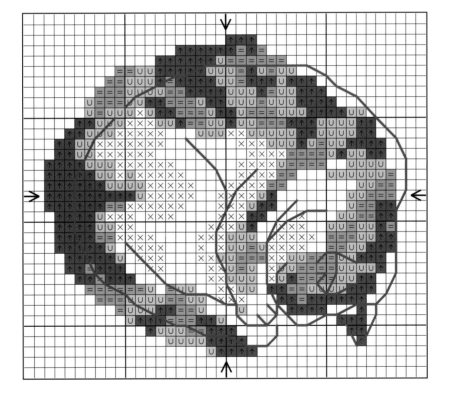

butterflies

With intricate patterns on their wings, butterflies have long been a popular decoration.

stitching the design

1 Overcast the edges of the fabric to prevent fraying. Mark the midpoint of the fabric both vertically and horizontally with basting stitches; mount the fabric in an embroidery hoop (or stretcher frame) (see Getting Started, page 18).

2 Use the size guide below to calculate the size of design that will result from using different fabric counts (see How to Use This Book, page 13). Refer to the cross-stitch chart and thread key, and stitch from the middle outward.

3 Remove the finished design from the hoop and press gently on the wrong side.

size guide			
fabric count	number of threads/blocks	number of strands	size of design
14	1	2	7¼ x 5½ in. (18.5 x 14 cm)
16	1	2	6¼ x 4¾ in. (16 x 12 cm)
18	1	2	5⅝ x 4¼ in. (14.25 x 10.75 cm)
28	2	2	7¼ x 5½ in. (18.5 x 14 cm)
28	3	3	10⅞ x 8¼ in. (27.5 x 21 cm)

materials

- The design shown here uses evenweave fabric, 28-count pale yellow linen, and tapestry needle size 26.

- Stranded cottons, one skein of each colour listed in key. Use two strands for cross-stitch and one for backstitch.

thread key

- ■ 310 black
- ☑ 726 daffodil yellow
- ☒ 741 tangerine
- ⊟ 742 pale sunshine yellow
- ▶ 797 French blue
- ⓢ 798 bright cornflower blue
- ⓤ 809 Delft blue
- ☒ 820 dark royal blue
- ▽ 3812 bright aqua
- ⬆ 3843 dark turquoise
- ⅍ 3844 deep turquoise
- ✳ 3845 bold turquoise

backstitch
- ◹ 310 black

◀ A delicate background fabric, adorned with satin ribbon bows, complements the fragility and shape of the butterflies. This effect is enhanced by the contrast of vivid turquoise against pale lemon. These motifs would also be ideal on a handkerchief or a pillowcase.

(top)

garden bugs

Characterized by black spots, these tiny insects combine well with accessories used outdoors.

stitching the design

1 Overcast the edges of the fabric to prevent fraying. Mark the midpoint of the fabric both vertically and horizontally with basting stitches; mount the fabric in an embroidery hoop (or stretcher frame) (see Getting Started, page 18).

2 Use the size guide below to calculate the size of design that will result from using different fabric counts (see How to Use This Book, page 13). Refer to the cross-stitch chart and thread key, and stitch from the middle outward.

3 Remove the finished design from the hoop and press gently on the wrong side.

size guide

fabric count	number of threads/blocks	number of strands	size of design
14	1	2	2⅛ x ⅞ in. (5.5 x 2.25 cm)
16	1	2	1⅞ x ¾ in. (4.75 x 2 cm)
18	1	2	1⅝ x ⅝ in. (4.25 x 1.5 cm)
28	2	2	2⅛ x ⅞ in. (5.5 x 2.25 cm)
28	3	3	3¼ x 1¼ in. (8.25 x 3.25 cm)

materials

- The design shown here uses evenweave fabric, 14-count white Aida, and tapestry needle size 24.

- Stranded cottons, one skein of each colour listed in key. Use two strands for cross-stitch and one for backstitch.

thread key

- 310 black
- 350 orange red
- 666 flame red
- 816 claret red

backstitch

- 310 black

◀ Two bugs—one still and one on the move—are stitched side by side to decorate a napkin holder. These motifs could also be used effectively in a child's room—imagine canvas shoe bags and padded hangers decorated with little garden bugs.

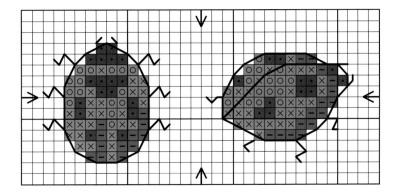

beach

Filled with summertime motifs, this sampler serves as a delightful memento of days at the beach.

stitching the design

1 Overcast the edges of the fabric to prevent fraying. Mark the midpoint of the fabric both vertically and horizontally with basting stitches; mount the fabric in an embroidery hoop (or stretcher frame) (see Getting Started, page 18).

2 Use the size guide below to calculate the size of design that will result from using different fabric counts (see How to Use This Book, page 13). Refer to the cross-stitch chart and thread key, and stitch from the middle outward.

3 Remove the finished design from the hoop and press gently on the wrong side.

size guide

fabric count	number of threads/blocks	number of strands	size of design
14	1	2	7¾ x 11⅜ in. (19.75 x 29 cm)
16	1	2	6¾ x 9⅞ in. (17.25 x 25 cm)
18	1	2	6 x 8⅞ in. (15.25 x 22.5 cm)
25	2	2	8¾ x 12¾ in. (22.25 x 32.5 cm)
28	2	2	7¾ x 11⅜ in. (19.75 x 29 cm)

materials

- The design shown here uses evenweave fabric, 25-count white, and tapestry needle, size 26.

- Stranded cottons, one skein of each colour listed in key. Use two strands for cross-stitch, backstitch, French knots, and bullion knots.

thread key

- 211 pale lilac
- 340 deep lilac
- 356 mid terra cotta
- 402 pale tan
- 552 mid violet
- 554 pale violet
- 728 bright gold
- 738 tan beige
- 741 tangerine
- 744 primrose yellow
- 746 buttermilk
- 792 lilac blue
- 959 mid aqua
- 991 dark green aqua
- 3706 candy
- 3747 ice lilac
- 3801 strawberry
- 3811 pale aqua

backstitch

- 340 deep lilac
- 356 mid terra cotta
- 402 pale tan
- 552 mid violet
- 741 tangerine
- 738 tan beige
- 792 lilac blue
- 991 dark green aqua
- 3801 strawberry
- 3811 pale aqua

French knots

- 552 mid violet
- 741 tangerine
- 792 lilac blue
- 959 mid aqua

◀ Bullion knots in 741, 959, and 3801 on the top left ice cream mimic sugar sprinkles. Shells add interest.

chapter seven:
kids' corner

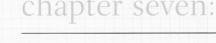

a, b, c . . .

The first letters of the alphabet can be used to create a fun early learning toy.

stitching the design

1 Overcast the edges of the fabric to prevent fraying. Mark the midpoint of the fabric both vertically and horizontally with basting stitches; mount the fabric in an embroidery hoop (or stretcher frame) (see Getting Started, page 18).

2 Use the size guide below to calculate the size of motif C that will result from using different fabric counts (see How to Use This Book, page 13). Refer to the cross-stitch chart and thread key, and stitch from the middle outward.

3 Remove the finished design from the hoop and press gently on the wrong side.

size guide

fabric count	number of threads/blocks	number of strands	size of design
14	1	2	2¾ x 3⅜ in. (7 x 8.5 cm)
16	1	2	2⅜ x 2⅞ in. (6 x 7.25 cm)
18	1	2	2⅛ x 2⅝ in. (5.5 x 6.75 cm)
28	2	2	2¾ x 3⅜ in. (7 x 8.5 cm)
28	3	3	4⅛ x 5⅛ in. (10.5 x 13 cm)

materials

- The design shown here uses evenweave fabric, 14-count yellow Aida, and tapestry needle, size 26.

- Stranded cottons, one skein of each colour listed in key. Use two strands for cross-stitch.

thread key

- ⊓ 209 pale lavender
- ■ 351 deep coral
- ⊞ 604 mid rose
- ⊟ 959 mid aqua
- ⊚ 996 mid turquoise
- Ⓤ 3341 mid melon

◄ Children can turn the play cube as they learn how to pronounce the different letters. Stitched onto any item—creative options include a wall hanging or a child's blanket— the motifs can be used to inspire simple word games.

(A)

(B)

(C)

(D)

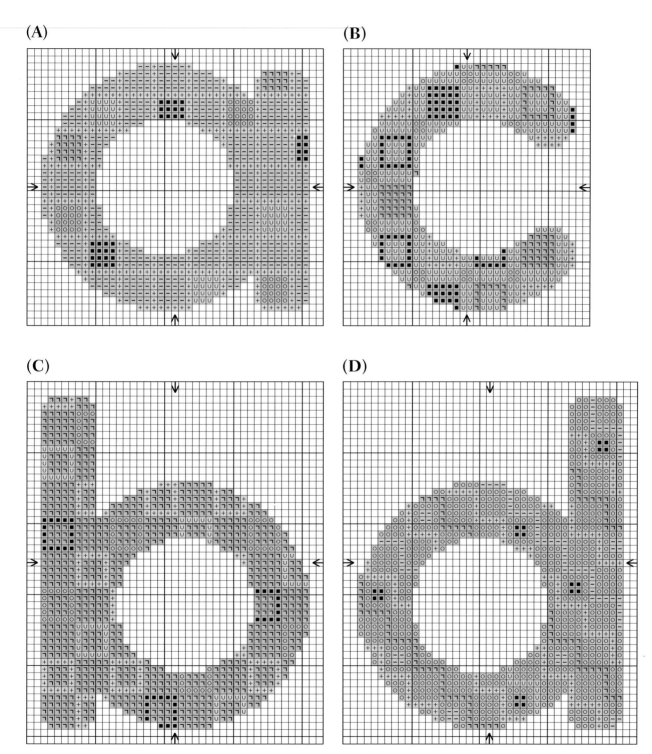

pets

A selection of pet animals and their favourite foods are ideal for decorating baby bibs.

stitching the design

1 Overcast the edges of the fabric to prevent fraying. Mark the midpoint of the fabric both vertically and horizontally with basting stitches; mount the fabric in an embroidery hoop (or stretcher frame) (see Getting Started, page 18).

2 Use the size guide below to calculate the size of design that will result from using different fabric counts (see How to Use This Book, page 13). Refer to the cross-stitch chart and thread key, and stitch from the middle outward.

3 Remove the finished design from the hoop and press gently on the wrong side.

size guide			
fabric count	number of threads/blocks	number of strands	size of design
14	1	2	6⅜ x 8⅛ in. (16.25 x 20.75 cm)
16	1	2	5⅝ x 7⅛ in. (14.25 x 18 cm)
18	1	2	5 x 6¼ in. (12.75 x 16 cm)
28	2	2	6⅜ x 8⅛ in. (16.25 x 20.75 cm)
28	3	3	9½ x 12¼ in. (24.25 x 31 cm)

materials

■ The design shown here uses evenweave fabric, 14-count white and baby pink Aida, and tapestry needle, size 26.

■ Stranded cottons, one skein of each colour listed in key. Use two strands for cross-stitch and three-quarter stitch and one for backstitch.

thread key

⊞ 301 mahogany
⊟ 318 dark pearl grey
▲ 402 pale tan
⊟ 761 pale dusty rose
⊠ 841 coffee
↑ 932 pale airforce blue
▨ 993 pale green aqua
■ 3031 dark brown
ᵁ 3865 soft white

backstitch
◺ 3031 dark brown

in detail

The cat and its dream cloud are outlined in backstitch. Vary the angle of the backstitches for the whiskers to give the cat a quizzical look.

◀ These different motifs can be used imaginatively to create a variety of lively compositions.

daisies

Simple to stitch, these pretty summer flowers will dress up both baby and toddler clothes.

stitching the design

1 To work on evenweave fabric, overcast the fabric edges and mark the midpoint vertically and horizontally with basting. Mount the fabric in a hoop (or frame) (see Getting Started, page 18). To work on knitted fabric, see page 27.

2 Use the size guide below to calculate the size of design that will result from using different fabric counts (see How to Use This Book, page 13). Refer to the cross-stitch chart and thread key, and stitch from the middle outward.

3 Remove the finished design from the hoop and press gently on the wrong side.

size guide

fabric count	number of threads/blocks	number of strands	size of design
14	1	6	1½ x 1¼ in. (4 x 3.25 cm)
16	1	6	1¼ x 1⅛ in. (3.25 x 2.75 cm)
18	1	6	1⅛ x 1 in. (2.75 x 2.5 cm)
28	2	6	1½ x 1¼ in. (4 x 3.25 cm)
28	3	6	2¼ x 1⅞ in. (5.75 x 4.75 cm)

materials

- The design shown here uses a baby's white knitted cardigan and tapestry needle, size 26.

- Stranded cottons, two skeins of 3846 and one skein of each of the other colours listed in key. Use six strands for cross-stitch, backstitch, and lazy daisy stitch.

thread key

- ⊞ 605 pale pink
- ◉ 721 rusty orange
- ⊡ 3846 light turquoise

backstitch and lazy daisy stitch
- ◨ 907 pale apple green

in detail

A pair of big lazy daisy stitches, worked on a slant, represents the leaves.

◁ Daisies are ideal for plain knitted accessories because they are composed of a small number of stitches. Instead of working a border onto a child's cardigan, you could work the daisies onto a knitted scarf or baby blanket.

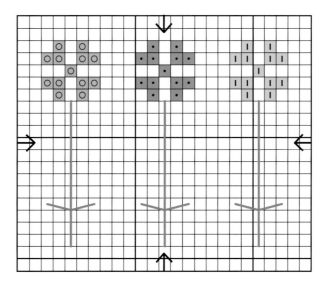

penguin

In calm shades of lavender and aqua, this scene from the South Pole is ideal for a child's bedroom.

stitching the design

1 Overcast the edges of the fabric to prevent fraying. Mark the midpoint of the fabric both vertically and horizontally with basting stitches; mount the fabric in an embroidery hoop (or stretcher frame) (see Getting Started, page 18).

2 Use the size guide below to calculate the size of design that will result from using different fabric counts (see How to Use This Book, page 13). Refer to the cross-stitch chart and thread key, and stitch from the middle outward.

3 Remove the finished design from the hoop and press gently on the wrong side.

size guide

fabric count	number of threads/blocks	number of strands	size of design
14	1	2	5⅝ in. (14.25 cm) square
16	1	2	5 in. (12.75 cm) square
18	1	2	4½ in. (11.5 cm) square
28	2	2	5⅝ in. (14.25 cm) square
28	3	3	8½ in. (21.5 cm) square

materials

- The design shown here uses evenweave fabric, 14-count white Aida, and tapestry needle, size 26.

- Stranded cottons, one skein of each colour listed in key. Use two strands for cross-stitch and one for backstitch.

thread key

- ⊞ blanc
- ▲ 211 pale lilac
- ■ 310 black
- ◉ 333 deep lavender
- ⊍ 340 deep lilac
- ⊟ 742 pale sunshine yellow
- ⊡ 747 pale baby blue
- ⊠ 958 aqua

backstitch

- ◸ 310 black

◂ Once framed, this design can be displayed on a shelf or a wall. Alternatively, it could be mounted on a greeting card to celebrate a birthday.

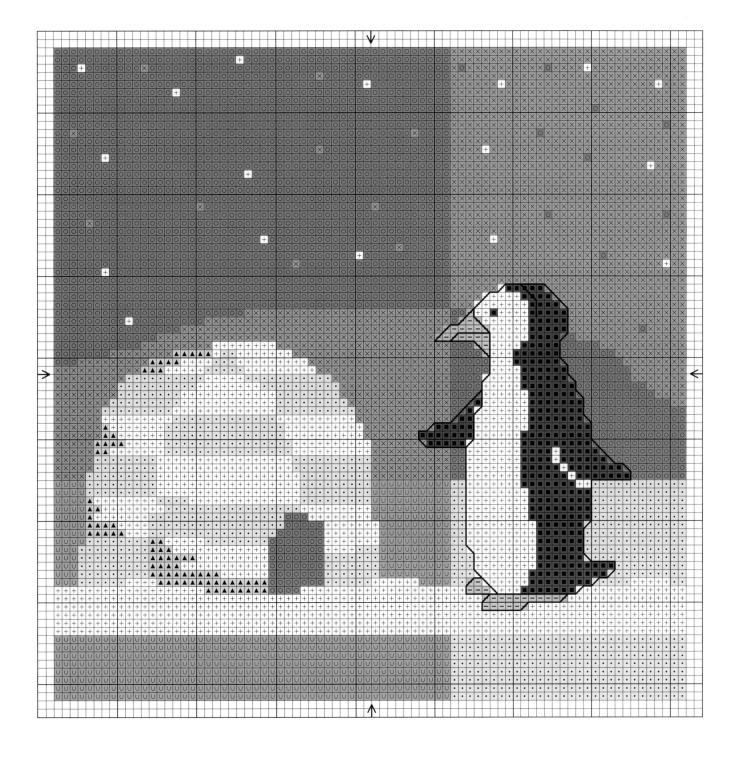

picture frame

A carefully stitched frame recalls the special care taken to display photographs in days gone by.

stitching the design

1 Overcast the edges of the fabric to prevent fraying. Mark the midpoint of the fabric both vertically and horizontally with basting stitches; mount the fabric in an embroidery hoop (or stretcher frame) (see Getting Started, page 18).

2 Use the size guide below to calculate the size of design that will result from using different fabric counts (see How to Use This Book, page 13). Refer to the cross-stitch chart and thread key, and stitch from the middle outward.

3 Remove the finished design from the hoop and press gently on the wrong side.

size guide

fabric count	number of threads/blocks	number of strands	size of design
14	1	2	5⅛ x 5¾ in. (13 x 14.5 cm)
16	1	2	4⅜ x 5⅛ in. (11 x 13 cm)
18	1	2	4 x 4½ in. (10.25 x 11.5 cm)
28	2	2	5⅛ x 5¾ in. (13 x 14.5 cm)
28	3	3	7⅝ x 8⅝ in. (19.25 x 22 cm)

materials

- The design shown here uses evenweave fabric, 14-count white Aida, and tapestry needle, size 26.

- Stranded cottons, one skein of the colour listed in key. Use two strands for cross-stitch.

◀ Worked in blue on white, this design is perfect for framing a cherished photograph of a baby or a young child. For an older child, stitch the frame in a brighter shade of pink or green onto a cream fabric.

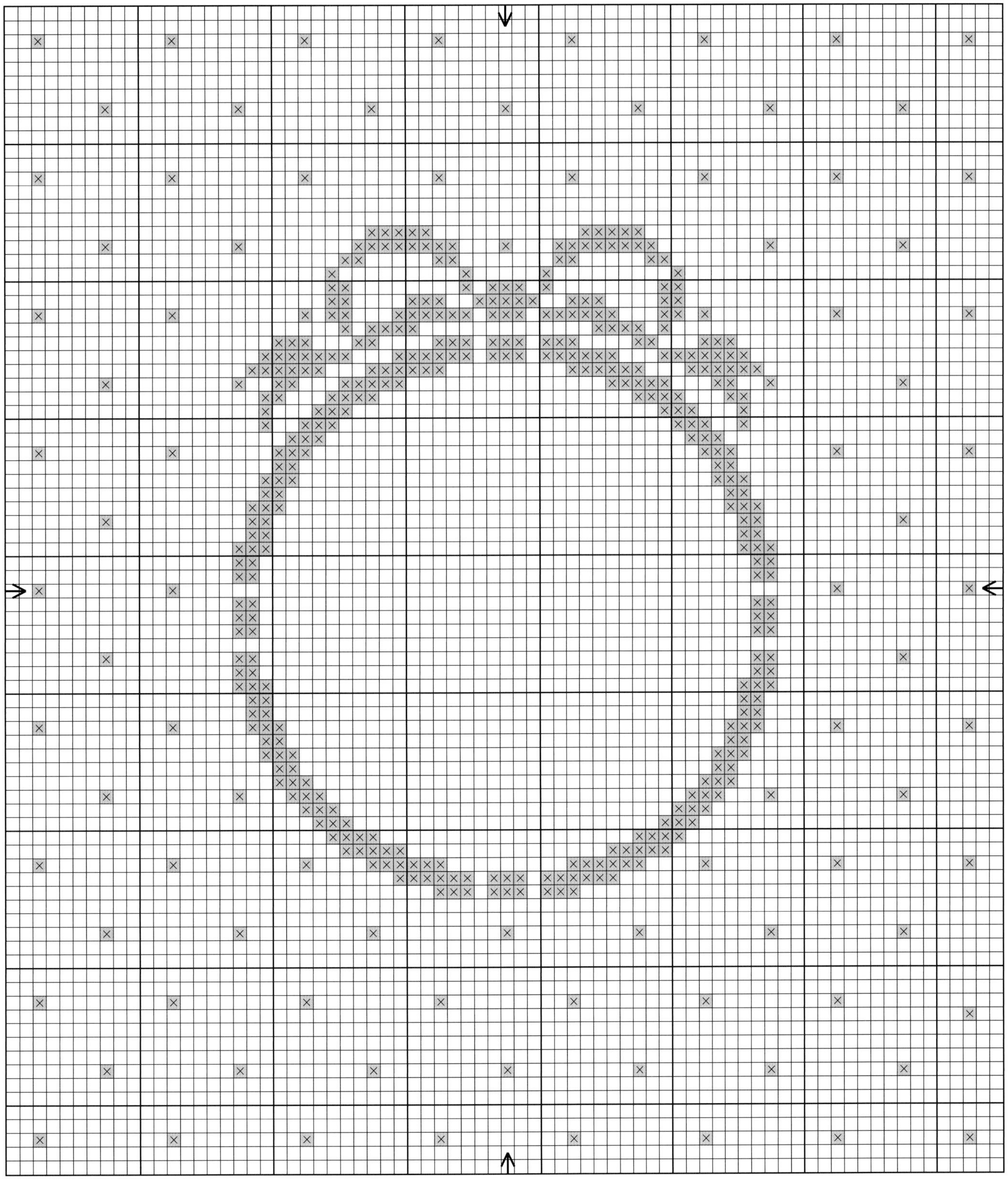

festive treats

Children will enjoy counting down to Christmas with the help of this delightful Advent calendar.

stitching the design

1 Overcast the edges of the fabric to prevent fraying. Mark the midpoint of the fabric both vertically and horizontally with basting stitches; mount the fabric in an embroidery hoop (or stretcher frame) (see Getting Started, page 18).

2 Use the size guide below to calculate the size of design that will result from using different fabric counts (see How to Use This Book, page 13). Refer to the cross-stitch chart and thread key, and stitch from the middle outward.

3 Remove the finished design from the hoop and press gently on the wrong side.

size guide

fabric count	number of threads/blocks	number of strands	size of design
14	1	2	5⅝ x 5⅞ in. (14.25 x 15 cm)
16	1	2	4⅞ x 5¼ in. (12.5 x 13.25 cm)
18	1	2	4⅜ x 4⅝ in. (11 x 11.75 cm)
28	2	2	5⅝ x 5⅞ in. (14.25 x 15 cm)
28	3	3	8⅜ x 8¾ in. (21.25 x 22.25 cm)

materials

- The design shown here uses evenweave fabric, 16-count white Aida band, 28-count biscuit raw linen and beige Quaker cloth, and tapestry needle, size 26.

- Stranded cottons, one skein of each colour listed in key. Use two strands for cross-stitch, three-quarter stitch, and French knots; one strand for backstitch and straight stitch.

thread key

- ⊡ blanc
- ☒ 150 berry pink
- ⊟ 561 dark leaf
- ◉ 676 pale old gold
- ▽ 869 hazel brown
- ▲ 951 pink cream
- ⊞ 3823 yellow cream
- Ⓤ 3852 dark gold

backstitch and straight stitch

- ◺ 801 dark brown
- ◺ 3852 dark gold

French knots

- ◉ 150 berry pink

◀ Stitched squares of fabric are sewn in rows to make miniature patch pockets into which sweets can be tucked and given to children each day from the beginning of December. Individual motifs could also be used to make gift tags or to decorate a child's Christmas stocking.

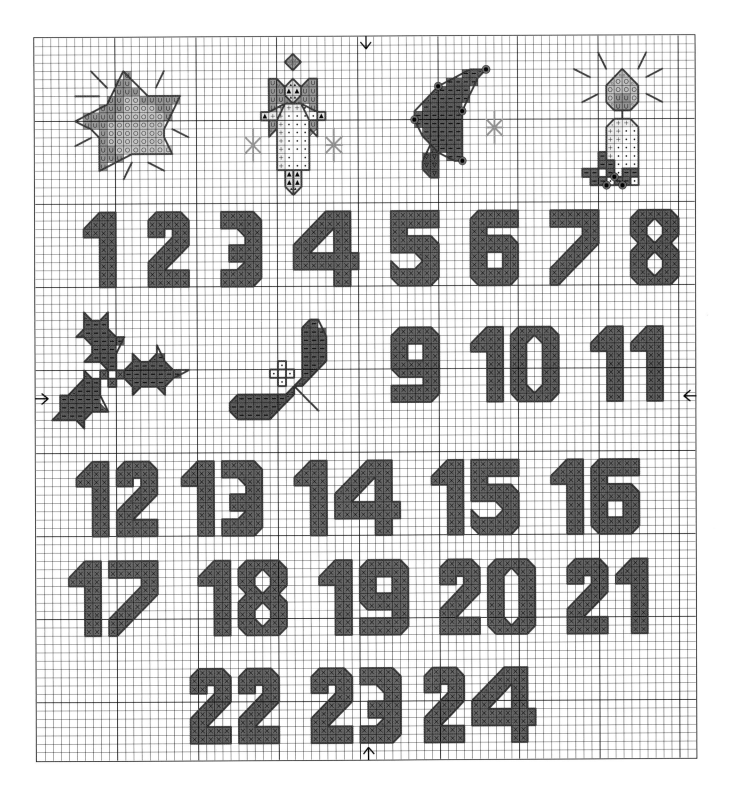

dinosaurs

A collection of whimsical prehistoric beasts never fails to stir young imaginations.

stitching the design

1 Overcast the edges of the fabric to prevent fraying. Mark the midpoint of the fabric both vertically and horizontally with basting stitches; mount the fabric in an embroidery hoop (or stretcher frame) (see Getting Started, page 18).

2 Use the size guide below to calculate the size of motif D that will result from using different fabric counts (see How to Use This Book, page 13). Refer to the cross-stitch chart and thread key, and stitch from the middle outward.

3 Remove the finished design from the hoop and press gently on the wrong side.

size guide

fabric count	number of threads/blocks	number of strands	size of design
11	1	3	7½ x 5⅞ in. (19 x 15 cm)
14	1	2	5⅞ x 4⅝ in. (15 x 11.75 cm)
16	1	2	5¼ x 4⅛ in. (13.25 x 10.5 cm)
18	1	2	4⅝ x 3⅝ in. (11.75 x 9.25 cm)
28	2	2	5⅞ x 4⅝ in. (15 x 11.75 cm)

materials

■ The design shown here uses evenweave fabric, 11-count white Aida, and tapestry needle, size 26.

■ Stranded cottons, one skein of each colour listed in key. Use three strands for cross-stitch and one for backstitch.

thread key

■ 310 black
⊞ 444 dark lemon
⊟ 553 violet
▲ 666 flame red
◉ 741 tangerine
⊠ 906 apple green
backstitch
◨ 310 black

◀ Here, four dinosaurs form a central panel, but they could also march in a line along the lower edge of curtains or shades. You could extend the theme to bed linen and stitch a dinosaur motif onto the corner of a pillowcase.

(A)

(B)

(C)

(D)

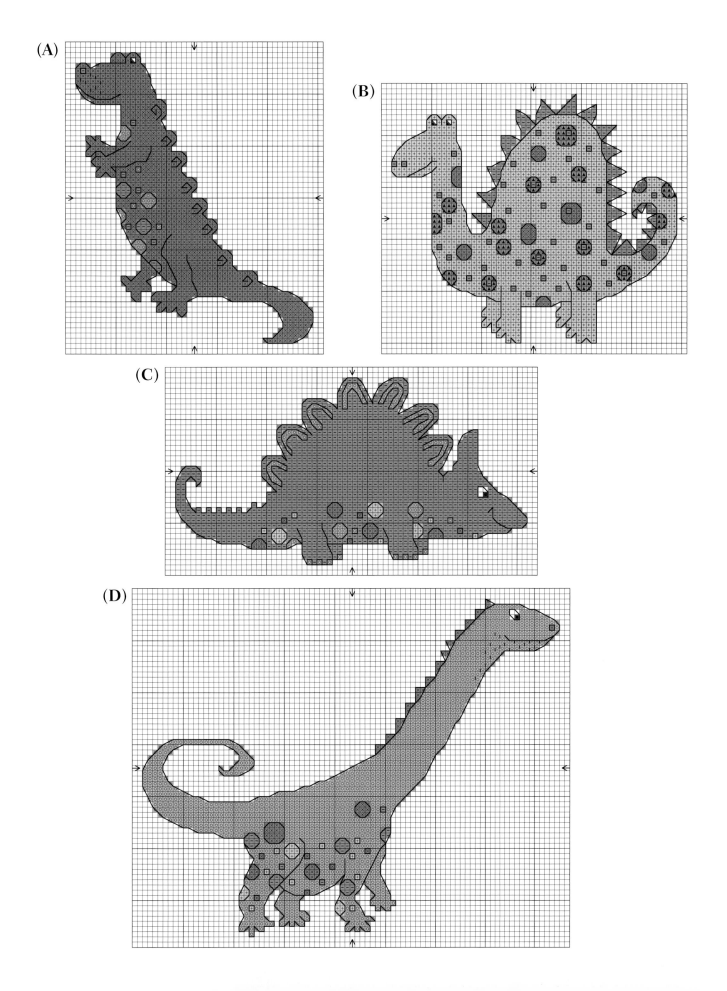

beach holiday

Happy memories of sea and sand create an upbeat holiday mood all year round.

stitching the design

1 Overcast the edges of the fabric to prevent fraying. Mark the midpoint of the fabric both vertically and horizontally with basting stitches; mount the fabric in an embroidery hoop (or stretcher frame) (see Getting Started, page 18).

2 Use the size guide below to calculate the size of design that will result from using different fabric counts (see How to Use This Book, page 13). Refer to the cross-stitch chart and thread key, and stitch from the middle outward.

3 Remove the finished design from the hoop and press gently on the wrong side.

size guide

fabric count	number of threads/blocks	number of strands	size of design
14	1	2	6½ x 11¼ in. (16.5 x 28.5 cm)
16	1	2	5⅝ x 9⅞ in. (14.25 x 25 cm)
18	1	2	5 x 8¾ in. (12.75 x 22.25 cm)
28	2	2	6½ x 11¼ in. (16.5 x 28.5 cm)
28	3	3	9¾ x 16⅞ in. (24.75 x 42.75 cm)

materials

- The design shown here uses evenweave fabric, 28-count white Quaker cloth, and tapestry needle, size 26.

- Stranded cottons, one skein of each colour listed in key. Use two strands for cross-stitch and one for backstitch.

thread key

- ⊡ blanc
- ■ 311 navy blue
- ▲ 517 deep sky blue
- ☑ 518 mid sky blue
- ▽ 519 sky blue
- ⊞ 676 pale old gold
- ⊠ 729 ochre
- ✳ 920 light brick
- ▽ 922 gold copper
- Ⓣ 928 silver grey
- ⓢ 977 mid fudge
- ⑂ 993 pale green aqua
- ◈ 3814 aquamarine

backstitch
- ◹ 311 navy blue

◀ In seaside shades of aquamarine and gold, the motifs on this sampler are worked in rows. Choose a frame for the design that enhances the beach theme, perhaps one with a weathered-paint effect or one made of driftwood or rope.

teddy bear

Along with a flower and heart, a cuddly bear can create an attractive theme for a little girl's room.

stitching the design

1 Overcast the edges of the fabric to prevent fraying. Mark the midpoint of the fabric both vertically and horizontally with basting stitches; mount the fabric in an embroidery hoop (or stretcher frame) (see Getting Started, page 18).

2 Use the size guide below to calculate the size of motif A that will result from using different fabric counts (see How to Use This Book, page 13). Refer to the cross-stitch chart and thread key, and stitch from the middle outward.

3 Remove the finished design from the hoop and press gently on the wrong side.

size guide

fabric count	number of threads/blocks	number of strands	size of design
14	1	2	3¾ x 4 in. (9.5 x 10.25 cm)
16	1	2	3¼ x 3½ in. (8.25 x 9 cm)
18	1	2	2⅞ x 3⅓ in. (7.25 x 8 cm)
28	2	2	3¾ x 4 in. (9.5 x 10.25 cm)
28	3	3	5⅝ x 6 in. (14.25 x 15.25 cm)

materials

- The design shown here uses evenweave fabric, 28-count baby blue linen, and tapestry needle, size 26.

- Stranded cottons, one skein of each colour listed in key. Use two strands for cross-stitch and one for backstitch.

thread key

- ▲ 422 light hazel
- ◉ 676 pale old gold
- ⊟ 677 cold cream
- ⊠ 819 ice pink
- ⬆ 955 pale spearmint
- ⊟ 963 cream pink
- Ⓤ 3838 Delft blue
- ⊞ 3839 pale Delft blue
- ⊠ 3840 palest Delft blue

backstitch
- ◹ 433 brown
- ◺ 3839 pale Delft blue

◀ Bedroom accessories, from a window shade to basketwork pots, can be linked by these complementary motifs. On the bear, brown backstitching defines its facial features. Pale blue backstitching helps to outline the flower and its leaves.

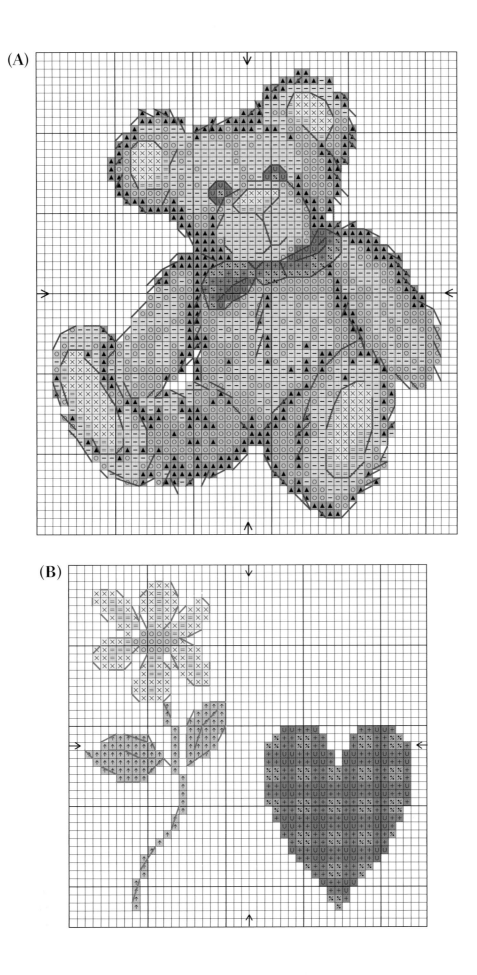

ice cream

An ever popular treat, scoops of ice cream always conjure up the joy of hot summer days.

stitching the design

1 Overcast the edges of the fabric to prevent fraying. Mark the midpoint of the fabric both vertically and horizontally with basting stitches; mount the fabric in an embroidery hoop (or stretcher frame) (see Getting Started, page 18).

2 Use the size guide below to calculate the size of design that will result from using different fabric counts (see How to Use This Book, page 13). Refer to the cross-stitch chart and thread key, and stitch from the middle outward.

3 Remove the finished design from the hoop and press gently on the wrong side.

size guide			
fabric count	number of threads/blocks	number of strands	size of design
14	1	2	2⅜ x 3⅞ in. (6 x 9.75 cm)
16	1	2	2⅛ x 3⅜ in. (5.5 x 8.5 cm)
18	1	2	1⅞ x 3 in. (4.75 x 7.5 cm)
28	2	2	2⅜ x 3⅞ in. (6 x 9.75 cm)
28	3	3	3½ x 5¾ in. (9 x 14.5 cm)

materials

- The design shown here uses evenweave fabric, 16-count white Aida, and tapestry needle, size 24.

- Stranded cottons, one skein of each colour listed in key. Use two strands for cross-stitch and one for backstitch.

thread key

- ▣ ecru
- ⊟ 894 carnation pink
- ◎ 3819 lime moss green
- ☒ 3820 gold
- ▲ 3823 yellow cream

◀ With a bright, spotted border, this design makes a decorative greeting card. It could also be stitched onto a bib, tablecloth, or place mats for a child's birthday party.

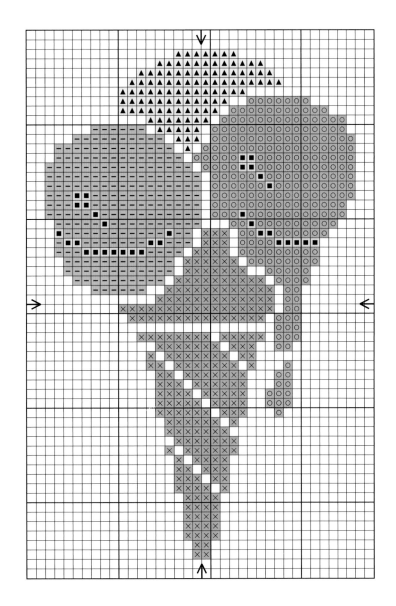

sailboat

Inspired by a child's drawing, this little boat is perfect as a bathroom decoration.

stitching the design

1 Overcast the edges of the fabric to prevent fraying. Mark the midpoint of the fabric both vertically and horizontally with basting stitches; mount the fabric in an embroidery hoop (or stretcher frame) (see Getting Started, page 18).

2 Use the size guide below to calculate the size of design that will result from using different fabric counts (see How to Use This Book, page 13). Refer to the cross-stitch chart and thread key, and stitch from the middle outward.

3 Remove the finished design from the hoop and press gently on the wrong side.

size guide

fabric count	number of threads/blocks	number of strands	size of design
14	1	2	3⅛ x 2¾ in. (8 x 7 cm)
16	1	2	2⅝ x 2⅜ in. (6.75 x 6 cm)
18	1	2	2⅜ x 2⅛ in. (6 x 5.5 cm)
28	2	2	3⅛ x 2¾ in. (8 x 7 cm)
28	3	3	4⅝ x 4⅛ in. (11.75 x 10.5 cm)

materials

- The design shown here uses evenweave fabric, 14-count white Aida, and tapestry needle, size 24.

- Stranded cottons, one skein of each colour listed in key. Use two strands for cross-stitch and one for backstitch.

thread key

- 436 light camel
- 666 flame red
- 726 daffodil yellow
- 798 bright cornflower blue
- 959 mid aqua

backstitch

- 310 black

◄ With jagged waves echoing the triangular shapes of the sails, the graphic design of this motif is complemented by clear, bright colours. The sailboat looks good displayed on a small easel, as here. You could also stitch a row of motifs onto a fabric window shade, using waste canvas.

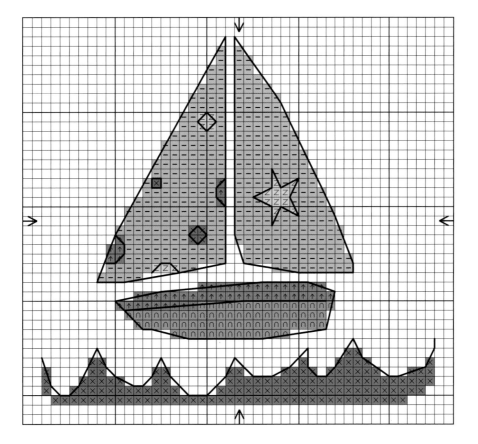

nursery set

Cute bottle and rattle motifs in pink, green, and blue decorate a bib's border and even baby toys.

stitching the design

1 Overcast the edges of the fabric to prevent fraying. Mark the midpoint of the fabric both vertically and horizontally with basting stitches; mount the fabric in an embroidery hoop (or stretcher frame) (see Getting Started, page 18).

2 Use the size guide below to calculate the size of design that will result from using different fabric counts (see How to Use This Book, page 13). Refer to the cross-stitch chart and thread key, and stitch from the middle outward.

3 Remove the finished design from the hoop and press gently on the wrong side.

size guide

fabric count	number of threads/blocks	number of strands	size of design
14	1	2	6⅞ x 1⅛ in. (17.5 x 2.75 cm)
16	1	2	6⅛ x ⅞ in. (15.5 x 2.25 cm)
18	1	2	5⅜ x ¾ in. (13.75 x 2 cm)
28	2	2	6⅞ x 1⅛ in. (17.5 x 2.75 cm)
28	3	3	10¼ x 1⅝ in. (26 x 4.25 cm)

materials

- The design shown here uses evenweave fabric, 14- and 18-count white Aida, and tapestry needle, size 26.

- Stranded cottons, one skein of each colour listed in key. Use two strands for cross-stitch.

thread key

- 813 iris blue
- 826 light rich blue
- 828 pale sky blue
- 842 beige coffee
- 911 pale emerald
- 913 spearmint
- 955 pale spearmint
- 962 dusty pink
- 963 cream pink
- 3731 dark old pink

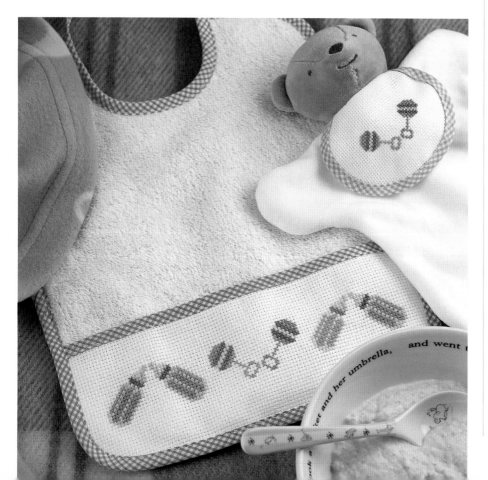

◀ For a new baby, stitch the design along the lower edge of a bib. To make the gift even more special, use one of the motifs, such as the pair of rattles, to decorate a matching bib for a soft toy.

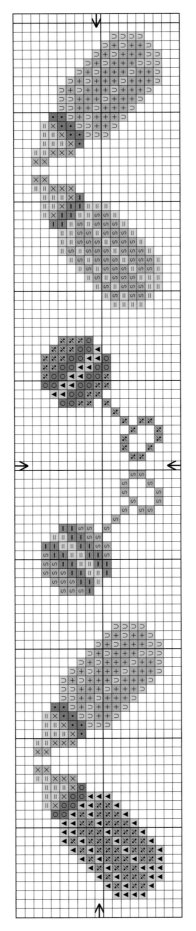

(top)

circus

Bright shades of blue, gold, and copper re-create the razzle-dazzle of a spectacular performance.

stitching the design

1 Overcast the edges of the fabric to prevent fraying. Mark the midpoint of the fabric both vertically and horizontally with basting stitches; mount the fabric in an embroidery hoop (or stretcher frame) (see Getting Started, page 18).

2 Use the size guide below to calculate the size of design that will result from using different fabric counts (see How to Use This Book, page 13). Refer to the cross-stitch chart and thread key, and stitch from the middle outward.

3 Remove the finished design from the hoop and press gently on the wrong side.

size guide

fabric count	number of threads/blocks	number of strands	size of design
14	1	2	6½ x 11¼ in. (16.5 x 28.5 cm)
16	1	2	5⅝ x 9⅞ in. (14.25 x 25 cm)
18	1	2	5 x 8¾ in. (12.75 x 22.25 cm)
28	2	2	6½ x 11¼ in. (16.5 x 28.5 cm)
28	3	3	9¾ x 16⅞ in. (24.75 x 42.75 cm)

materials

- The design shown here uses evenweave fabric, 28-count white Quaker cloth, and tapestry needle, size 26.

- Stranded cottons, two skeins of 519 and one skein of each of the other colours listed in key. Use two strands for cross-stitch and three-quarter stitch and one for backstitch.

thread key

- ⊡ blanc
- Ⓤ 169 slate grey
- ▲ 517 deep sky blue
- ☑ 518 mid sky blue
- ◁ 519 sky blue
- ⊞ 676 pale old gold
- Ⓒ 728 bright gold
- Ⓜ 729 ochre
- ✳ 920 light brick
- ▽ 922 gold copper
- ▬ 924 dark grey blue
- ⊠ 927 pale grey blue
- Ⓣ 928 silver grey
- ⬤ 976 toffee
- Ⓢ 977 mid fudge
- ↑ 988 mid grass green
- ◆ 3814 aquamarine

backstitch
- ◲ 801 dark brown
- ◲ 920 light brick

◀ Outlining the animals in backstitch makes them stand out clearly against the background. Backstitching is also used for the animals' tails and the ropes of the circus tents. Any panel of this sampler could be stitched onto Aida band to form a border edging for curtains.

robot

Children are mesmerized by robots, especially a friendly one that presents a birthday cake.

stitching the design

1 Overcast the edges of the fabric to prevent fraying. Mark the midpoint of the fabric both vertically and horizontally with basting stitches; mount the fabric in an embroidery hoop (or stretcher frame) (see Getting Started, page 18).

2 Use the size guide below to calculate the size of design that will result from using different fabric counts (see How to Use This Book, page 13). Refer to the cross-stitch chart and thread key, and stitch from the middle outward.

3 Remove the finished design from the hoop and press gently on the wrong side.

size guide

fabric count	number of threads/blocks	number of strands	size of design
14	1	2	1¾ x 3½ in. (4.5 x 9 cm)
16	1	2	1½ x 3⅛ in. (4 x 8 cm)
18	1	2	1⅜ x 2¾ in. (3.5 x 7 cm)
28	2	2	1¾ x 3½ in. (4.5 x 9 cm)
28	3	3	2⅝ x 5¼ in. (6.75 x 13.25 cm)

materials

- The design shown here uses evenweave fabric, 14-count white Aida, and tapestry needle, size 26.

- Stranded cottons, one skein of each colour listed in key. Use two strands for cross-stitch and one for backstitch.

thread key

- ⊞ blanc
- ■ 310 black
- ⊟ 352 salmon
- ▲ 415 steel grey
- ▣ 435 camel
- ⊠ 742 pale sunshine yellow
- ⊟ 744 primrose yellow
- ● 930 dark airforce blue
- ◎ 931 metal blue
- ⊞ 932 pale airforce blue
- ⊡ 3756 pale duck egg
- ⬆ 5283 metallic silver

backstitch

- ◫ 310 black
- ◻ 5283 metallic silver

◀ Black and silver backstitching define the edges of the robot. This design makes an ideal birthday card for a science-fiction enthusiast. For items that will be seen all year round, you could simply stitch the robot without the cake, varying the colours according to personal choice.

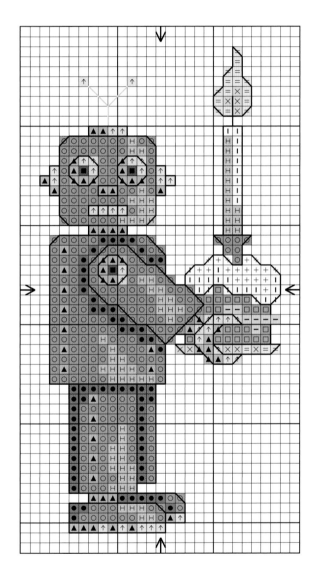

toy collection

A mixture of toys and letters makes this sampler an ideal educational tool for a young child.

stitching the design

1 Overcast the edges of the fabric to prevent fraying. Mark the midpoint of the fabric both vertically and horizontally with basting stitches; mount the fabric in an embroidery hoop (or stretcher frame) (see Getting Started, page 18).

2 Use the size guide below to calculate the size of design that will result from using different fabric counts (see How to Use This Book, page 13). Refer to the cross-stitch chart and thread key, and stitch from the middle outward.

3 Remove the finished design from the hoop and press gently on the wrong side.

size guide

fabric count	number of threads/blocks	number of strands	size of design
14	1	2	6 x 9⅛ in. (15.25 x 23.25 cm)
16	1	2	5¼ x 8 in. (13.25 x 20.25 cm)
18	1	2	4⅝ x 7⅛ in. (11.75 x 18 cm)
25	2	2	6¾ x 10¼ in. (17.25 x 26 cm)
28	2	2	6 x 9⅛ in. (15.25 x 23.25 cm)

materials

- The design shown here uses evenweave fabric, 25-count white, and tapestry needle, size 26.

- Stranded cottons, one skein of each colour listed in key. Use two strands for cross-stitch and French knots and one for backstitch.

thread key

- ⊡ B5200 bright white
- ▣ ecru
- ☒ 310 black
- ⊟ 351 deep coral
- ◎ 402 pale tan
- ● 435 camel
- ⊞ 517 deep sky blue
- ⊎ 518 mid sky blue
- ⊟ 519 sky blue
- ↑ 605 pale pink
- ▲ 646 mud grey
- ⫴ 648 pale mud green
- ⊠ 704 pale lime green
- ▽ 721 rusty orange
- ⑤ 725 bright yellow
- ✳ 747 pale baby blue
- ㇐ 772 pale leaf green
- ⋔ 819 ice pink
- ⊤ 3024 pale grey
- ◩ 3804 fuchsia
- Ⓝ 3806 pale fuchsia
- ☑ 3827 pale fudge
- ➡ 3832 mid brick pink

backstitch
- ◣ 310 black
- ◢ 351 deep coral

French knots
- ▨ 310 black

◀ Any of these motifs could be used as a decorative clothing patch, and letters could be stitched to form the initials of a child's name.

sheep

Adorned with brightly patterned fleece, pairs of black-faced sheep line up in a decorative border.

stitching the design

1 Overcast the edges of the fabric to prevent fraying. Mark the midpoint of the fabric both vertically and horizontally with basting stitches; mount the fabric in an embroidery hoop (or stretcher frame) (see Getting Started, page 18).

2 Use the size guide below to calculate the size of design that will result from using different fabric counts (see How to Use This Book, page 13). Refer to the cross-stitch chart and thread key, and stitch from the middle outward.

3 Remove the finished design from the hoop and press gently on the wrong side.

size guide

fabric count	number of threads/blocks	number of strands	size of design
14	1	2	5¾ x 2¼ in. (14.5 x 5.75 cm)
16	1	2	5 x 1⅞ in. (12.75 x 4.75 cm)
18	1	2	4½ x 1¾ in. (11.5 x 4.5 cm)
28	2	2	5¾ x 2¼ in. (14.5 x 5.75 cm)
28	3	3	8⅞ x 3⅜ in. (22.5 x 8.5 cm)

materials

- The design shown here uses evenweave fabric, 14-count white Aida, and tapestry needle, size 26.

- Stranded cottons, one skein of each colour listed in key. Use two strands for cross-stitch and three-quarter stitch and one for backstitch.

thread key

- ⊡ blanc
- ⊡ 151 palest old pink
- ⊞ 153 palest violet
- △ 604 mid rose
- ☑ 722 tango
- ⊡ 744 primrose yellow
- ⊟ 913 spearmint
- ↑ 959 mid aqua
- ⊠ 967 pale melon
- ■ 3031 dark brown
- ⊡ 3607 mid raspberry
- ⊞ 3811 pale aqua
- ▣ 3839 pale Delft blue

backstitch
- ◩ 3031 dark brown
- ◪ 3607 mid raspberry

◀ Repeat the sheep motifs to form a band around a toy sack, or use just one pair to decorate a smaller item, such as a laundry bag. Work the design on gingham or floral fabrics that echo the patterns on the sheep's fleece.

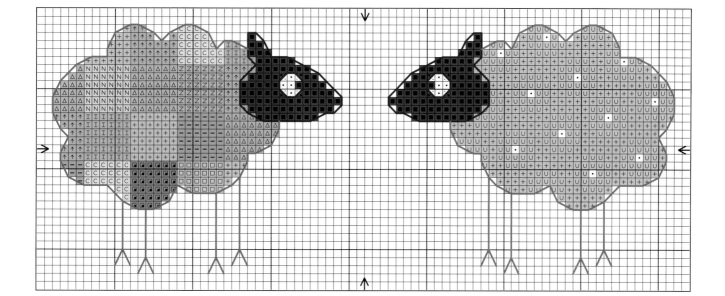

ballerina

Any aspiring prima ballerina will love accessories decorated with ballet shoes and a dancer's wrap top.

stitching the design

1 Overcast the edges of the fabric to prevent fraying. Mark the midpoint of the fabric both vertically and horizontally with basting stitches; mount the fabric in an embroidery hoop (or stretcher frame) (see Getting Started, page 18).

2 Use the size guide below to calculate the size of design that will result from using different fabric counts (see How to Use This Book, page 13). Refer to the cross-stitch chart and thread key, and stitch from the middle outward.

3 Remove the finished design from the hoop and press gently on the wrong side.

size guide

fabric count	number of threads/blocks	number of strands	size of design
14	1	2	2¾ x 7⅜ in. (7 x 18.75 cm)
16	1	2	2⅜ x 6½ in. (6 x 16.5 cm)
18	1	2	2⅛ x 5¾ in. (5.5 x 14.5 cm)
28	2	2	2¾ x 7⅜ in. (7 x 18.75 cm)
28	3	3	4⅛ x 11⅛ in. (10.5 x 28.25 cm)

materials

- The design shown here uses evenweave fabric, 14-count white Aida, and tapestry needle, size 26.

- Stranded cottons, one skein of each colour listed in key. Use two strands for cross-stitch and for backstitch on the wands. Use one strand for the remaining backstitch.

thread key

- ◉ 316 pale old mauve
- ▲ 451 dark putty
- ⊞ 819 ice pink
- ⊟ 963 cream pink
- ⊠ 3716 mid ice pink
- **backstitch**
- ◻ 3803 mauve

◀ A single pair of ballet shoes is perfect for a patch on a girl's drawstring shoe bag. Stitched vertically onto an Aida band, the design could be applied to a pale pink towel or bed linen. The stars symbolize the dreams of every young ballerina.

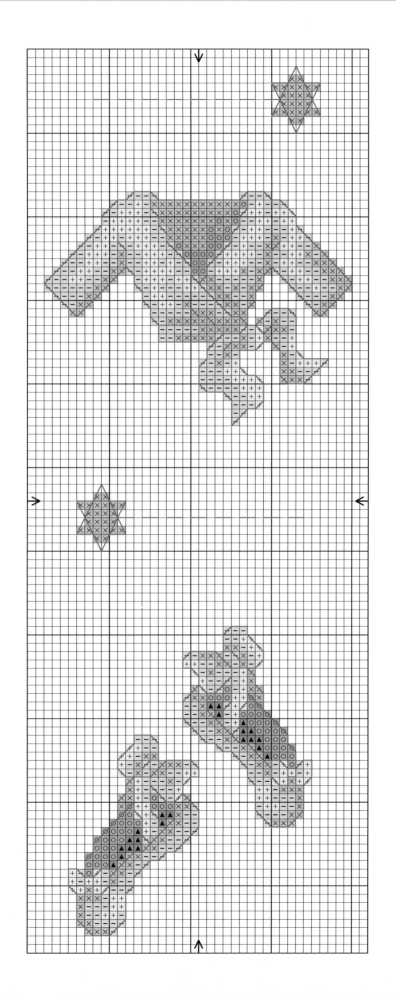

spring bear

This happy little bear holding a primrose can be added to many baby accessories.

stitching the design

1 Overcast the edges of the fabric to prevent fraying. Mark the midpoint of the fabric both vertically and horizontally with basting stitches; mount the fabric in an embroidery hoop (or stretcher frame) (see Getting Started, page 18).

2 Use the size guide below to calculate the size of motif A that will result from using different fabric counts (see How to Use This Book, page 13). Refer to the cross-stitch chart and thread key, and stitch from the middle outward.

3 Remove the finished design from the hoop and press gently on the wrong side.

size guide

fabric count	number of threads/blocks	number of strands	size of design
14	1	2	1⅞ x 2⅛ in. (4.75 x 5.5 cm)
16	1	2	1⅝ x 1⅞ in. (4.25 x 4.75 cm)
18	1	2	1½ x 1⅝ in. (4 x 4.25 cm)
28	2	2	1⅞ x 2⅛ in. (4.75 x 5.5 cm)
28	3	3	2¾ x 3¼ in. (7 x 8.25 cm)

materials

- The design shown here uses evenweave fabric, 18-count antique white Aida, and tapestry needle, size 26.

- Stranded cottons, one skein of each colour listed in key. Use two strands for cross-stitch and one for backstitch.

thread key

- ▲ 433 brown
- ◈ 436 light camel
- ☒ 437 old gold
- ⊟ 677 cold cream
- ◎ 738 tan beige
- ↑ 744 primrose yellow
- ⊠ 745 pale buttercup yellow
- ■ 761 pale dusty rose
- Ⓤ 913 spearmint
- ▽ 955 pale spearmint

backstitch

- ◩ 433 brown

◄ These booties would make a lovely gift for a new baby. The bear is used on the sole, with a single primrose added to the upper toe. Use one bear for a greeting card, or facing pairs for a window shade in a nursery. Alternatively, decorate child-size padded hangers with a row of the flowers.

(A)

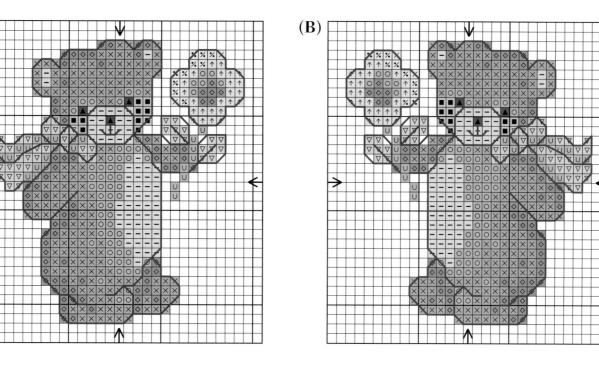

(B)

(C)

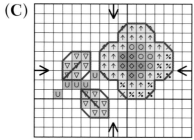

(D)

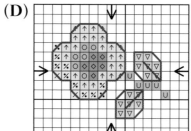

balloon

A small balloon bobbing in the air over dainty flowers makes a versatile motif for toys and clothes.

stitching the design

1 Overcast the edges of the fabric to prevent fraying. Mark the midpoint of the fabric both vertically and horizontally with basting stitches; mount the fabric in an embroidery hoop (or stretcher frame) (see Getting Started, page 18).

2 Use the size guide below to calculate the size of motif A that will result from using different fabric counts (see How to Use This Book, page 13). Refer to the cross-stitch chart and thread key, and stitch from the middle outward.

3 Remove the finished design from the hoop and press gently on the wrong side.

size guide

fabric count	number of threads/blocks	number of strands	size of design
14	1	2	4⅞ x 3⅜ in. (12.5 x 8.5 cm)
16	1	2	4¼ x 2⅞ in. (10.75 x 7.25 cm)
18	1	2	3¾ x 2⅝ in. (9.5 x 6.75 cm)
28	2	2	4⅞ x 3⅜ in. (12.5 x 8.5 cm)
28	3	3	7¼ x 5⅛ in. (18.5 x 13 cm)

materials

- The design shown here uses evenweave fabric, 14- and 18-count white Aida, and tapestry needle, size 26.

- Stranded cottons, one skein of each colour listed in key. Use two strands for cross-stitch and one for backstitch.

thread key

- ■ 210 lilac
- Ⅱ 605 pale pink
- ▬ 704 pale lime green
- ◎ 744 primrose yellow
- ⊞ 961 deep rusty pink
- ↑ 3746 purple

backstitch
- ◩ 961 deep rusty pink
- ◪ 3746 purple

◀ The delicacy of these motifs makes them suitable for small accessories, such as this simple dress for a rag doll and a scented sachet for a padded hanger. You could also enliven a girl's knitted pullover or cardigan by stitching the flower border along the neckline or a balloon near the shoulder.

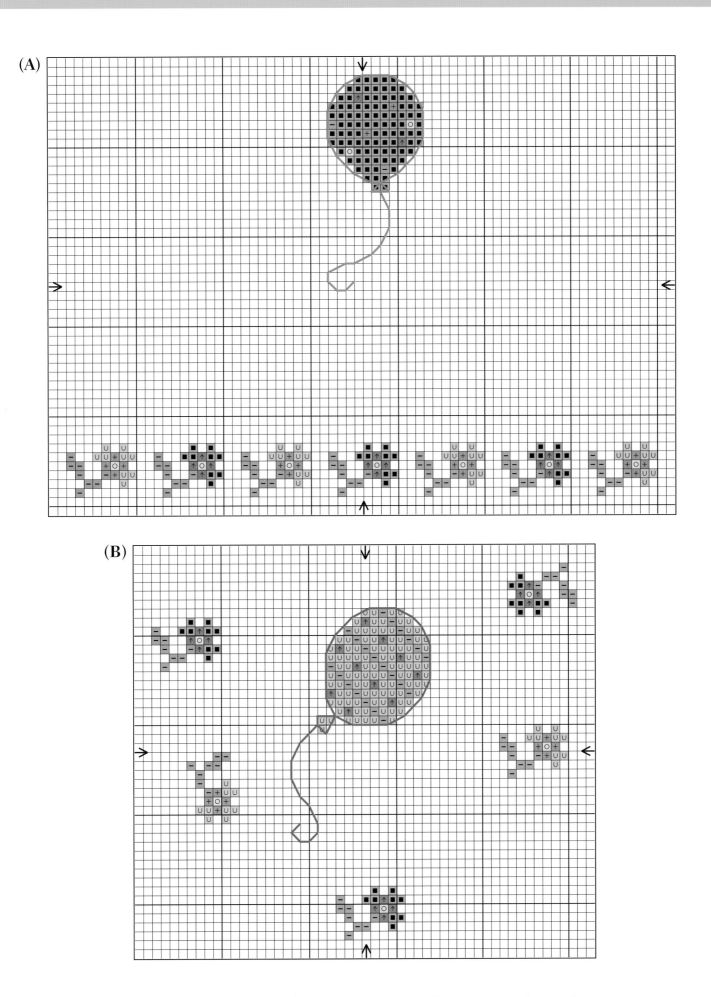

floral trellis

In soft shades of yellow, lilac, and aqua, this floral trellis can be repeated to create a pretty border.

stitching the design

1 Overcast the edges of the fabric to prevent fraying. Mark the midpoint of the fabric both vertically and horizontally with basting stitches; mount the fabric in an embroidery hoop (or stretcher frame) (see Getting Started, page 18).

2 Use the size guide below to calculate the size of design that will result from using different fabric counts (see How to Use This Book, page 13). Refer to the cross-stitch chart and thread key, and stitch from the middle outward.

3 Remove the finished design from the hoop and press gently on the wrong side.

materials

- The design shown here uses evenweave fabric, 11-count white Aida, and tapestry needle, size 26.

- Stranded cottons, one skein of each colour listed in key. Use three strands for cross-stitch and one for backstitch.

size guide			
fabric count	number of threads/blocks	number of strands	size of design
11	1	3	7⅞ x 2⅞ in. (20 x 7.25 cm)
14	1	2	6¼ x 2¼ in. (16 x 5.75 cm)
16	1	2	5⅜ x 1⅞ in. (13.75 x 4.75 cm)
18	1	2	4⅞ x 1¾ in. (12.5 x 4.5 cm)
28	2	2	6¼ x 2¼ in. (16 x 5.75 cm)

thread key

- ⊠ 209 pale lavender
- ⊠ 210 lilac
- ▽ 341 mid lilac
- ⊟ 353 peach
- ⊞ 772 pale leaf green
- ■ 958 aqua
- ◎ 964 ice aqua
- ⊡ 3078 pale yellow
- ▲ 3854 pale carrot orange
- Ⓤ 3855 pale apricot
- Ⓘ 3865 soft white

backstitch

- ◻ 958 aqua
- ◻ 3854 pale carrot orange

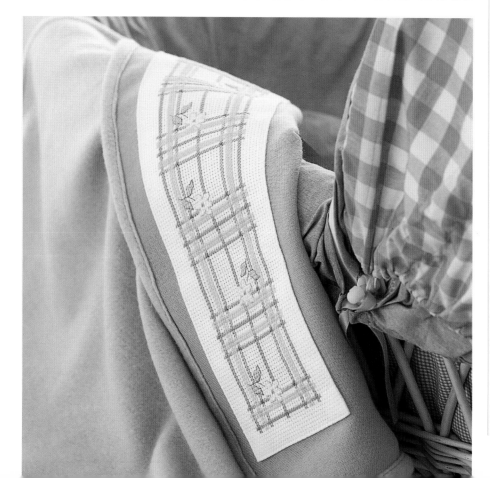

◄ Stitch the design onto white fabric to form a contrasting strip between the floral trellis and the lilac baby blanket. You could also work the design directly onto the edge of a baby coverlet, using waste canvas, for a more subtle effect.

(top)

baby keepsake

Symbols of childhood in pale pastels create a sampler that is a perfect gift for a new baby.

stitching the design

1 Overcast the edges of the fabric to prevent fraying. Mark the midpoint of the fabric both vertically and horizontally with basting stitches; mount the fabric in an embroidery hoop (or stretcher frame) (see Getting Started, page 18).

2 Use the size guide below to calculate the size of design that will result from using different fabric counts (see How to Use This Book, page 13). Refer to the cross-stitch chart and thread key, and stitch from the middle outward.

3 Remove the finished design from the hoop and press gently on the wrong side.

size guide

fabric count	number of threads/blocks	number of strands	size of design
14	1	2	9 x 7¼ in. (22.75 x 18.5 cm)
16	1	2	7⅞ x 6¼ in. (20 x 16 cm)
18	1	2	7 x 5⅝ in. (17.75 x 14.25 cm)
25	2	2	10⅛ x 8⅛ in. (25.75 x 20.75 cm)
28	2	2	9 x 7¼ in. (22.75 x 18.5 cm)

materials

- The design shown here uses evenweave fabric, 25-count white, and tapestry needle, size 26.

- Stranded cottons, one skein of each colour listed in key. Use two strands for cross-stitch and French knots and one for backstitch.

thread key

- ☑ 162 pale ice blue
- ▣ 435 camel
- ▤ 554 pale violet
- ◉ 603 pink
- ◎ 676 pale old gold
- ▲ 744 primrose yellow
- ⊞ 746 buttermilk
- Ⓤ 772 pale leaf green
- ⊟ 819 ice pink
- ↑ 955 pale spearmint
- ◈ 977 mid fudge
- ⊠ 3078 pale yellow
- ▽ 3325 ice blue
- Ⓢ 3713 ivory pink
- ✳ 3756 pale duck egg
- Ⓥ 3823 yellow cream
- ⓒ 3827 pale fudge

backstitch
- ◺ 435 camel
- ◺ 553 violet
- ◺ 801 dark brown

French knots
- Ⓣ 603 pink

◀ **All the letters of the alphabet are included in this sampler, so that any name can be formed at the top of the design. For a longer name, just work fewer ducks on each side. Frame the design to turn it into a commemorative picture, or make it into a bag for baby accessories.**

(top)

flower fairy

With wings outlined in glistening gold thread, this adorable fairy will captivate any little girl.

stitching the design

1 Overcast the edges of the fabric to prevent fraying. Mark the midpoint of the fabric both vertically and horizontally with basting stitches; mount the fabric in an embroidery hoop (or stretcher frame) (see Getting Started, page 18).

2 Use the size guide below to calculate the size of design that will result from using different fabric counts (see How to Use This Book, page 13). Refer to the cross-stitch chart and thread key, and stitch from the middle outward.

3 Remove the finished design from the hoop and press gently on the wrong side.

size guide

fabric count	number of threads/blocks	number of strands	size of design
14	1	2	4⅜ x 7⅜ in. (11 x 18.75 cm)
16	1	2	3¾ x 6⅜ in. (9.5 x 16.25 cm)
18	1	2	3⅜ x 5¾ in. (8.5 x 14.5 cm)
28	2	2	4⅜ x 7⅜ in. (11 x 18.75 cm)
28	3	3	6½ x 11⅛ in. (16.5 x 28.25 cm)

materials

■ The design shown here uses evenweave fabric, 16-count antique white Aida, and tapestry needle, size 26.

■ Stranded cottons and metallic thread, one skein of each colour listed in key. Use two strands for cross-stitch and one for backstitch.

thread key

▼ 301 mahogany
● 400 mid mahogany
Z 471 pale avocado
U 472 light avocado
⊟ 744 primrose yellow
☒ 950 rose beige
⊟ 3770 warm cream
⊡ 3823 yellow cream
N 3854 pale carrot orange
H 3855 pale apricot
▣ 3863 suede
◥ 3864 pale suede
③ 5282 metallic gold

backstitch
◻ 3772 dark maple sugar
◻ 3787 grey brown
◻ 3863 suede
◻ 5282 metallic gold

◀ **Mounted and framed, this delicate fairy makes a charming picture for a girl's bedroom. You could decorate other items in the bedroom as well—for instance, try stitching a fairy onto either end of a dressing-table cover.**

groovy girl

This fashionably dressed young girl has a spring in her step and a smile on her face.

stitching the design

1 Overcast the edges of the fabric to prevent fraying. Mark the midpoint of the fabric both vertically and horizontally with basting stitches; mount the fabric in an embroidery hoop (or stretcher frame) (see Getting Started, page 18).

2 Use the size guide below to calculate the size of design that will result from using different fabric counts (see How to Use This Book, page 13). Refer to the cross-stitch chart and thread key, and stitch from the middle outward.

3 Remove the finished design from the hoop and press gently on the wrong side.

size guide

fabric count	number of threads/blocks	number of strands	size of design
14	1	2	6¾ x 7¾ in. (17.25 x 19.75 cm)
16	1	2	5⅞ x 6¾ in. (15 x 17.25 cm)
18	1	2	5¼ x 6 in. (13.25 x 15.25 cm)
28	2	2	6¾ x 7¾ in. (17.25 x 19.75 cm)
28	3	3	10⅛ x 11⅝ in. (25.75 x 29.5 cm)

materials

- The design shown here uses evenweave fabric, 28-count white, and tapestry needle, size 26.

- Stranded cottons, one skein of each colour listed in key. Use two strands for cross-stitch.

thread key

- ■ 310 black
- ◎ 703 lime green
- ⊟ 951 pink cream
- ▣ 970 orange
- ⊠ 973 yellow

◀ A crisp white background enhances the fresh appeal of this motif. It is used here to form the central panel of a carryall with yellow side panels. On its own, the design is just the right shape for a small tote bag.

chapter eight:

traditional arts

Shaker hearts

Heart and flower motifs in a patchwork panel are unified by a cheerful red-and-white scheme.

stitching the design

1 Overcast the edges of the fabric to prevent fraying. Mark the midpoint of the fabric both vertically and horizontally with basting stitches; mount the fabric in an embroidery hoop (or stretcher frame) (see Getting Started, page 18).

2 Use the size guide below to calculate the size of design that will result from using different fabric counts (see How to Use This Book, page 13). Refer to the cross-stitch chart and thread key, and stitch from the middle outward.

3 Remove the finished design from the hoop and press gently on the wrong side.

materials

- The design shown here uses evenweave fabric, 28-count natural linen, and tapestry needle, size 26.

- Stranded cottons, one skein of each colour listed in key. Use two strands for cross-stitch and backstitch. Attach fabric shapes and stitch on buttons as shown in photograph.

size guide			
fabric count	number of threads/blocks	number of strands	size of design
14	1	2	7½ x 10 in. (19 x 25.5 cm)
16	1	2	6½ x 8¾ in. (16.5 x 22.25 cm)
18	1	2	5⅞ x 7¾ in. (15 x 19.75 cm)
28	2	2	7½ x 10 in. (19 x 25.5 cm)
28	3	3	11¼ x 15 in. (28.5 x 38 cm)

thread key

- ⊠ 351 deep coral
- ■ 498 red wine
- ◉ 666 flame red
- ▲ 817 poppy red
- ⊞ 3705 deep candy
- ⊡ 3865 soft white
- **backstitch**
- ◻ 351 deep coral
- ◪ 498 red wine

◀ The outline of the patchwork design is worked in red running stitches. A fabric heart and flower add textural contrast, as do the buttons stitched onto some of the motifs. Two roughly carved, heart-shaped buttons are interesting enough to stand alone.

calligraphy

The medieval art of using a variety of quills to create different scripts inspired this alphabet design.

stitching the design

1 Overcast the edges of the fabric to prevent fraying. Mark the midpoint of the fabric both vertically and horizontally with basting stitches; mount the fabric in an embroidery hoop (or stretcher frame) (see Getting Started, page 18).

2 Use the size guide below to calculate the size of design that will result from using different fabric counts (see How to Use This Book, page 13). Refer to the cross-stitch chart and thread key, and stitch from the middle outward.

3 Remove the finished design from the hoop and press gently on the wrong side.

size guide

fabric count	number of threads/blocks	number of strands	size of design
14	1	2	8⅝ x 10⅜ in. (22 x 26.25 cm)
16	1	2	7½ x 9⅛ in. (19 x 23.25 cm)
18	1	2	6¾ x 8 in. (17.25 x 20.25 cm)
28	2	2	8⅝ x 10⅜ in. (22 x 26.25 cm)
28	3	3	12⅞ x 16¼ in. (32.75 x 41.25 cm)

materials

- The design shown here uses evenweave fabric, 28-count slate blue linen, and tapestry needle, size 26.

- Stranded cottons, one skein of each colour listed in key. Use two strands for cross-stitch.

thread key

- ■ blanc
- ◉ 162 pale ice blue
- ⊠ 211 pale lilac
- Ⅰ 225 pale shell pink
- ▲ 369 pale green
- ⊞ 677 cold cream
- ⊟ 964 ice aqua

◀ Using a slate blue fabric and pale embroidery threads adds to the decorative appeal of this sampler. Modern, blocklike letters contrast with the older flowing and ornate ones. Display the sampler near bookshelves to emphasize the literary theme.

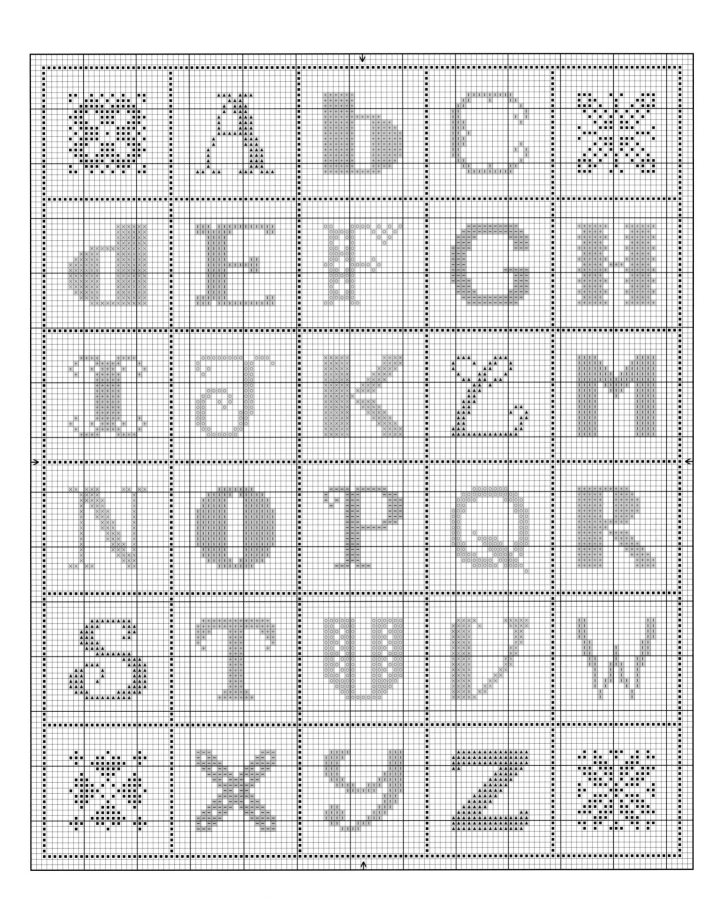

Moroccan tile

An interlocking grid contains a geometric pattern characteristic of painted tiles from North Africa.

stitching the design

1 Overcast the edges of the fabric to prevent fraying. Mark the midpoint of the fabric both vertically and horizontally with basting stitches; mount the fabric in an embroidery hoop (or stretcher frame) (see Getting Started, page 18).

2 Use the size guide below to calculate the size of design that will result from using different fabric counts (see How to Use This Book, page 13). Refer to the cross-stitch chart and thread key, and stitch from the middle outward.

3 Remove the finished design from the hoop and press gently on the wrong side.

size guide

fabric count	number of threads/blocks	number of strands	size of design
14	1	2	9¾ in. (24.75 cm) square
16	1	2	8½ in. (21.5 cm) square
18	1	2	7⅝ in. (19.25 cm) square
28	2	2	9¾ in. (24.75 cm) square
28	3	3	14⅝ in. (37.25 cm) square

materials

- The design shown here uses evenweave fabric, 16-count white Aida, and tapestry needle, size 26.

- Stranded cottons, two skeins of 959 and one skein of each of the other colours listed in key. Use two strands for cross-stitch.

thread key

- ☑ 959 mid aqua
- Ⓢ 3607 mid raspberry
- ■ 3609 ice raspberry
- ⊟ 3812 bright aqua
- ☒ 3821 pale gold

◄ This design makes an ideal frame for a square mirror. It would also look good in the middle of a tablecloth, perhaps on a pink or green fabric, in a Moroccan-style decor.

African styles

A bold design in terra cotta, beige, and gold suggests the look of some African textiles.

stitching the design

1 Overcast the edges of the fabric to prevent fraying. Mark the midpoint of the fabric both vertically and horizontally with basting stitches; mount the fabric in an embroidery hoop (or stretcher frame) (see Getting Started, page 18).

2 Use the size guide below to calculate the size of design that will result from using different fabric counts (see How to Use This Book, page 13). Refer to the cross-stitch chart and thread key, and stitch from the middle outward.

3 Remove the finished design from the hoop and press gently on the wrong side.

size guide

fabric count	number of threads/blocks	number of strands	size of design
14	1	2	11 x 7⅝ in. (28 x 19.25 cm)
16	1	2	9⅝ x 6⅝ in. (24.5 x 16.75 cm)
18	1	2	8½ x 5⅞ in. (21.5 x 15 cm)
28	2	2	11 x 7⅝ in. (28 x 19.25 cm)
28	3	3	16½ x 11⅜ in. (42 x 29 cm)

materials

- The design shown here uses evenweave fabric, 28-count cream Quaker cloth, and tapestry needle, size 26.

- Stranded cottons, three skeins of 3857, two skeins of 355 and 738, and one skein of each of the other colours listed in key. Use two strands for cross-stitch.

thread key

- ▣ 355 dark terra cotta
- ⊡ 437 old gold
- ◎ 738 tan beige
- Ⓝ 977 mid fudge
- ⬤ 3857 burnt brick

◀ Choose threads in the earthy tones typical of African fabrics. This design has many possibilities—for example, it could be displayed under glass on a low wooden coffee table.

(top)

folk-art hearts

This intricate pattern of hearts forms loops that meet around a central point.

stitching the design

1 Overcast the edges of the fabric to prevent fraying. Mark the midpoint of the fabric both vertically and horizontally with basting stitches; mount the fabric in an embroidery hoop (or stretcher frame) (see Getting Started, page 18).

2 Use the size guide below to calculate the size of design that will result from using different fabric counts (see How to Use This Book, page 13). Refer to the cross-stitch chart and thread key, and stitch from the middle outward.

3 Remove the finished design from the hoop and press gently on the wrong side.

materials

■ The design shown here uses evenweave fabric, 32-count natural linen band, and tapestry needle, size 26.

■ Stranded cottons, one skein of the colour listed in key. Use two strands for cross-stitch.

thread key

■ 3857 burnt brick

size guide

fabric count	number of threads/blocks	number of strands	size of design
14	1	2	2⅝ x 5½ in. (6.75 x 14 cm)
16	1	2	2¼ x 4¾ in. (5.75 x 12 cm)
18	1	2	2 x 4¼ in. (5 x 10.75 cm)
28	2	2	2⅝ x 5½ in. (6.75 x 14 cm)
32	2	2	2¼ x 4¾ in. (5.75 x 12 cm)

◄ Ideally shaped for a bookmark, this design is finished here with a matching beaded tassel. For curtain tiebacks, extend the hearts as required, working the stitching in a shade that complements the curtain fabric.

Roman figures

To complement a classic interior theme, Roman numerals stand out in white on a natural fabric.

stitching the design

1 Overcast the edges of the fabric to prevent fraying. Mark the midpoint of the fabric both vertically and horizontally with basting stitches; mount the fabric in an embroidery hoop (or stretcher frame) (see Getting Started, page 18).

2 Use the size guide below to calculate the size of design that will result from using different fabric counts (see How to Use This Book, page 13). Refer to the cross-stitch chart and thread key, and stitch from the middle outward.

3 Remove the finished design from the hoop and press gently on the wrong side.

materials

- The design shown here uses evenweave fabric, 28-count raw linen, and tapestry needle, size 26.

- Stranded cottons, one skein of the colour listed in key. Use two strands for cross-stitch.

size guide			
fabric count	number of threads/blocks	number of strands	size of design
14	1	2	4¾ x 2⅛ in. (12 x 5.5 cm)
16	1	2	4⅛ x 1⅞ in. (10.5 x 4.75 cm)
18	1	2	3⅝ x 1⅝ in. (9.25 x 4.25 cm)
28	2	2	4¾ x 2⅛ in. (12 x 5.5 cm)
28	3	3	7⅛ x 3¼ in. (18 x 8.25 cm)

◀ Made into a table runner, this design suits a formal dining setting. It would also work well on raw linen curtains, either bordering the lower edge or repeated at intervals all over the fabric.

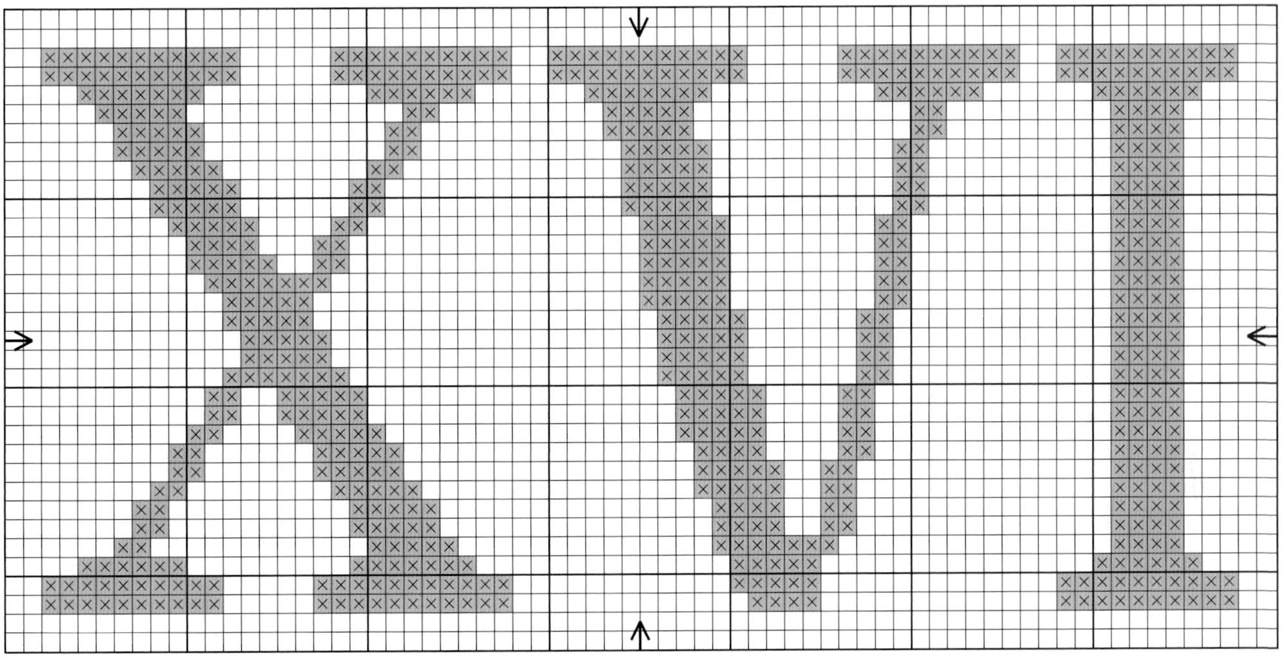

modern Kelim

A bright palette of aqua, teal, and yellow brings a classic Turkish design up to date.

stitching the design

1 Overcast the edges of the fabric to prevent fraying. Mark the midpoint of the fabric both vertically and horizontally with basting stitches; mount the fabric in a stretcher frame (see Getting Started, page 18).

2 Use the size guide below to calculate the size of design that will result from using different fabric counts (see How to Use This Book, page 13). Refer to the cross-stitch chart and thread key, and stitch from the middle outward.

3 Remove the finished design from the frame and press gently on the wrong side.

materials

■ The design shown here uses 10-count white interlock canvas, and tapestry needle, size 20.

■ DMC tapestry yarn, 12 skeins of ecru; three skeins of 7019; two skeins of 7055, 7725, 7861, and 7952; and one skein of 7011 and 7956. Use one strand for half cross-stitch.

Note that each half cross-stitch is worked over one intersection of canvas threads. The stitch is worked basically as described in "Half cross-stitch" on page 20, but a better finish will be achieved if you bring the needle up in an empty hole and take it down in one that is partly filled.

size guide

fabric count	number of threads/blocks	number of strands	size of design
8	1	1	8¾ x 18 in. (22.25 x 45.75 cm)
10	1	1	7 x 14⅜ in. (17.75 x 36.5 cm)
12	1	1	5⅞ x 12 in. (15 x 30.5 cm)
14	1	1	5 x 10¼ in. (12.75 x 26 cm)
18	1	1	3⅞ x 8 in. (9.75 x 20.25 cm)

thread key

half cross-stitch

⊟ ecru
▲ 7011 light terra cotta
◼ 7019 lavender blue
⊡ 7055 daffodil yellow
◎ 7952 pale aqua
▲ 7725 deep yellow
▯ 7861 teal
⊞ 7956 mid aqua

◄ Worked in half cross-stitch on canvas using tapestry yarn, this design is perfect for a shopping bag that is both practical and stylish. It can also be used to cover other items in the home, such as a footstool or chair-back cover.

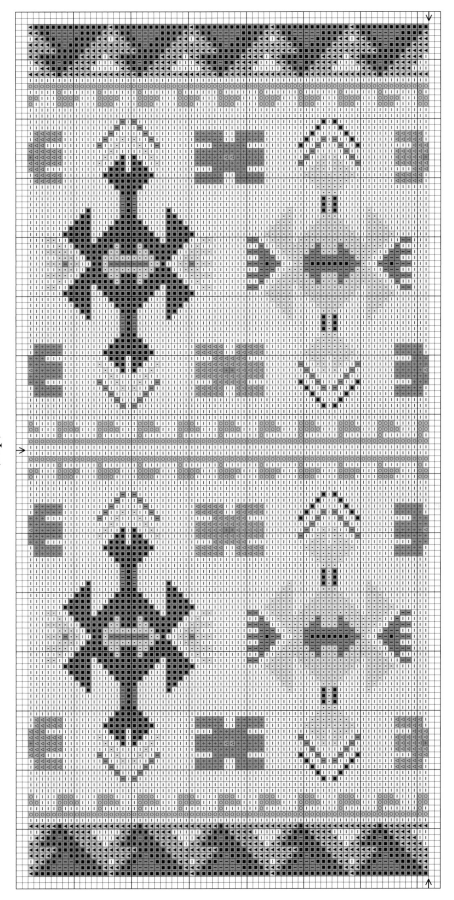

(top)

Repeat this cross-stitch chart to stitch the bottom half of the design.

Indian flowers

From India's rich tradition of embroidered textiles comes a sampler displaying exotic floral patterns.

stitching the design

1 Overcast the edges of the fabric to prevent fraying. Mark the midpoint of the fabric both vertically and horizontally with basting stitches; mount the fabric in an embroidery hoop (or stretcher frame) (see Getting Started, page 18).

2 Use the size guide below to calculate the size of design that will result from using different fabric counts (see How to Use This Book, page 13). Refer to the cross-stitch chart and thread key, and stitch from the middle outward.

3 Remove the finished design from the hoop and press gently on the wrong side.

size guide

fabric count	number of threads/blocks	number of strands	size of design
14	1	2	11 x 7½ in. (28 x 19 cm)
16	1	2	9⅝ x 6½ in. (24.5 x 16.5 cm)
18	1	2	8½ x 5⅞ in. (21.5 x 15 cm)
28	2	2	11 x 7½ in. (28 x 19 cm)
28	3	3	16½ x 11¼ in. (42 x 28.5 cm)

materials

- The design shown here uses evenweave fabric, 28-count raw linen, and tapestry needle, size 26.
- Stranded cottons, one skein of each colour listed in key. Use two strands for cross-stitch and three-quarter stitch and one for backstitch.

thread key

- 151 palest old pink
- 310 black
- 600 dark pink
- 783 pale caramel
- 791 purple blue
- 818 pale baby pink
- 955 pale spearmint
- 3731 dark old pink
- 3733 mid old pink
- 3807 cornflower blue
- 3820 gold
- 3821 pale gold
- 3822 palest gold
- 3839 pale Delft blue
- 3840 palest Delft blue
- 3847 deep aqua
- 3849 teal
- 3865 soft white

backstitch

- 310 black
- 3821 pale gold
- 3847 deep aqua

◀ **This design combines a range of floral and border motifs. Backstitching provides the fine detailing on these motifs characteristic of Indian embroidered textiles. The sampler would look good framed, or stitched onto a bag or window-seat covering.**

(top)

festive stars

Motifs symbolic of the Christmas season are stitched in berry red on a snowy white background.

stitching the design

1 Overcast the edges of the fabric to prevent fraying. Mark the midpoint of the fabric both vertically and horizontally with basting stitches; mount the fabric in an embroidery hoop (or stretcher frame) (see Getting Started, page 18).

2 Use the size guide below to calculate the size of design that will result from using different fabric counts (see How to Use This Book, page 13). Refer to the cross-stitch chart and thread key, and stitch from the middle outward.

3 Remove the finished design from the hoop and press gently on the wrong side.

size guide			
fabric count	number of threads/blocks	number of strands	size of design
14	1	2	7⅝ x 10⅞ in. (19.25 x 27.5 cm)
16	1	2	6⅝ x 9½ in. (16.75 x 24.25 cm)
18	1	2	6 x 8½ in. (15.25 x 21.5 cm)
27	2	2	7⅞ x 11⅜ in. (20 x 29 cm)
27	3	3	11¾ x 17⅛ in. (30 x 43.5 cm)

materials

- The design shown here uses evenweave fabric, 27-count white, and tapestry needle, size 26.

- Stranded cottons, three skeins of the colour listed in key. Use two strands for cross-stitch.

thread key

⊠ 347 berry red

in detail
Some of the eight-pointed stars in the sampler are worked in positive and negative forms so that red and white are reversed. This style is inspired by traditional patchwork quilts.

◀ Included on this sampler are a pair of doves, a Christmas tree, holly, hearts, and chrysanthemums.

Tibetan textile

Taken from designs found in northern Tibet, these jewel-bright motifs look superb set against black.

stitching the design

1 Overcast the edges of the fabric to prevent fraying. Mark the midpoint of the fabric both vertically and horizontally with basting stitches; mount the fabric in an embroidery hoop (or stretcher frame) (see Getting Started, page 18).

2 Use the size guide below to calculate the size of design that will result from using different fabric counts (see How to Use This Book, page 13). Refer to the cross-stitch chart and thread key, and stitch from the middle outward.

3 Remove the finished design from the hoop and press gently on the wrong side.

size guide

fabric count	number of threads/blocks	number of strands	size of design
14	1	3	7½ x 10½ in. (19 x 26.75 cm)
16	1	2	6½ x 9¼ in. (16.5 x 23.5 cm)
18	1	2	5⅞ x 8⅛ in. (15 x 20.75 cm)
28	2	2	7½ x 10½ in. (19 x 26.75 cm)
28	3	3	11¼ x 15¾ in. (28.5 x 40 cm)

materials

- The design shown here uses evenweave fabric, 16-count black Aida, and tapestry needle size 26.

- Stranded cottons, one skein of each colour listed in key. Use two strands for cross-stitch.

thread key

- ■ 666 flame red
- ⊟ 726 daffodil yellow
- ☒ 907 pale apple green
- ◉ 996 mid turquoise

in detail

Two strands of thread cover the 16-count black Aida perfectly. If you work on 14-count fabric, you will need to use three strands to cover it adequately, as shown here.

◀ An advantage of these square designs is their versatility. All six could be easily repeated to decorate larger items, such as a footstool. Alternatively, a single motif could be used for a small pincushion.

Navajo motifs

Replicating the colours of Native American dyes, this design adds an ethnic touch to table accessories.

stitching the design

1 Overcast the edges of the fabric to prevent fraying. Mark the midpoint of the fabric both vertically and horizontally with basting stitches; mount the fabric in an embroidery hoop (or stretcher frame) (see Getting Started, page 18).

2 Use the size guide below to calculate the size of design that will result from using different fabric counts (see How to Use This Book, page 13). Refer to the cross-stitch chart and thread key, and stitch from the middle outward.

3 Remove the finished design from the hoop and press gently on the wrong side.

size guide

fabric count	number of threads/blocks	number of strands	size of design
14	1	2	3⅜ x 1⅜ in. (8.5 x 3.5 cm)
16	1	2	2⅞ x 1¼ in. (7.25 x 3.25 cm)
18	1	2	2⅝ x 1 in. (6.75 x 2.5 cm)
28	2	2	3⅜ x 1⅜ in. (8.5 x 3.5 cm)
28	3	3	5⅛ x 2⅛ in. (13 x 5.5 cm)

materials

- The design shown here uses evenweave fabric, 28-count white, and tapestry needle, size 26.

- Stranded cottons, one skein of each colour listed in key. Use two strands for cross-stitch.

thread key

- T 666 flame red
- U 729 ochre
- ◣ 824 rich blue
- ◉ 912 deep spearmint
- ☒ 3810 dark aqua

◀ Flame red and ochre are two of the main colours used in traditional Navajo designs. With a simple border, reminiscent of a row of semiprecious stones, this bright design looks good on a napkin ring. Without the border, it makes a decorative motif for a set of matching napkins.

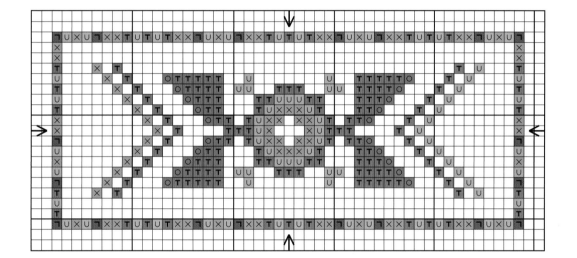

medieval cross

A patterned cross borrowed from the Middle Ages takes on a modern look in pink and blue.

stitching the design

1 Overcast the edges of the fabric to prevent fraying. Mark the midpoint of the fabric both vertically and horizontally with basting stitches; mount the fabric in an embroidery hoop (or stretcher frame) (see Getting Started, page 18).

2 Use the size guide below to calculate the size of design that will result from using different fabric counts (see How to Use This Book, page 13). Refer to the cross-stitch chart and thread key, and stitch from the middle outward.

3 Remove the finished design from the hoop and press gently on the wrong side.

size guide

fabric count	number of threads/blocks	number of strands	size of design
14	1	2	2⅞ in. (7.25 cm) square
16	1	2	2½ in. (6.25 cm) square
18	1	2	2¼ in. (5.75 cm) square
28	2	2	2⅞ in. (7.25 cm) square
28	3	3	4¼ in. (10.75 cm) square

materials

- The design shown here uses evenweave fabric, 28-count pale yellow linen, and tapestry needle, size 26.

- Stranded cottons, one skein of each colour listed in key. Use two strands for cross-stitch.

thread key

- ⬆ 3806 pale fuchsia
- ⧄ 3843 dark turquoise

◀ This design makes an attractive pincushion and could also be used to create a matching needle case.

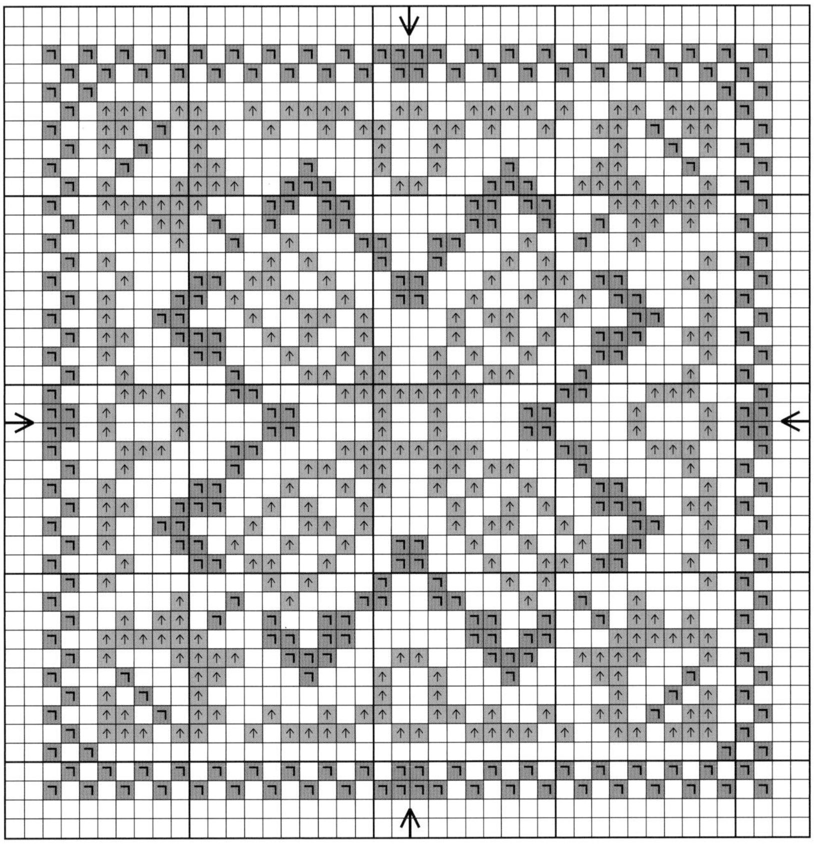

paisley

With intricate teardrop shapes, this attractive paisley design originated in India.

stitching the design

1 Overcast the edges of the fabric to prevent fraying. Mark the midpoint of the fabric both vertically and horizontally with basting stitches; mount the fabric in an embroidery hoop (or stretcher frame) (see Getting Started, page 18).

2 Use the size guide below to calculate the size of design that will result from using different fabric counts (see How to Use This Book, page 13). Refer to the cross-stitch chart and thread key, and stitch from the middle outward.

3 Remove the finished design from the hoop and press gently on the wrong side.

size guide

fabric count	number of threads/blocks	number of strands	size of design
14	1	2	6⅞ in. (17.5 cm) square
16	1	2	6⅛ in. (15.5 cm) square
18	1	2	5⅜ in. (13.75 cm) square
28	2	2	6⅞ in. (17.5 cm) square
28	3	3	10¼ in. (26 cm) square

materials

- The design shown here uses evenweave fabric, 28-count biscuit linen, and tapestry needle, size 26.

- Stranded cottons, one skein of each colour listed in key. Use two strands for cross-stitch and backstitch.

thread key

- ■ 777 plum
- Ⓤ 3045 yellow beige
- ⊞ 3047 pale putty
- ◉ 3814 aquamarine
- ⊠ 3831 brick pink
- ▲ 3834 dark grape
- Ⓒ 3836 pale grape

backstitch
- ◩ 3814 aquamarine

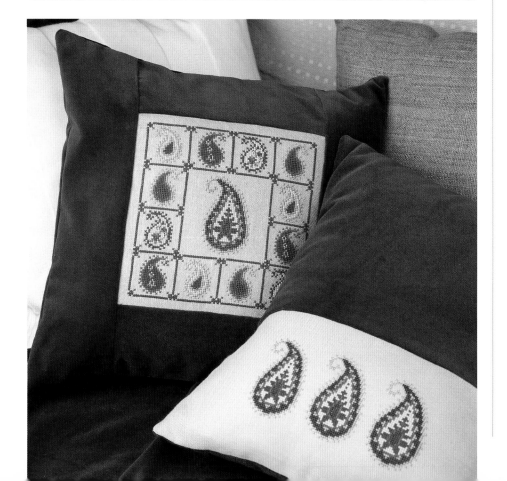

◀ Here, the design is used in its entirety on one fabric panel, while the main motif is repeated on the other. Purple velvet enhances the deep, rich colours of the paisley teardrops.

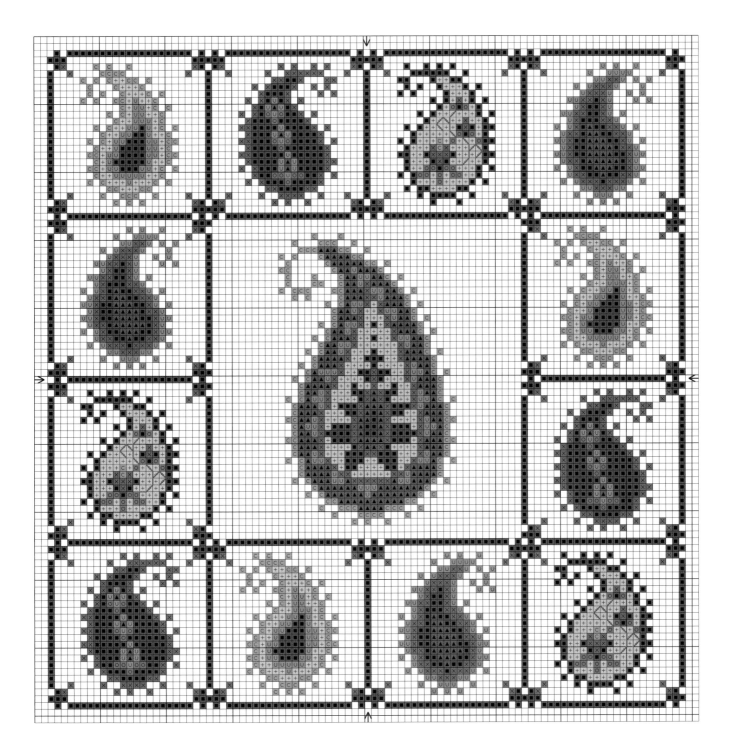

patchwork

For early American settlers, patchwork quilts were a much-loved means of creative expression.

stitching the design

1 Overcast the edges of the fabric to prevent fraying. Mark the midpoint of the fabric both vertically and horizontally with basting stitches; mount the fabric in an embroidery hoop (or stretcher frame) (see Getting Started, page 18).

2 Use the size guide below to calculate the size of design that will result from using different fabric counts (see How to Use This Book, page 13). Refer to the cross-stitch chart and thread key, and stitch from the middle outward.

3 Remove the finished design from the hoop and press gently on the wrong side.

materials

- The design shown here uses evenweave fabric, 28-count dark fawn, and tapestry needle, size 26.

- Stranded cottons, one skein of each colour listed in key. Use two strands for cross-stitch and backstitch.

thread key

- ☒ 517 deep sky blue
- ⊟ 677 cold cream
- ◩ 832 deep lime gold
- ⊞ 920 light brick
- ⓤ 3815 deep jade
- **backstitch**
- ◹ 517 deep sky blue

size guide

fabric count	number of threads/blocks	number of strands	size of design
14	1	2	6⅛ x 8⅞ in. (15.5 x 22.5 cm)
16	1	2	5¼ x 7¾ in. (13.25 x 19.75 cm)
18	1	2	4¾ x 6⅞ in. (12 x 17.5 cm)
28	2	2	6⅛ x 8⅞ in. (15.5 x 22.5 cm)
28	3	3	9¼ x 13¼ in. (23.5 x 33.75 cm)

in detail

Using two strands of 517 for backstitching the alphabet and numbers gives the design a bolder effect.

◀ The cross-stitch on this sampler is easy to work because each patch is a solid block of colour. The design would look decorative on a rectangular tablecloth. Each motif could also be stitched individually to create matching place mats.

Greek vase

Elaborate scrolling and geometric patterns are typically found on vases from ancient Greece.

materials

- The design shown here uses evenweave fabric, 28-count natural, and tapestry needle, size 26.

- Stranded cottons, three skeins of 310 and one skein of each of the other colours listed in key. Use two strands for cross-stitch and one for backstitch.

stitching the design

1 Overcast the edges of the fabric to prevent fraying. Mark the midpoint of the fabric both vertically and horizontally with basting stitches; mount the fabric in an embroidery hoop (or stretcher frame) (see Getting Started, page 18).

2 Use the size guide below to calculate the size of design that will result from using different fabric counts (see How to Use This Book, page 13). Refer to the cross-stitch chart and thread key, and stitch from the middle outward.

3 Remove the finished design from the hoop and press gently on the wrong side.

thread key

- ▲ 310 black
- ● 355 dark terra cotta
- ☒ 356 mid terra cotta
- ◎ 758 mid rose brown
- Ⓤ 783 pale caramel
- ⊞ 3820 gold
- ⊟ 3822 palest gold

backstitch

- ◥ 310 black
- ◥ 355 dark terra cotta
- ◥ 783 pale caramel
- ◻ 3822 palest gold

size guide

fabric count	number of threads/blocks	number of strands	size of design
14	1	2	11⅛ x 8¼ in. (28.25 x 21 cm)
16	1	2	9⅝ x 7¼ in. (24.5 x 18.5 cm)
18	1	2	8⅝ x 6½ in. (22 x 16.5 cm)
28	2	2	11⅛ x 8¼ in. (28.25 x 21 cm)
28	3	3	16⅝ x 12⅜ in. (42.25 x 31.5 cm)

in detail
Backstitch worked in 3822 gleams brightly against the 310 cross-stitch. You could use a single strand of metallic gold thread in places to add a real shine to the design.

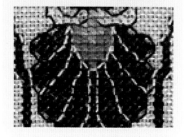

◀ Ancient Greek vases featured either black designs on a terra cotta base or terra cotta designs reversed out of a black background. This design looks good as a table runner, or it could equally be framed as a sampler.

(top)

Asian script

Far Eastern calligraphy has a graphic quality that makes it perfect for minimalist settings.

stitching the design

1 Overcast the edges of the fabric to prevent fraying. Mark the midpoint of the fabric both vertically and horizontally with basting stitches; mount the fabric in an embroidery hoop (or stretcher frame) (see Getting Started, page 18).

2 Use the size guide below to calculate the size of design that will result from using different fabric counts (see How to Use This Book, page 13). Refer to the cross-stitch chart and thread key, and stitch from the middle outward.

3 Remove the finished design from the hoop and press gently on the wrong side.

size guide

fabric count	number of threads/blocks	number of strands	size of design
12	1	2	2¼ x 7 in. (5.75 x 17.75 cm)
14	1	2	1⅞ x 6 in. (4.75 x 15.25 cm)
16	1	2	1⅝ x 5¼ in. (4.25 x 13.25 cm)
18	1	2	1½ x 4⅝ in. (4 x 11.75 cm)
28	2	2	1⅞ x 6 in. (4.75 x 15.25 cm)

materials

- The design shown here uses 12-count waste canvas, and embroidery needle, size 9.

- Stranded cottons, one skein of the colour listed in key. Use two strands for cross-stitch.

 822 light stone

◄ Here, waste canvas is used so that the design can be worked directly onto a black napkin. For the place mat, light-stone stitching on a dark-stone background provides subtle contrasts in tone and texture. A black border links the place mat to the napkin.

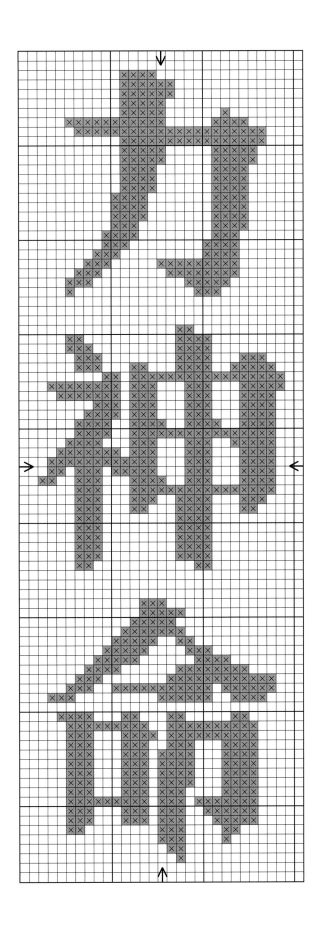

Mexican style

Fiery peppers, a sombrero, and prickly cacti make lively motifs for kitchen accessories.

stitching the design

1 Overcast the edges of the fabric to prevent fraying. Mark the midpoint of the fabric both vertically and horizontally with basting stitches; mount the fabric in an embroidery hoop (or stretcher frame) (see Getting Started, page 18).

2 Use the size guide below to calculate the size of motif A that will result from using different fabric counts (see How to Use This Book, page 13). Refer to the cross-stitch chart and thread key, and stitch from the middle outward.

3 Remove the finished design from the hoop and press gently on the wrong side.

size guide

fabric count	number of threads/blocks	number of strands	size of design
14	1	2	11¼ x 1⅝ in. (28.5 x 4.25 cm)
16	1	2	9¾ x 1⅜ in. (24.75 x 3.5 cm)
18	1	2	8¾ x 1¼ in. (22.25 x 3.25 cm)
28	2	2	11¼ x 1⅝ in. (28.5 x 4.25 cm)
28	3	3	16⅞ x 2⅜ in. (42.75 x 6 cm)

materials

- The design shown here uses evenweave fabric, 14-count ochre Aida band and Christmas red Aida, and tapestry needle, size 26.

- Stranded cottons, one skein of each colour listed in key. Use two strands for cross-stitch and one for backstitch.

thread key

- ⊞ blanc
- ⬤ 321 red
- ▼ 400 mid mahogany
- ■ 498 red wine
- ⊠ 518 mid sky blue
- ↑ 676 pale old gold
- ⊟ 677 cold cream
- N 702 spring green
- S 703 lime green
- U 722 tango
- ◁ 729 ochre
- 1 744 primrose yellow
- T 987 grass green
- Z 3760 dark sky blue
- ◎ 3776 tan
- ⊓ 3787 grey brown
- 4 3855 pale apricot

backstitch
- ◻ 321 red
- ☐ 744 primrose yellow
- ◻ 907 pale apple green
- ◻ 3760 dark sky blue
- ◻ 3787 grey brown

◀ The key to creating this design successfully is to use hot Mexican shades of Aida, such as bright red and golden ochre.

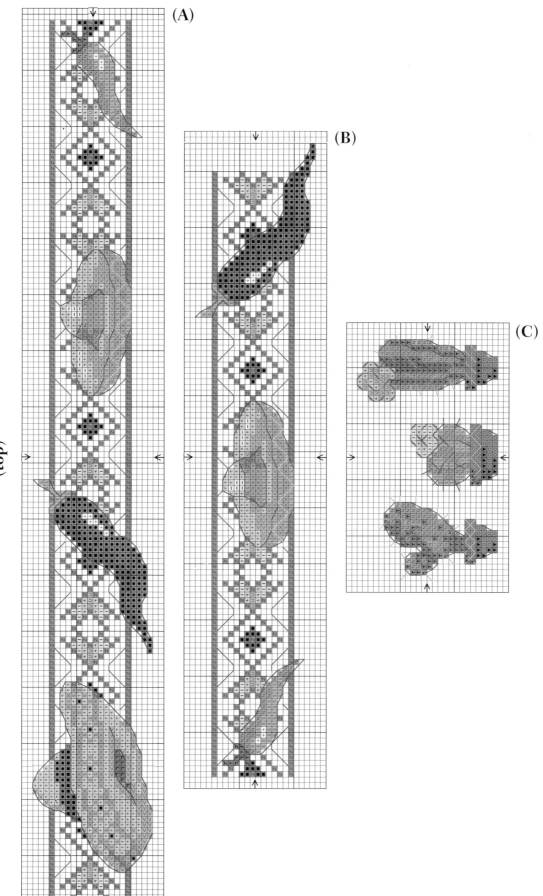

(top)

(A)

(B)

(C)

Delft tiles

Blue-and-white tiles from Delft, painted with designs like these, were fashionable in 17th-century Holland.

stitching the design

1 Overcast the edges of the fabric to prevent fraying. Mark the midpoint of the fabric both vertically and horizontally with basting stitches; mount the fabric in an embroidery hoop (or stretcher frame) (see Getting Started, page 18).

2 Use the size guide below to calculate the size of design that will result from using different fabric counts (see How to Use This Book, page 13). Refer to the cross-stitch chart and thread key, and stitch from the middle outward.

3 Remove the finished design from the hoop and press gently on the wrong side.

size guide

fabric count	number of threads/blocks	number of strands	size of design
14	1	2	6¾ x 9¾ in. (17.25 x 24.75 cm)
16	1	2	5⅞ x 8½ in. (15 x 21.5 cm)
18	1	2	5¼ x 7½ in. (13.25 x 19 cm)
27	2	2	7 x 10⅛ in. (17.75 x 25.75 cm)
27	3	3	10½ x 15¼ in. (26.75 x 38.75 cm)

materials

- The design shown here uses evenweave fabric, 27-count white, and tapestry needle, size 26.

- Stranded cottons, one skein of each colour listed in key. Use two strands for cross-stitch and one for backstitch.

thread key

- ◉ 312 light navy blue
- ⊠ 334 azure aqua
- ▽ 775 pale ice blue
- ▼ 803 navy blue
- **backstitch**
- ◲ 803 navy blue

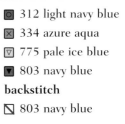

◀ Originally, Delft tiles were often used to surround fireplaces, so a firescreen might be a fitting application for this design. Its delicacy also makes it a perfect dressing-table cover, particularly for a blue-and-white bedroom.

African textile

Centuries of rug weaving in Africa have produced a rich variety of patterns and motifs.

stitching the design

1 Overcast the edges of the fabric to prevent fraying. Mark the midpoint of the fabric both vertically and horizontally with basting stitches; mount the fabric in an embroidery hoop (or stretcher frame) (see Getting Started, page 18).

2 Use the size guide below to calculate the size of motif A that will result from using different fabric counts (see How to Use This Book, page 13). Refer to the cross-stitch chart and thread key, and stitch from the middle outward.

3 Remove the finished design from the hoop and press gently on the wrong side.

size guide			
fabric count	number of threads/blocks	number of strands	size of design
14	1	2	4½ in. (11.5 cm) square
16	1	2	3⅞ in. (9.75 cm) square
18	1	2	3½ in. (9 cm) square
28	2	2	4½ in. (11.5 cm) square
28	3	3	6¾ in. (17.25 cm) square

materials

- The design shown here uses evenweave fabric, 14-count antique white Aida, and tapestry needle, size 26.

- Stranded cottons, one skein of each colour listed in key. Use two strands for cross-stitch and one for backstitch.

thread key

- ☒ 300 dark mahogany
- ◼ 310 black
- ▲ 782 mid mustard
- ▬ 869 hazel brown
- ☑ 919 dark copper
- ◉ 938 deep chocolate
- ⊡ 3823 yellow cream
- ⊞ 3852 dark gold
- Ⓢ 3853 carrot orange
- Ⓤ 3855 pale apricot

◀ Warm, earthy tones and natural fabrics best complement an African theme. The designs are attached to a sandy-brown throw with a simple border of black running stitch. A matching footstool would complete the look.

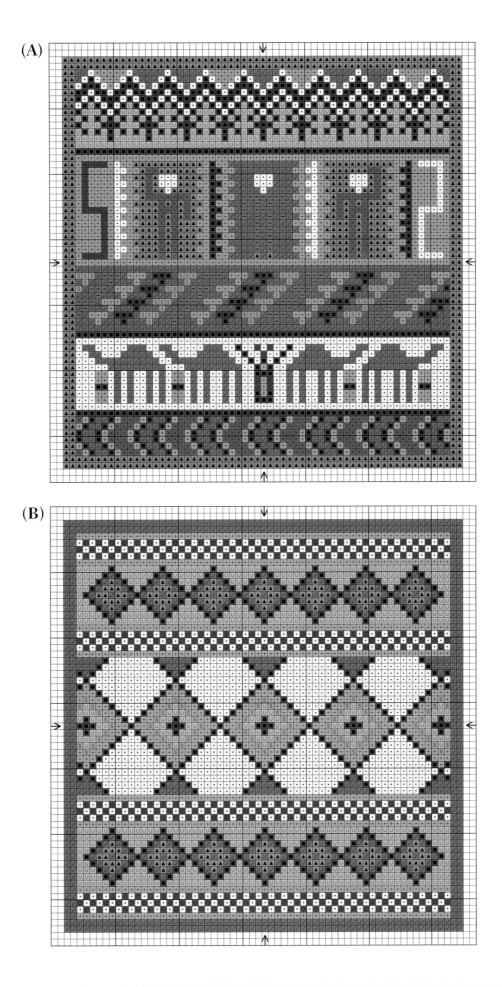

(A)

(B)

classic scrolls

Often seen on ornate cornices in grand houses, scrolls are reminiscent of an elegant age.

stitching the design

1 Overcast the edges of the fabric to prevent fraying. Mark the midpoint of the fabric both vertically and horizontally with basting stitches; mount the fabric in an embroidery hoop (or stretcher frame) (see Getting Started, page 18).

2 Use the size guide below to calculate the size of design that will result from using different fabric counts (see How to Use This Book, page 13). Refer to the cross-stitch chart and thread key, and stitch from the middle outward.

3 Remove the finished design from the hoop and press gently on the wrong side.

size guide

fabric count	number of threads/blocks	number of strands	size of design
14	1	2	8¼ in. (21 cm) square
16	1	2	7¼ in. (18.5 cm) square
18	1	2	6⅜ in. (16.25 cm) square
28	2	2	8¼ in. (21 cm) square
28	3	3	12⅜ in. (31.5 cm) square

materials

- The design shown here uses evenweave fabric, 28-count antique white Quaker cloth, and tapestry needle, size 26.

- Stranded cottons, one skein of each colour listed in key. Use two strands for cross-stitch.

thread key

 304 dark red
 347 berry red
816 claret red

◀ Here used as a decorative panel, the design is stitched in stylish shades of red and claret. Within a classic-style home interior, square scroll motifs could work well on ivory curtains. In this case, repeat the motifs as a border, leaving a square of plain fabric between each stitched one.

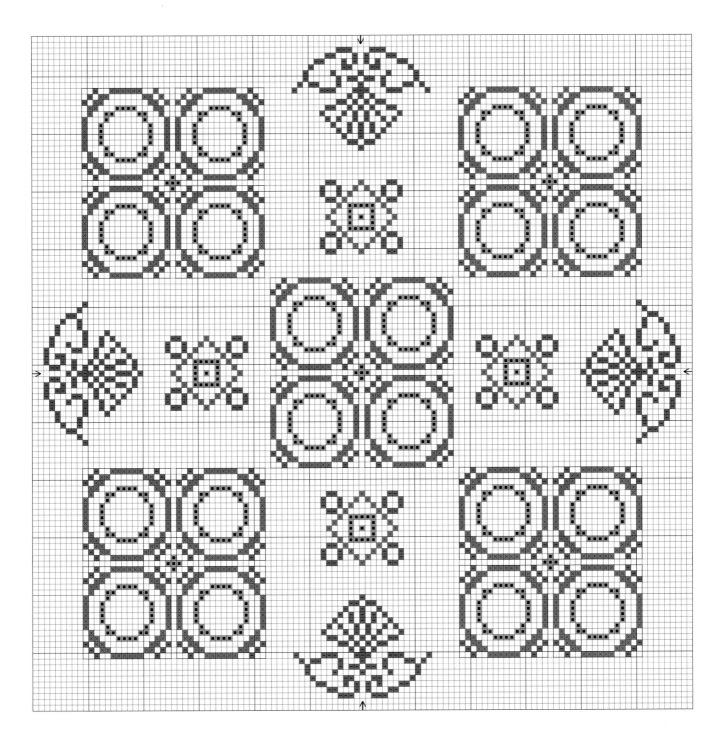

geometric art

This modern design juxtaposes different colours, shapes, and sizes to create striking compositions.

stitching the design

1 Overcast the edges of the fabric to prevent fraying. Mark the midpoint of the fabric both vertically and horizontally with basting stitches; mount the fabric in an embroidery hoop (or stretcher frame) (see Getting Started, page 18).

2 Use the size guide below to calculate the size of design that will result from using different fabric counts (see How to Use This Book, page 13). Refer to the cross-stitch chart and thread key, and stitch from the middle outward.

3 Remove the finished design from the hoop and press gently on the wrong side.

size guide

fabric count	number of threads/blocks	number of strands	size of design
14	1	2	10⅛ x 4¾ in. (25.75 x 12 cm)
16	1	2	8¾ x 4⅛ in. (22.25 x 10.5 cm)
18	1	2	7⅞ x 3⅝ in. (20 x 9.25 cm)
27	2	2	10½ x 4⅞ in. (26.75 x 12.5 cm)
27	3	3	15¾ x 7¼ in. (40 x 18.5 cm)

materials

- The design shown here uses evenweave fabric, 27-count Christmas red, and tapestry needle, size 26.

- Stranded cottons, one skein of each colour listed in key. Use two strands for cross-stitch.

thread key

- 905 mid apple green
- 3799 charcoal
- 3820 gold
- 3865 soft white

◀ Geometric bands have the advantage of being extremely adaptable. Each band can be repeated horizontally or vertically to create complementary designs. Using red fabric, as here, ensures that the motifs look bright and bold, because the fabric shows through parts of the design.

(top)

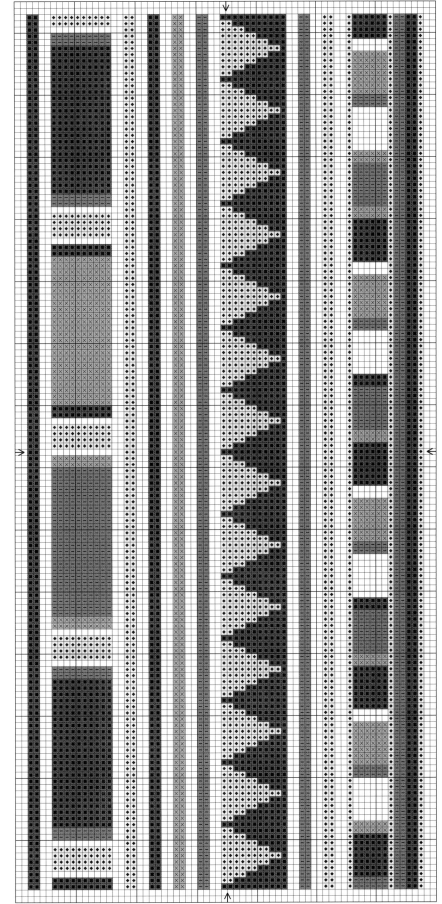

initials

Adorned with French knots, letters in a curling script can be combined to make elegant monograms.

stitching the design

1 Overcast the edges of the fabric to prevent fraying. Mark the midpoint of the fabric both vertically and horizontally with basting stitches; mount the fabric in an embroidery hoop (or stretcher frame) (see Getting Started, page 18).

2 Use the size guide below to calculate the size of design that will result from using different fabric counts (see How to Use This Book, page 13). Refer to the cross-stitch chart and thread key, and stitch from the middle outward.

3 Remove the finished design from the hoop and press gently on the wrong side.

size guide

fabric count	number of threads/blocks	number of strands	size of design
14	1	2	15⅜ x 11½ in. (39 x 29.25 cm)
16	1	2	13⅜ x 10⅛ in. (34 x 25.75 cm)
18	1	2	12 x 9 in. (30.5 x 22.75 cm)
28	2	2	15⅜ x 11½ in. (39 x 29.25 cm)
28	3	3	23⅛ x 17¼ in. (58.75 x 43.75 cm)

materials

- The design shown here uses evenweave fabric, 28-count baby blue linen, and tapestry needle, size 26.

- Stranded cottons, one skein of the colour listed in key. Use two strands for cross-stitch, three-quarter stitch, and French knots.

thread key

⊠ 841 coffee

French knots
◉ 841 coffee

◀ All types of bedroom and bathroom clothing and accessories can be embroidered with initials. Match the colour of the thread to the fabric, but choose a slightly lighter or darker tone so that the monogram stands out against the background.

(top)

heart quartet

A cluster of little hearts framed by red and blue squares creates a perfectly symmetrical pattern.

stitching the design

1 Overcast the edges of the fabric to prevent fraying. Mark the midpoint of the fabric both vertically and horizontally with basting stitches; mount the fabric in an embroidery hoop (or stretcher frame) (see Getting Started, page 18).

2 Use the size guide below to calculate the size of design that will result from using different fabric counts (see How to Use This Book, page 13). Refer to the cross-stitch chart and thread key, and stitch from the middle outward.

3 Remove the finished design from the hoop and press gently on the wrong side.

size guide

fabric count	number of threads/blocks	number of strands	size of design
14	1	2	3¼ in. (8.25 cm) square
16	1	2	2¾ in. (7 cm) square
18	1	2	2½ in. (6.25 cm) square
28	2	2	3¼ in. (8.25 cm) square
28	3	3	4⅞ in. (12.5 cm) square

materials

- The design shown here uses evenweave fabric, 14-count pale blue Aida, and tapestry needle, size 24.

- Stranded cottons, one skein of each colour listed in key. Use two strands for cross-stitch.

thread key

- ☒ 321 red
- ⊟ 3750 army blue

◀ As well as making a stylish pincushion when stitched onto pale blue Aida, this design can be worked on a variety of fabric counts to make different-sized hearts. For example, use an 18-count fabric to make a smaller version for decorating other sewing-kit equipment, such as a needle case or thread box.

Kelim

Hand-woven Turkish carpets that use natural dyes inspired a beautifully balanced design in rustic tones.

stitching the design

1 Overcast the edges of the fabric to prevent fraying. Mark the midpoint of the fabric both vertically and horizontally with basting stitches; mount the fabric in a stretcher frame (see Getting Started, page 18).

2 Use the size guide below to calculate the size of design that will result from using different fabric counts (see How to Use This Book, page 13). Refer to the cross-stitch chart and thread key, and stitch from the middle outward.

3 Remove the finished design from the frame and press gently on the wrong side.

size guide

fabric count	number of threads/blocks	number of strands	size of design
8	1	1	10 x 15¼ in. (25.5 x 38.75 cm)
10	1	1	8 x 12¼ in. (20.25 x 31 cm)
12	1	1	6⅝ x 10⅛ in. (16.75 x 25.75 cm)
14	1	1	5¾ x 8¾ in. (14.5 x 22.25 cm)
18	1	1	4½ x 6¾ in. (11.5 x 17.25 cm)

materials

■ The design shown here uses 10-count white interlock canvas, and tapestry needle, size 20.

■ DMC tapestry yarn, seven skeins of 7059 and 7503; six skeins of 7032; three skeins of ecru; and two skeins of 7504. Use one strand for half cross-stitch.

Note that each half cross-stitch is worked over one intersection of canvas threads. The stitch is worked basically as described in "Half cross-stitch" on page 20, but a better finish will be achieved if you bring the needle up in an empty hole and take it down in one that is partly filled.

thread key

half cross-stitch
⊞ ecru
▲ 7032 deep blue
✳ 7059 golden brown
◎ 7503 pale gold
■ 7504 mustard

◀ This Kelim design has been trimmed with a cream twisted cord. An alternative way of embellishing the design would be to make four tassels, using threads that complement or contrast with the tapestry yarn colours, and attach a tassel to each corner.

To stitch the right-hand side of the design, you must flip the cross-stitch chart.

resources

United States

Coats & Clark
Consumer Services
P.O. Box 12229
Greenville, SC 29612-0229
1-800-648-1479

The DMC Corporation
South Hackensack Avenue
Port Kearny Bldg. 10F
South Kearney, NJ 07032-4688
www.dmc-usa.com

Jo-Ann Stores
2361 Rosencrans Avenue
Suite 360
El Segundo, CA 90245
1-800-525-4951
www.joann.com

Australia

Tapestry Craft
50 York Street
Sydney NSW 2000
1800 222 155
www.tapestrycraft.com.au

Cross Stitch World
PO Box 1355
Burpengary Qld 4505
07 3888 1877
www.crosstitchworld.com

New Zealand

Golding Handcrafts
17 Marion Street
Wellington
04 801 5855
www.goldingcraft.com

Canada

Thread & Eye
699 Wilkins St Unit 37
London, ON, N6C 5C8
(519) 685-1444
www.threadneye.com

Golden Threads Imports Inc.
556 Upper James Street
Hamilton, ON, L9C 2Y4
(905) 318-8254
www.gthreads.com

Stitcher's Heaven Ltd.
3731-98 St
Edmonton, AB, T6E 5N2
(780) 435-0795
www.stitchersheaven.com

Cross-Stitch Cupboard
2181 Carling Ave.
Ottawa, ON K2B 7E8
(613) 729-9744
(613) 729-0212
www.cross-stitch.ca

Loving Stitch
10566 King George Hwy
Surrey, BC, V3T 2X5
(604) 584-9022
(604) 584-7089
www.lovingstitch.com

United Kingdom

Coats Crafts UK
P.O. Box 22
Lingfield Estate
McMullen Road
Darlington
County Durham DL1 1YQ
01325 365457
www.coatscrafts.co.uk

DMC Creative World
62 Pullman Road
Wigston
Leicestershire LE18 2DY
0116 281 1040
www.dmc.com

Framecraft Miniatures Ltd.
Unit 3 Isis House
Lindon Road
Brownhills
Walsall
West Midlands WS8 6LH
01543 373 076
www.framecraft.com

Madeira Threads (UK) Ltd.
12 Hallikeld Close
Barker Business Park
Melmerby
Ripon
North Yorkshire HG4 5GZ
01765 641 705
www.madeira.co.uk